IMAGES
of America

ANSON

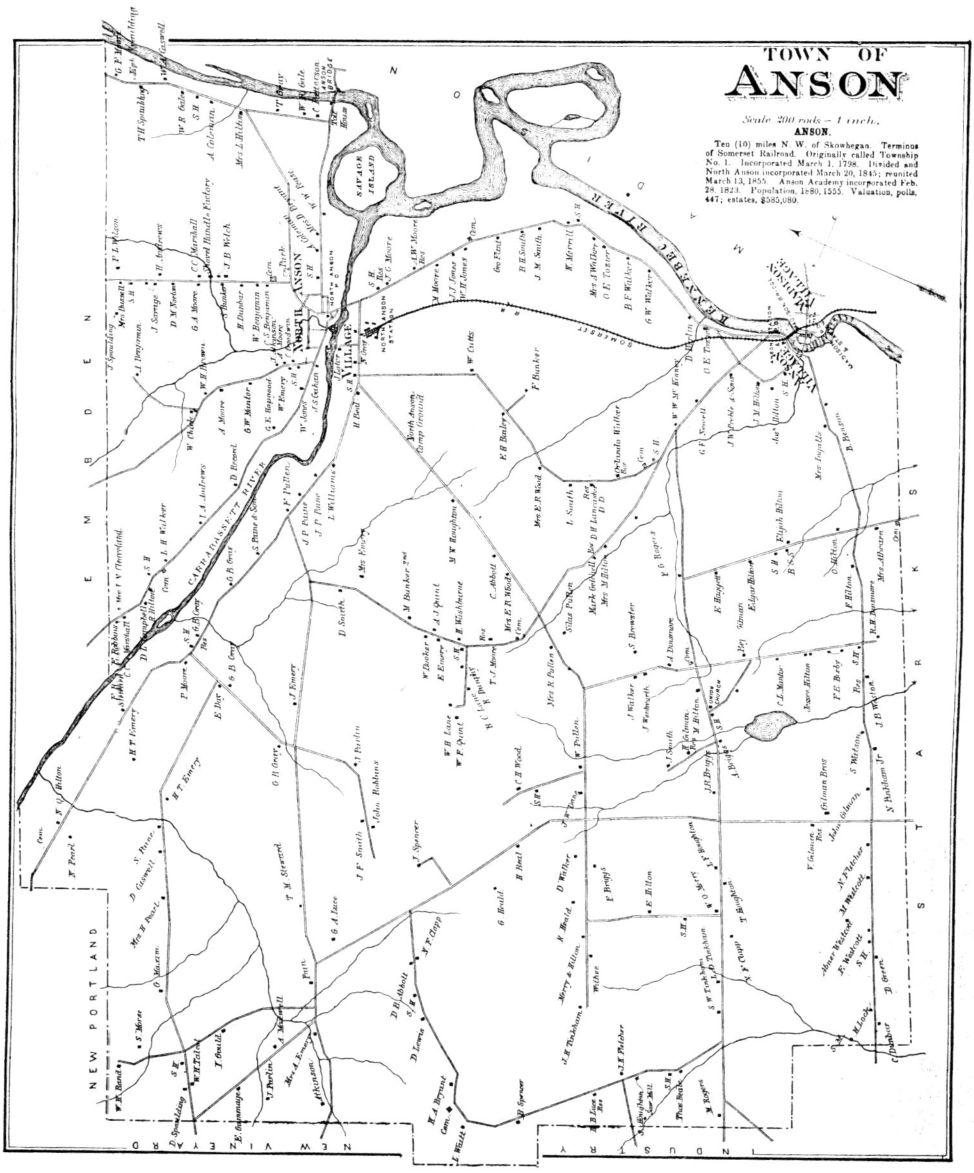

TOWN OF
ANSON
Scale 200 rods = 1 inch.
ANSON.
Ten (10) miles N. W. of Skowhegan. Terminus of Somerset Railroad. Originally called Township No. 1. Incorporated March 1, 1798. Divided and North Anson incorporated March 20, 1845; reunited March 13, 1855. Anson Academy incorporated Feb. 28, 1823. Population, 1880, 1555. Valuation, polls, 447; estates, $585,080.
SAVAGE ISLAND
KENNEBEC RIVER
CARRABASSETT RIVER
NORTH ANSON VILLAGE
SOMERSET R.R.
EMBDEN
NEW PORTLAND
NEW VINEYARD
INDUSTRY
STARKS
MADISON

IMAGES
of America

ANSON

Anson Bicentennial Committee

ARCADIA
PUBLISHING

ISBN 978-0-7385-8240-5

Published by Arcadia Publishing,
Charleston, South Carolina

Printed in the United States of America

Library of Congress Catalog Card Number: 98-86556

For all general information contact Arcadia Publishing at:
Telephone 843-853-2070
Fax 843-853-0044
E-mail sales@arcadiapublishing.com
For customer service and orders:
Toll-Free 1-888-313-2665

Visit us on the Internet at www.arcadiapublishing.com

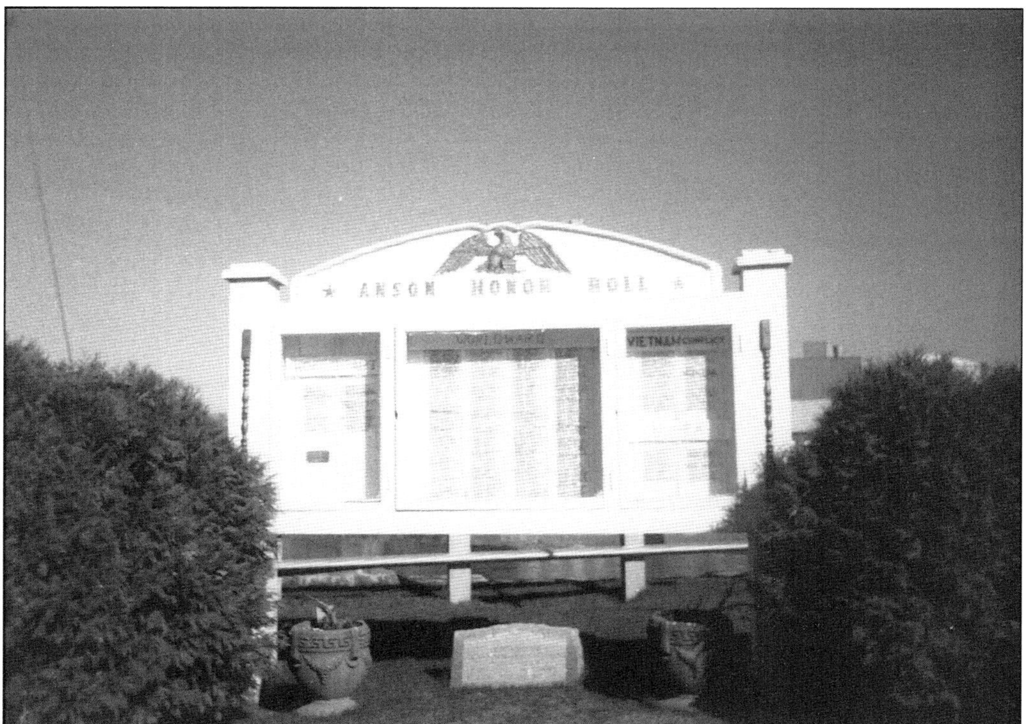

The honor roll in Anson, built by the Anson Community Club in 1944. This memorial honors veterans of World War I, World War II, and the Korean and Vietnam Wars. It will soon be replaced with a new modern structure honoring the veterans of both villages.

Contents

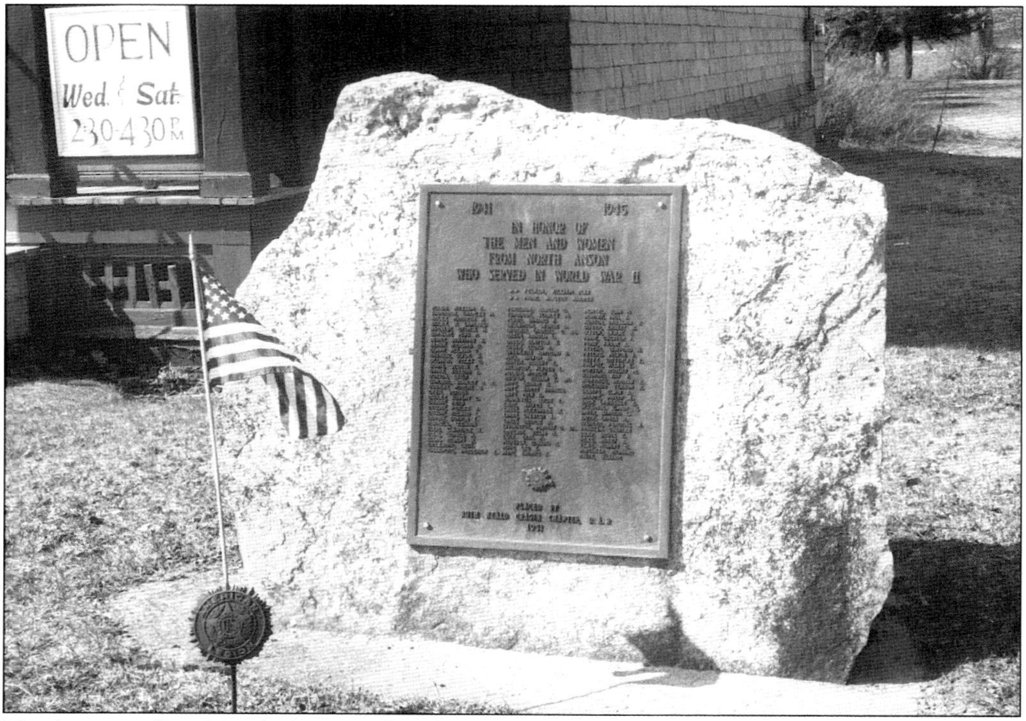

The honor roll in North Anson, placed at the Stewart Public Library by the DAR to honor veterans of WW II.

ACKNOWLEDGMENTS

We have spent many hours pondering over old photographs and articles submitted by many generous individuals and groups. If we found two similar photos with the same date we knew our information was accurate . . . with all of the others, we've done the best that we could. This entire project would not be the wonderful book that you are about to enjoy, and add to your history collection, without the help of the following people:

Earle Shettleworth from Maine Historic Preservation Commission, Albert Morrell, Isabelle Carlson, Barbara Qualey, the Stewart Public Library, Marjorie Morrell, Shirley Goodwin, Gary Agren, Blanche Nichols, Robert Garland, Ivan Hoyt, Dorothy Flanders, Ramona Everett, Charlene Davis, Claudia Viles, Bradford Brown, Avis Luce, Joyce Bishop, Shirley Bessey, Keith Partridge, Carol McLaughlin, Nancy McLean, Frances Savage, Bertha Welch, Trudy Hayes, Florence Lovejoy, John Bryant, Harold Sterling, Frances Gould, Beatrice King, Tom Billing, Doug Cahill, Carol Dolan from the Embden Historical Society, Frances Merrill, Hilda Witham, Virginia Wing Moore, TDS Telecom, Laton Edwards, Mahlon Hilton, Donald Ray, Jamie Doiron, Jan Welch, Florence Welch, Erlon Barron, Hurley Fletcher, Betty Dawes, Raymond Moody, Terry Petley of the Anson Fire Department, Barbara Hoyt, Georgia Dodson, Colby Seams, Rosalie Nason, Almon Watson, Patricia Mayo, Luce's Sap House, and Ellsworth Spencer. We gratefully acknowledge any other contributors that we have omitted from this list.

INTRODUCTION

The town of Anson is celebrating its 200th birthday this year. Its history is both complex and unique, in part because it is composed of two villages which in many years had different characteristics, and, in some ways, different styles of living.

The town was named after Lord George Anson, an English navigator. Prior to incorporation, the area had been known by several names, including Township No. 1, Brookfield, Seven Mile Brook Plantation, and Titcomb Town. On March 20, 1845, the town was divided, and North Anson—5 miles up the river—was incorporated as a separate town. The towns were reunited on March 13, 1855.

When settlers from Massachusetts, New Hampshire, and southern Maine first arrived, our area was inhabited by Abenaki Indians. The fertile soil and direct access to the Kennebec and Carrabassett Rivers, which served as important transportation corridors, were attractive to the settlers.

Among the first settlers who came to clear the land and build homes were the Moores, the Dinsmores, the Rogers, and the Fletchers. Elemuel Williams came in 1791 and helped organize the town in 1798.

There were no fast trains or automobiles to transport people to other places; even a wagon was probably a great curiosity then, so the children and the children's children for the most part cleared more land and settled down on nearby farms. They soon began to realize the potential of harvesting the woodlands and the water power offered by the rivers. About 1780, sawmills, gristmills, and fulling mills were built on the rivers.

By the late 1870s, North Anson had become the trading center for a large number of farming communities. It was also the terminus of the Somerset Railroad, which made it the center of business for a wide extent of country.

During the 1900s the economy in South Anson was affected significantly by the woolen mills and the paper mill. A substantial increase in the population obliged the town of Anson to increase its school facilities.

Thanks to the generosity of the people who were willing to search their attics and share their pictures we have made an attempt to show in this book the changes made through the years in our two villages. It is our hope that it may inspire our children to record the continuing history of our small town for future generations and perhaps inspire someone to publish a written history.

Where Two Rivers Meet

The Town of Anson sitteth
Where two rivers meet,
Along the Kennebec River
And by Carrabassett's feet.

Memories linger in our minds
Of the horse and buggy days,
As life has changed, down through
The years, many things are now passee.

Many, many years ago
A windstorm swept through town,
And took the flagpole on Main Street,
In North Anson, to the ground.

One-room schoolhouses are no more,
Also, the blacksmith shops,
And telephone lines are private now,
No party lines, we can't eavesdrop.

Ice was cut from the Kennebec
And stored along the shore,
In an icehouse on the River Road,
With sawdust covered floors.

A wagon drawn by horses,
Delivered ice from door to door,
And milkmen delivered eggs and
Juice, and bottled milk galore.

The train no longer rambles
On the tracks we used to trek,
Logs floating to the paper mills
Are gone from the Kennebec.

Smudge pots keeping vigil
O'er potholes, through the night,
And wood-slat snowfences in the fields,
Were ordinary sights.

Spanning the Carrabassett
The old green bridge of yore, was
Replaced by the Robert Garland Bridge
That now connects the shores.

The huge old barns are few today
Upon family lots in town,
They either fell by nature's hand
Or by mans they were torn down.

The Anson Bridge was further down and
When crossed would happily croon,
And a whistle blown from the Power
House, told us it was noon.

When a fire occurred we counted
The lengths a whistle blew,
Two long, one short, we checked a
Chart, what street it was, we knew.

Folks hardly ever locked their homes,
Used a "skeleton" key if they did,
Over the door or under the mat,
Is where it was usually hid.

If lost a neighbor had a spare,
Through a junk drawer they would sort,
Or for a nickel at the hardware store
Another could be bought.

Now these things we took for granted
That they would always be,
Not thinking time would bring
Them, to turn into memories.

The cycle will repeat itself,
Times now, will be memories sweet,
About the Town of Anson that sitteth
Where two rivers meet.

—Charlene Preble Davis

One

ANSON

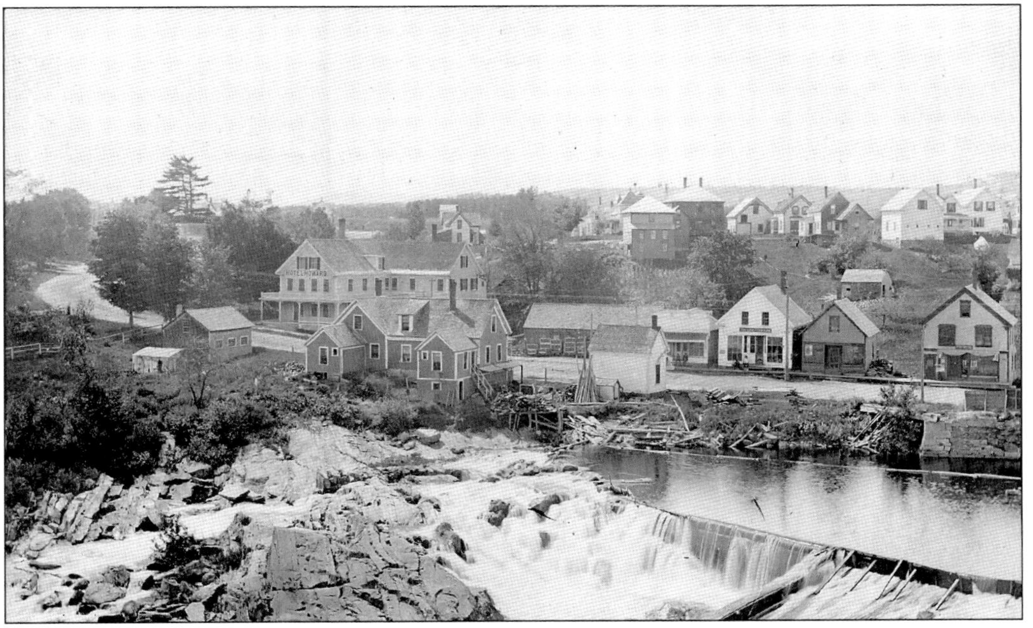

A view of Main Street, Anson, 1898. The dam and sluice in the foreground were used by the Kennebec Log Driving Company. The buildings on the river side were Baxter's Furniture Shop and the Bennett house. Across the street from the left is the Hotel Howard, the livery stable, a blacksmith shop, the Tinkham and Tinkham General Store, C.C. Moore Meat Shop, and the post office. The postmaster was S.G. Tinkham.

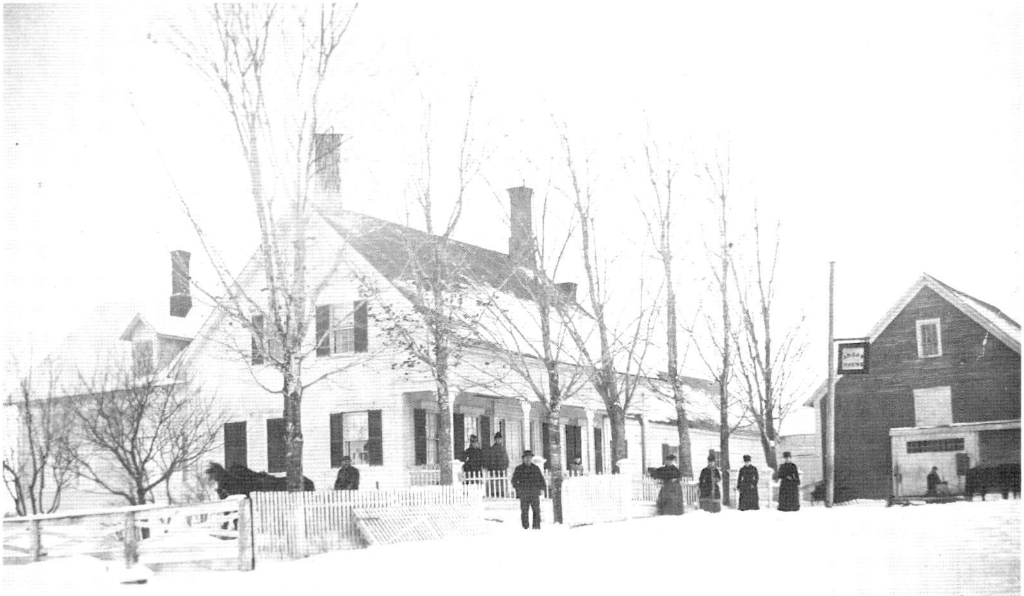

The first hotel in Anson, the Anson House, c. 1880. Its keeper was John Tinkham. The main house still exists and is the home of William and Jan Lynds.

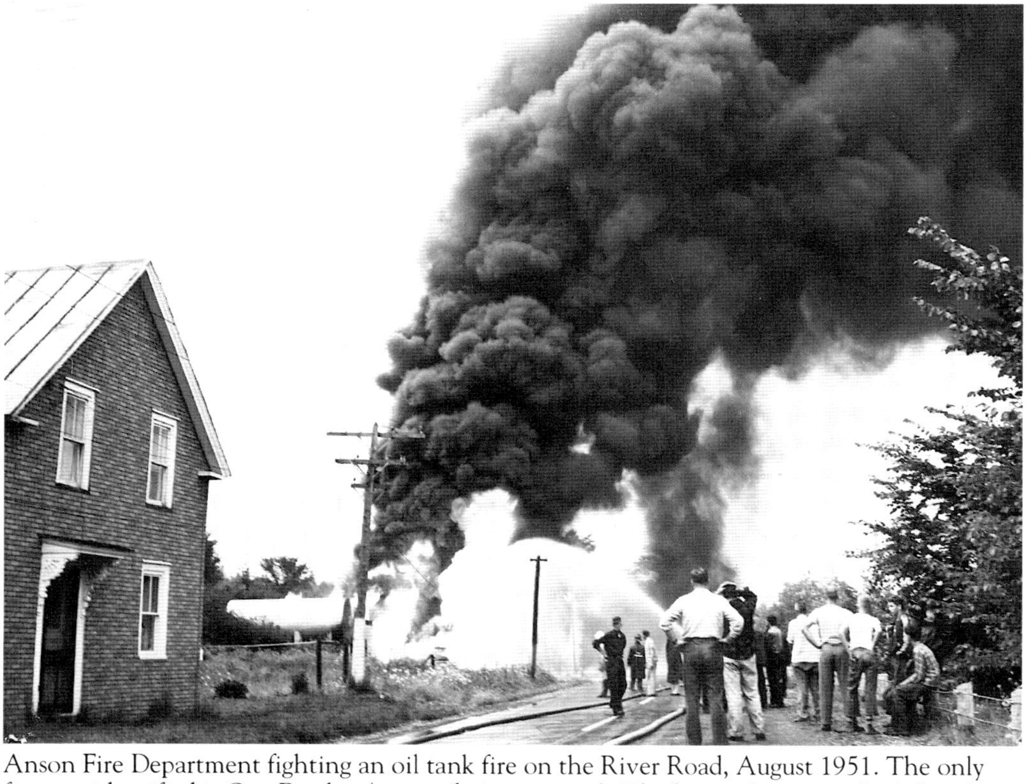

Anson Fire Department fighting an oil tank fire on the River Road, August 1951. The only fireman identified is Guy Dunlap (center facing camera). The house shown on the left is the former Kate Henry house.

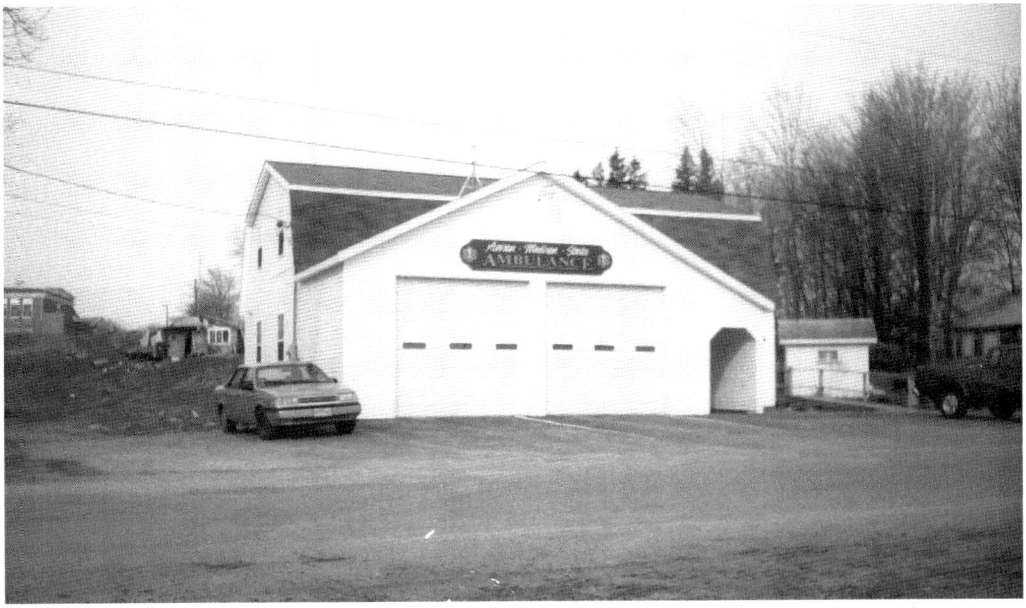

The Anson, Madison, Starks Ambulance service building erected in 1996 on Arnolds Lane. Organized in 1989 under Anson and Madison, it was originally housed in the old firehouse at the town hall. Starks joined them in 1992.

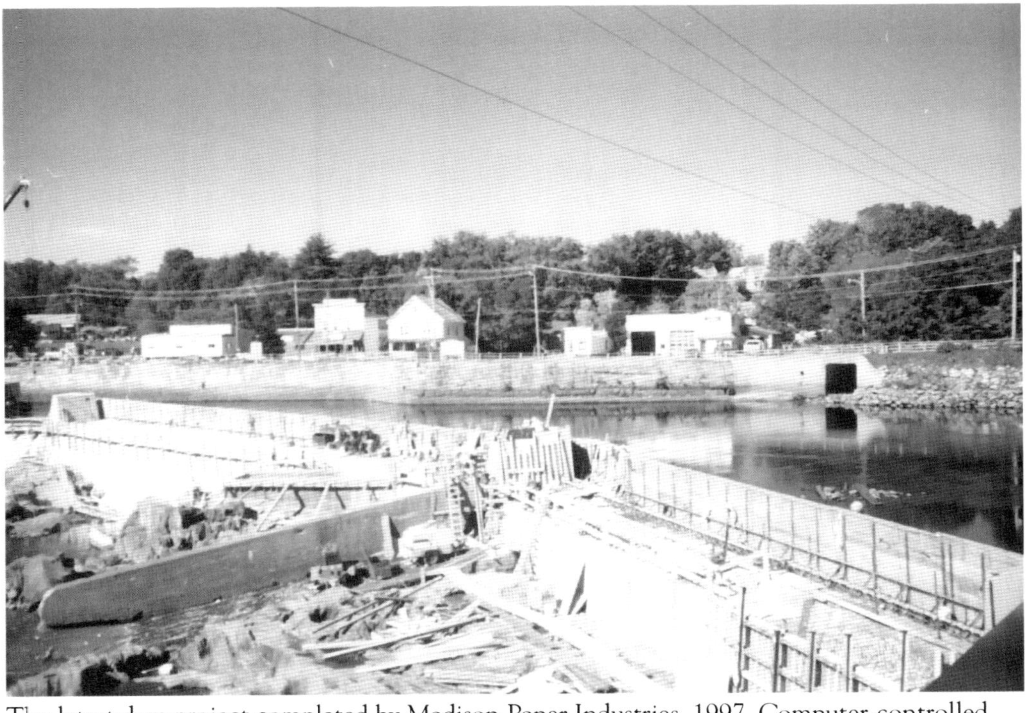

The latest dam project completed by Madison Paper Industries, 1997. Computer-controlled rubber bladders replaced the wooden splashboards.

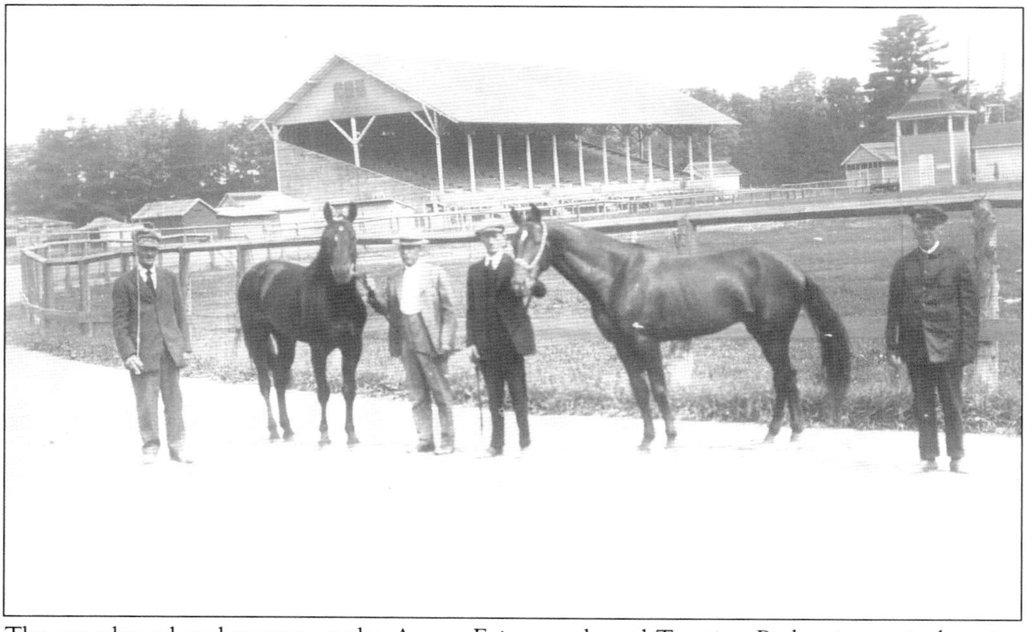

The grandstand and trotters at the Anson Fairgrounds and Trotting Park prior to its burning in 1936, located on Route 148, west of Anson Village. The following verse is from a poem depicting the "Good Old Anson Fair:" *When the horses get to scorin', And J. Withee mounts the stand, When the race is gettin' closer And the favorites sure to land, 'Tis some grand and glorious feelin', As the horses rip and tear, And your ticket wins the money, At the Good Old Anson Fair.*

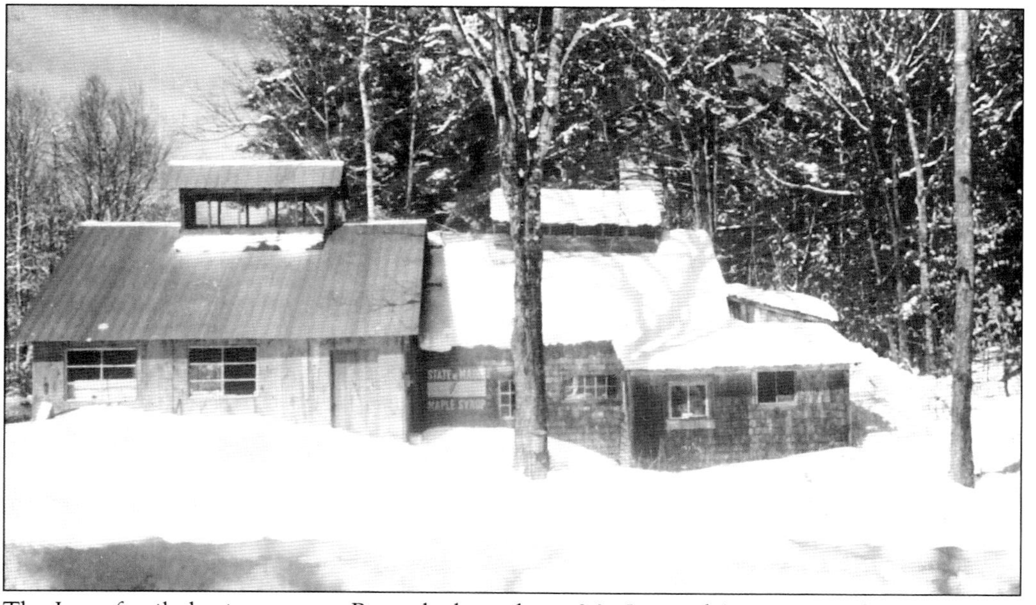

The Luce family business—sap. Records show that a Mr. Luce of Anson tapped 900 trees and made 100 gallons of syrup in six days in 1902. In 1915 Morrill Luce built the sap house that is still used today. His fourth son of five sons, Raymond, took over in 1947, and his ninth child of 11 children, Arnold P. Luce, lives on the farm with his family today and continues to run the sap business located on the West Mills Road.

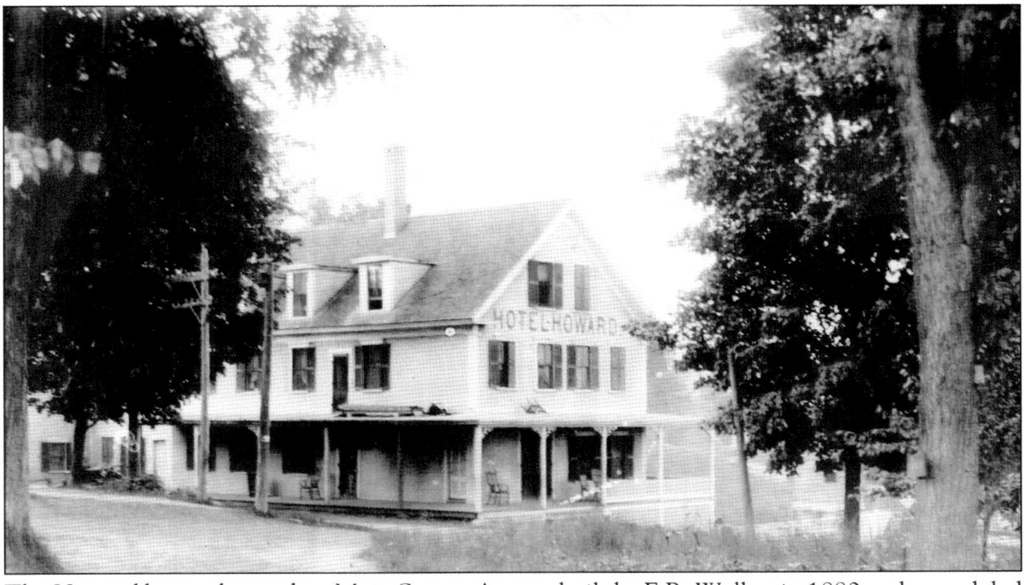

The Howard house, located on Main Street, Anson, built by E.R. Walker in 1880 and remodeled to become the Hotel Howard. A disastrous fire on November 11, 1910, burned the hotel, an adjoining house, a blacksmith shop, and a livery stable.

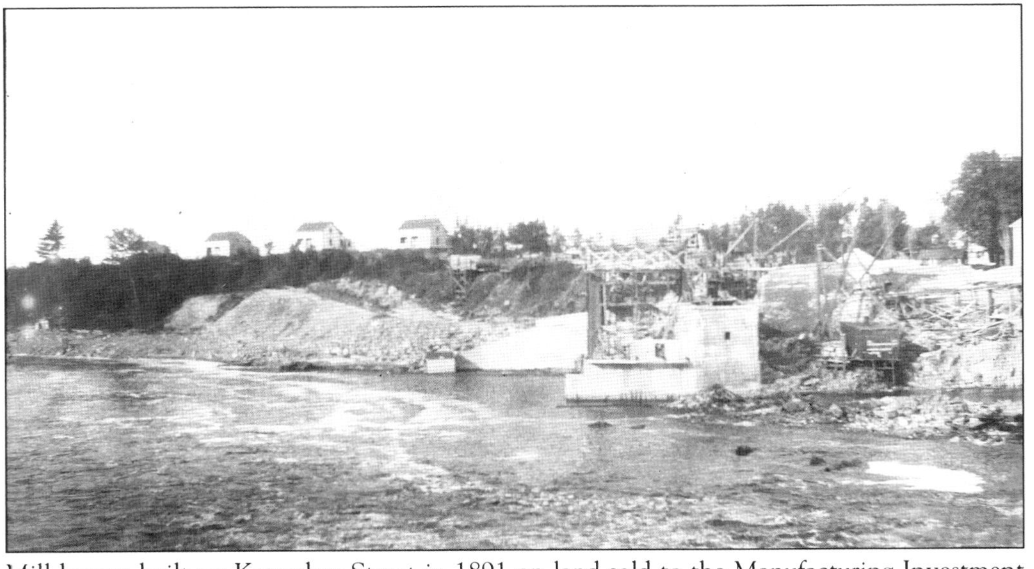

Mill houses built on Kennebec Street in 1891 on land sold to the Manufacturing Investment Co. to rent to their employees.

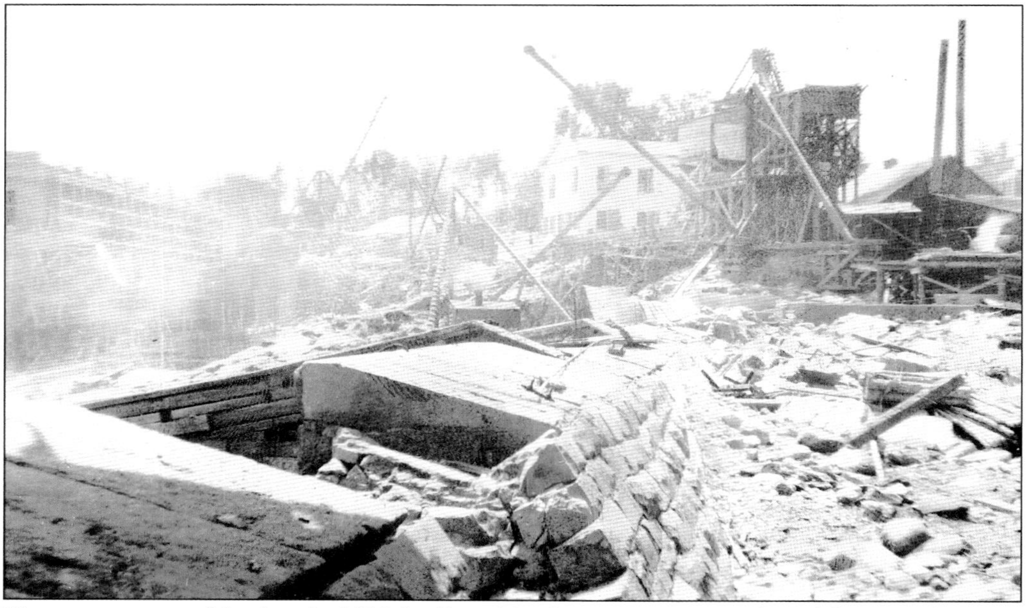

The construction of the dam. In 1899 the Great Northern Paper Co. purchased the Manufacturing Investment Co. of Madison and in 1923 began construction of a large powerhouse and dam on the Anson side. With sufficient water, all the power used at the mill was generated here.

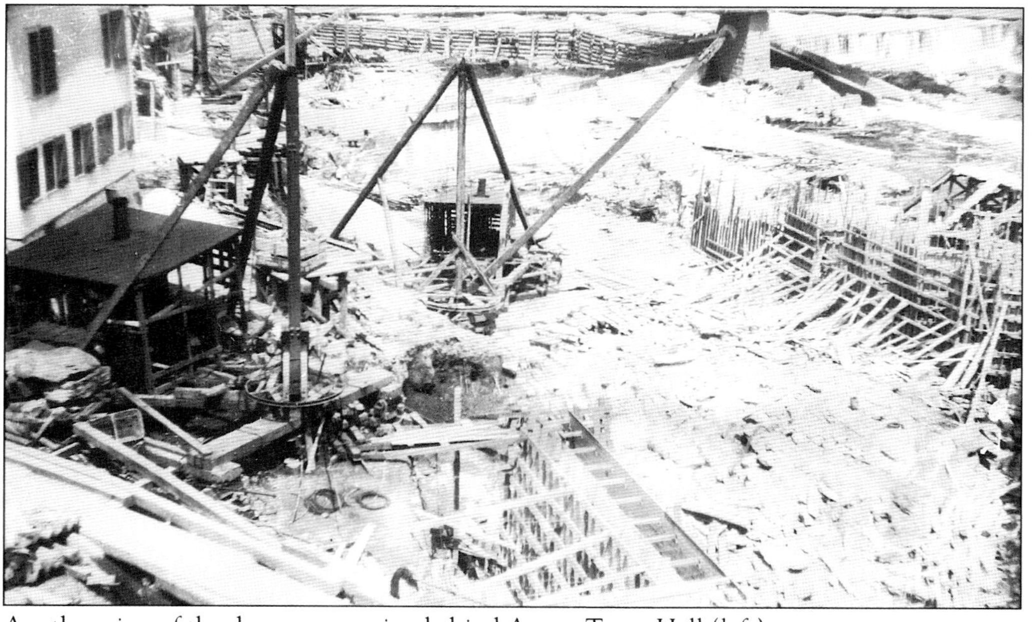

Another view of the dam construction behind Anson Town Hall (left).

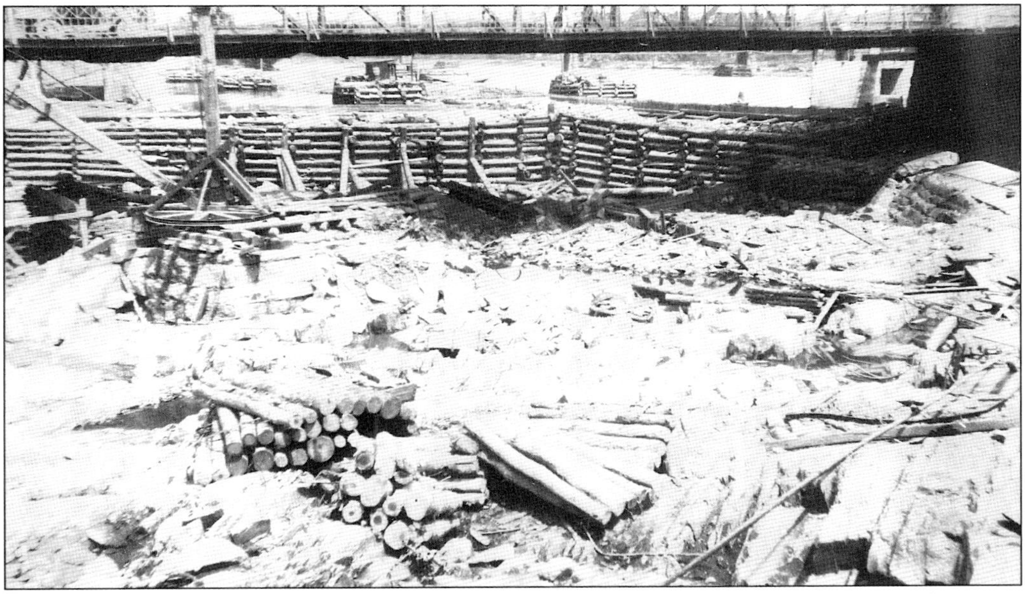

A 1923 view under the bridge showing construction of the dam. Note the piers in the river, many of which are still visible today.

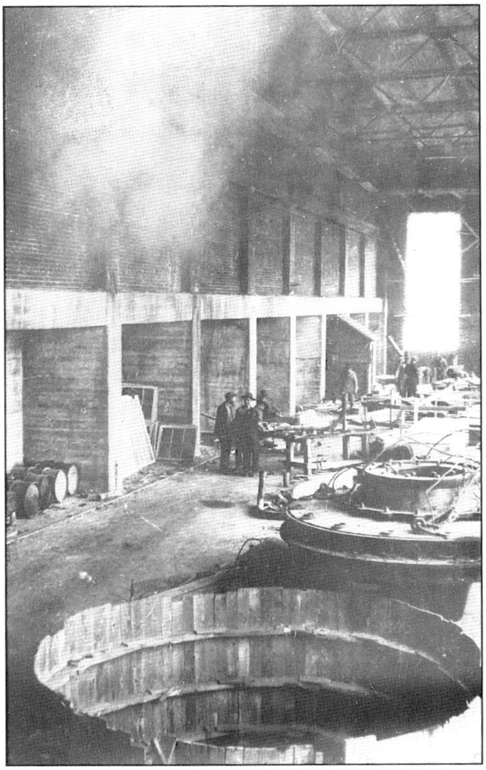

The 1,500-h.p. waterwheels under construction in 1923. These would eventually generate power for the Great Northern Paper Co.

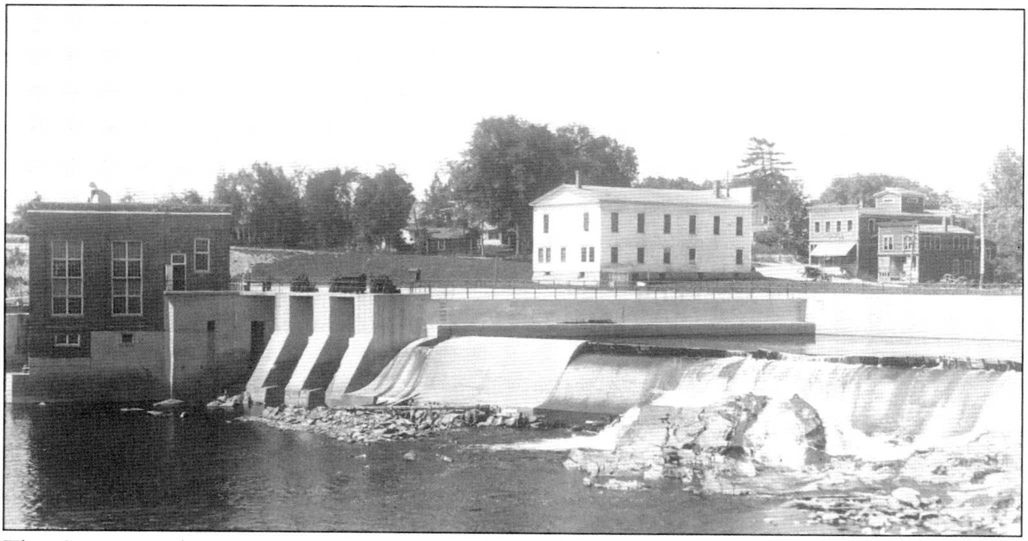

The Great Northern Paper Co. Power Station, completed in 1923. The town office and the Anson Fire Department were housed in the town hall. The Walter Rays General Store is on the right.

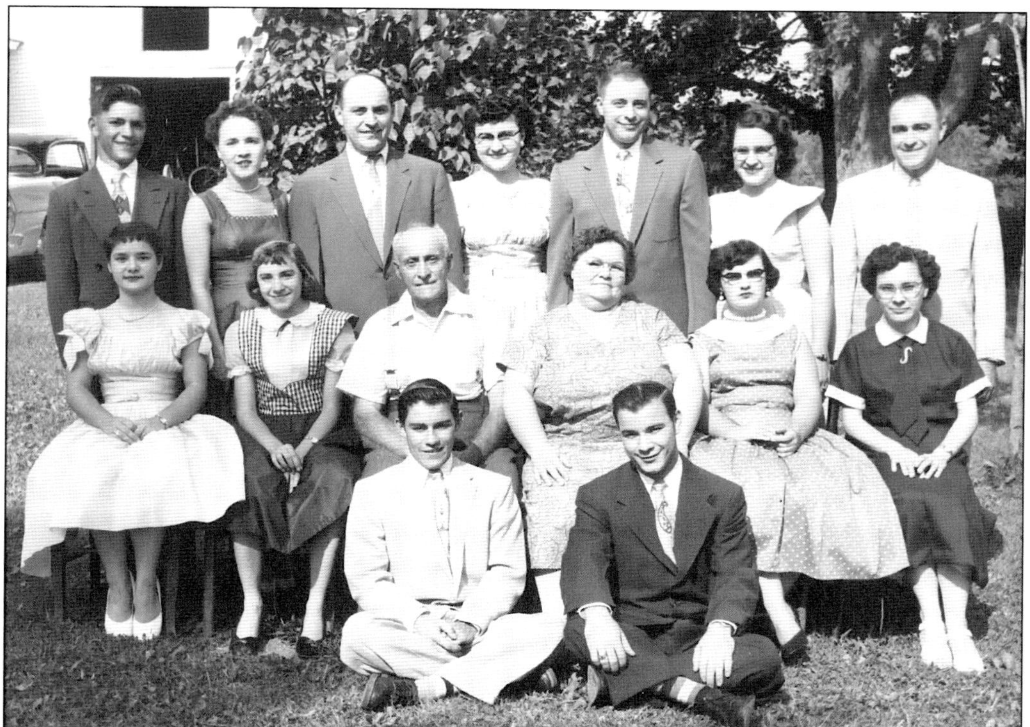

A 1960 photograph of the family of Jerry & Leana (Coron) Thebarge. The family moved in 1938 from Browns Hill in Anson to their present residence on Preble Avenue, Anson, the home of Eva Thebarge. From left to right, they are as follows: (front row) Edmund and Jeffrey (twins); (middle row) Florence, Evangeline, Jerry (father), Leana (mother), Grace, and Eva; (back row) Edwin, Lydia, Ernest, Lena, Walter, Evelyn, and Armond.

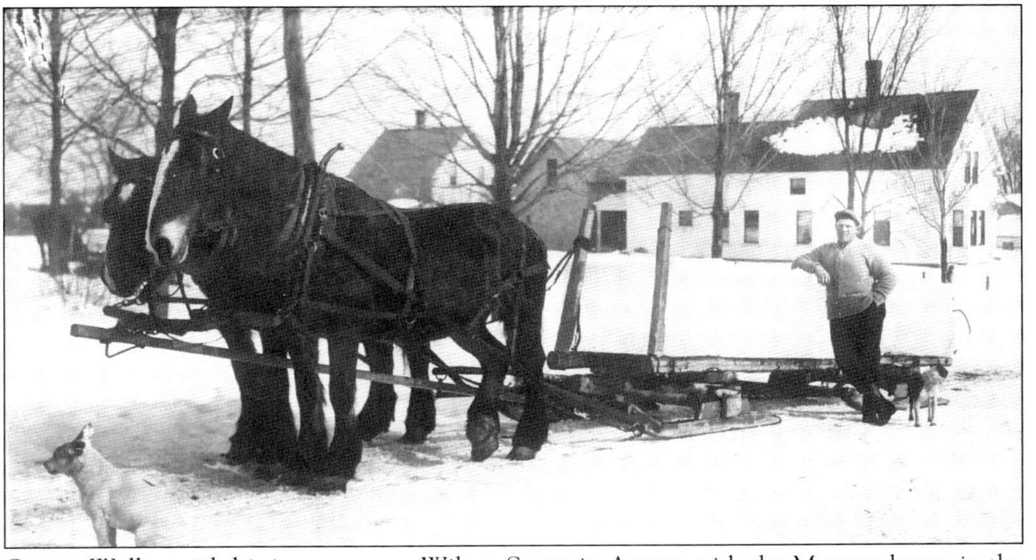

George Walker with his ice wagon on Wilson Street in Anson, with the Mungen house in the background, *c.* early 1930s. It later became Jacobs Store.

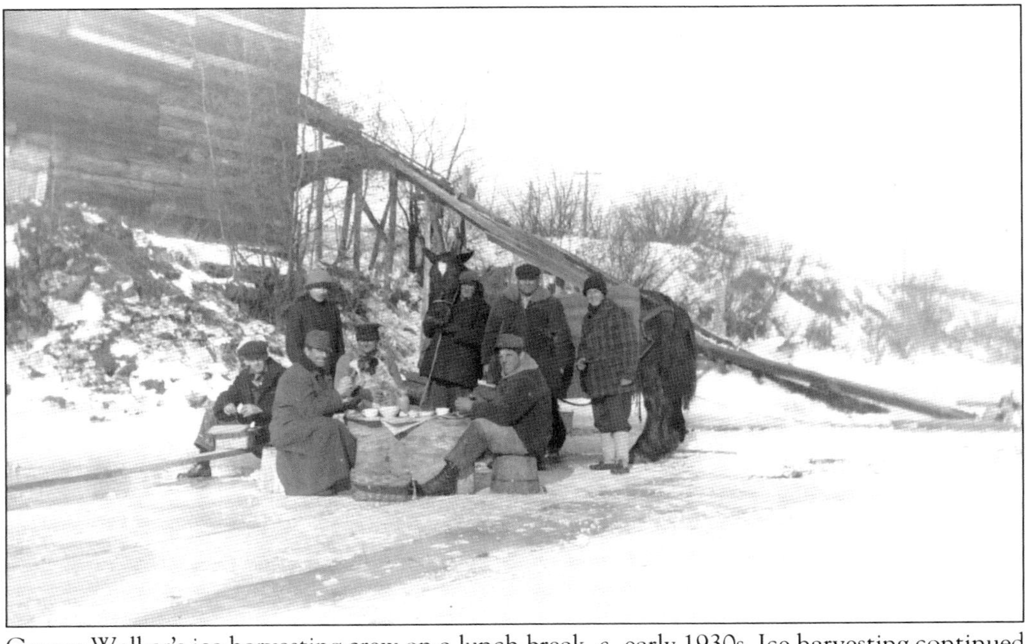

George Walker's ice harvesting crew on a lunch break, *c.* early 1930s. Ice harvesting continued through the early 1950s.

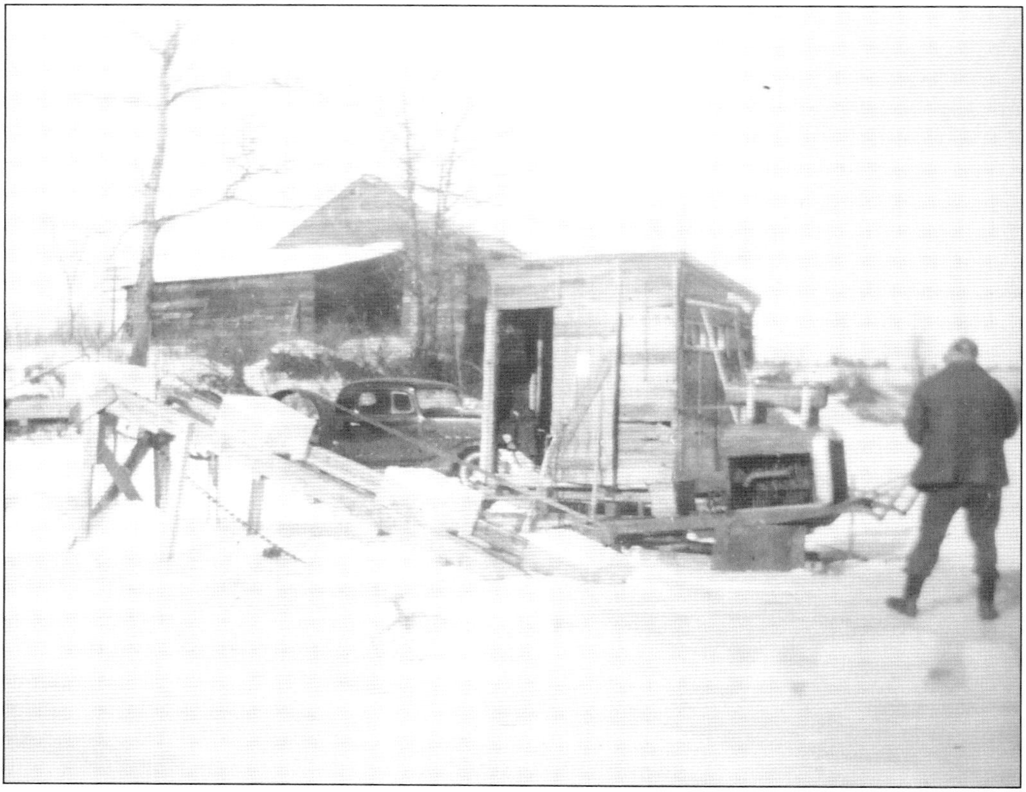

George Walker's ice harvesting machinery. This conveyor was used to load ice on the trucks or wagons.

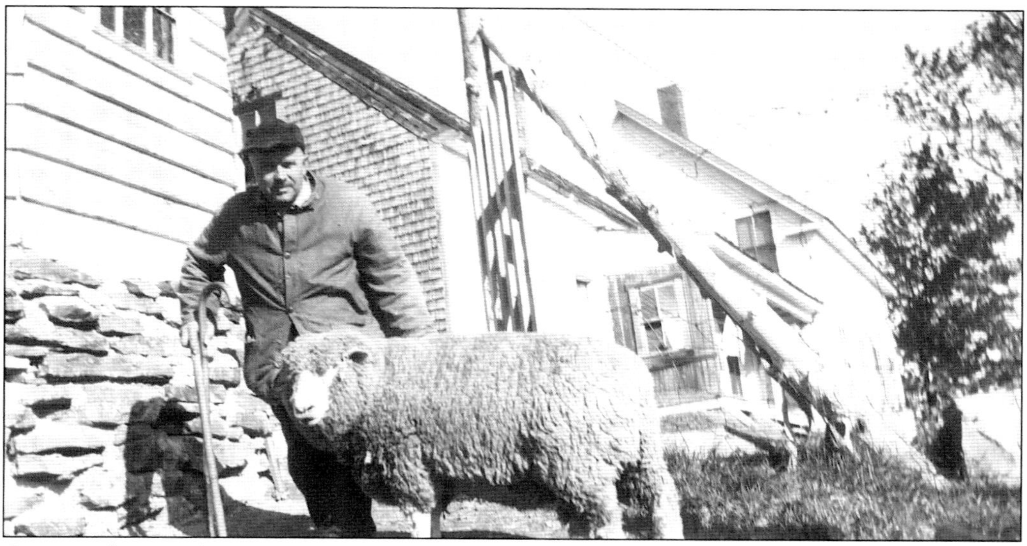

George Johnson of Anson with his Grand Champion Corriedale Ram in 1948. Mr. Johnson was a former selectman in Anson.

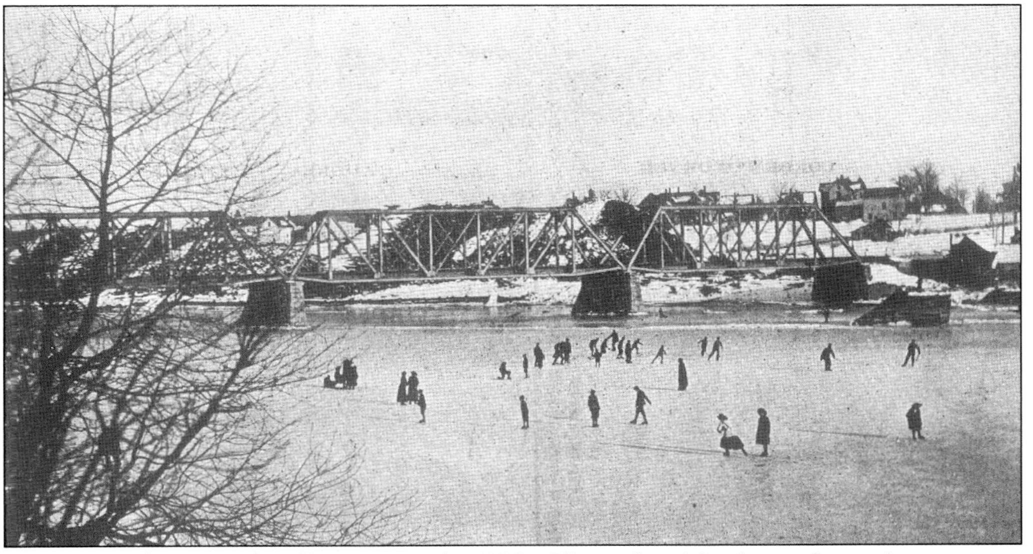

Skating on the Kennebec River, *c.* early 1900s. The railroad bridge is shown here as seen from Anson.

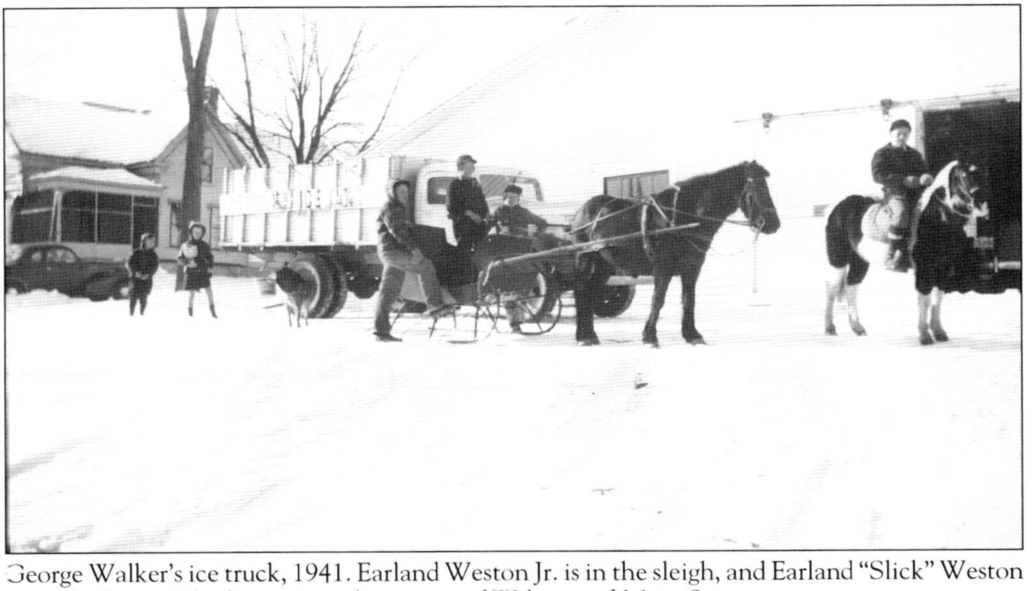

George Walker's ice truck, 1941. Earland Weston Jr. is in the sleigh, and Earland "Slick" Weston is on the horse. The house is at the corner of Wilson and Main Streets.

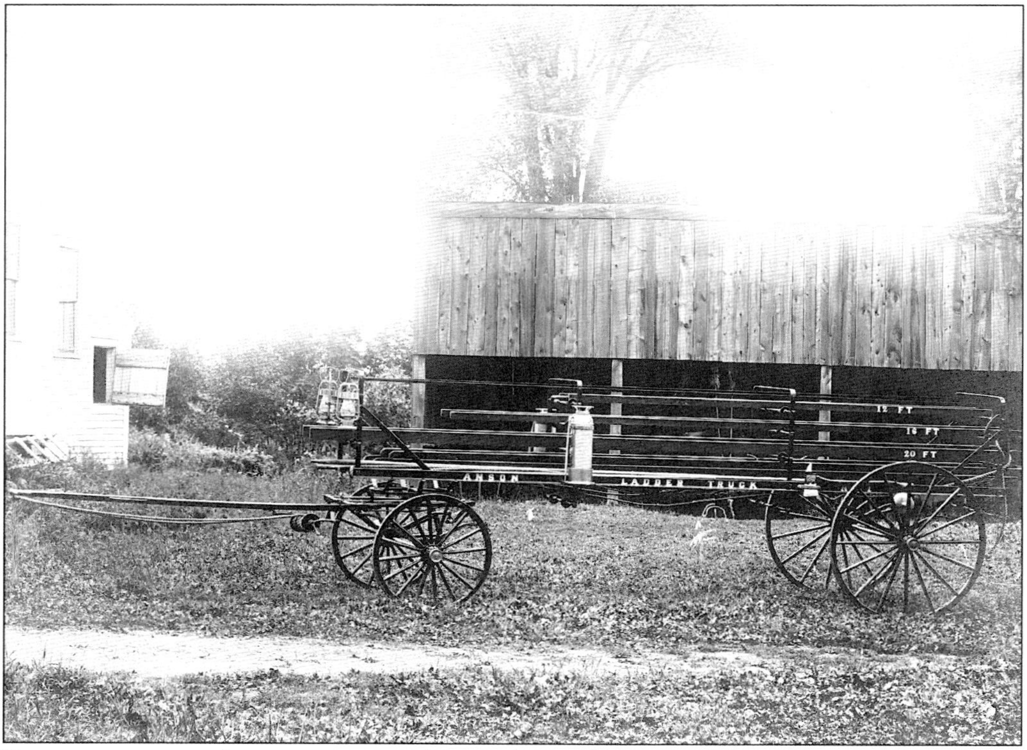

Fire equipment used prior to and with the chemical pumpers in 1907, probably until the purchase of a motorized fire truck. Firemen would line up on each side and run when the alarm rang. It must have required some organization to form a bucket brigade.

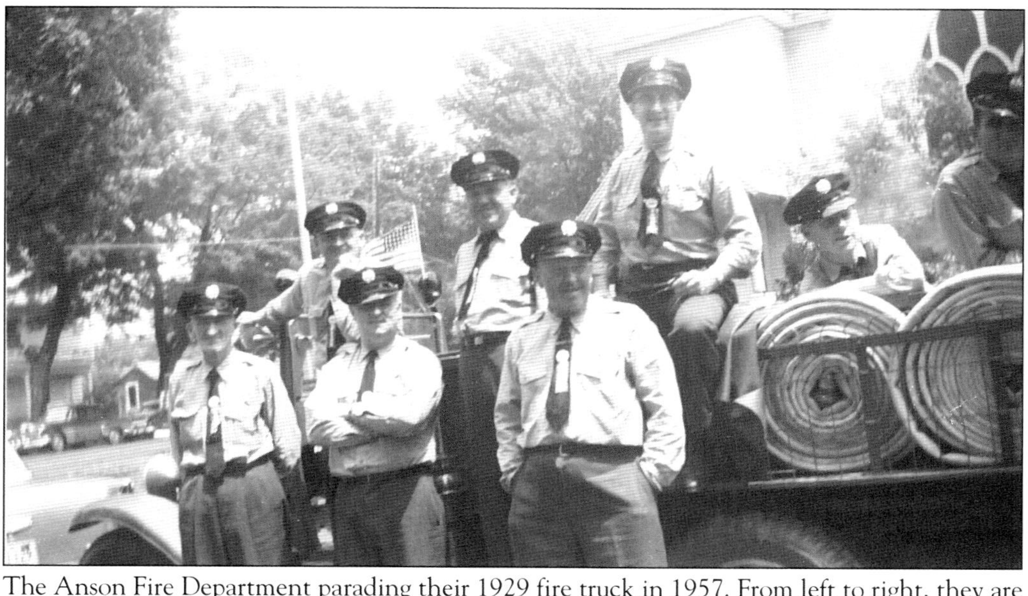

The Anson Fire Department parading their 1929 fire truck in 1957. From left to right, they are as follows: (front row) Wallace Moody, Leon Young, and Charles Conners; (back row) Charles MacDonald, Charles Petley, Elwood Bearor, Raymond Barron, and Harold "Dud" Bragg.

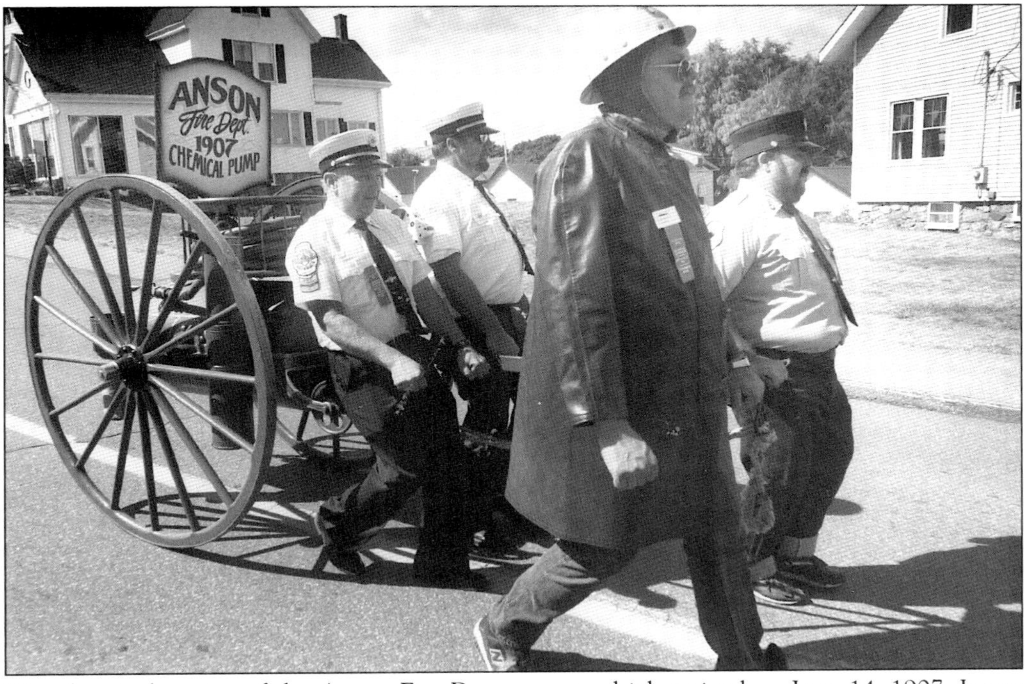

The chemical engine of the Anson Fire Department, which arrived on June 14, 1907. It was often proudly paraded in many area towns. Shown here are Terry Petley, Jody Manzer, David Hayward, and Peter Paine (in rain gear).

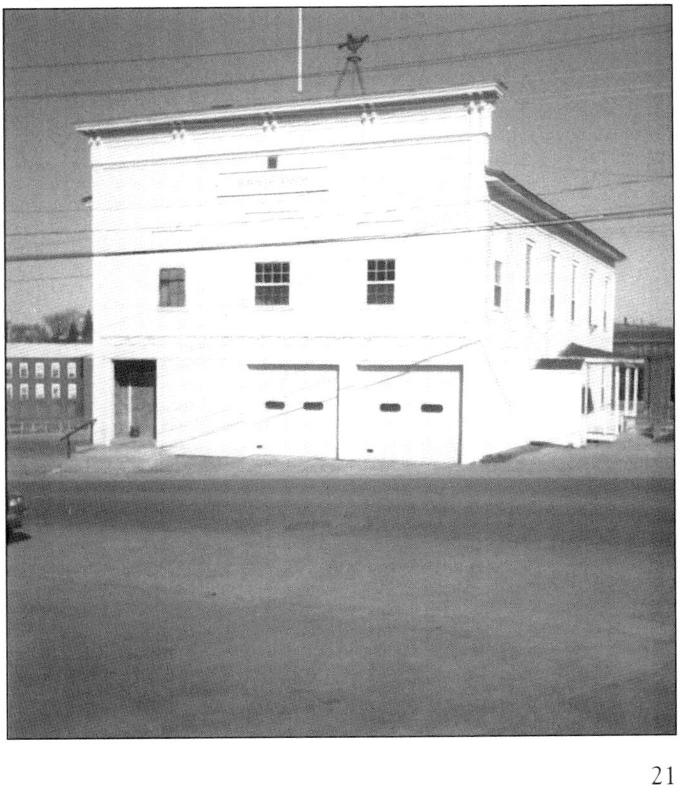

The new town hall, erected in 1918. The first town hall in Anson, built in 1910 and destroyed by fire in 1917, was located on Wilson Street. The new structure has served the community well, housing the town office, the old firehouse, the ambulance, meeting place, and supply room of the Sunshine Society. The second-floor hall has been a well-used gathering place for many occasions, and was even used as a basketball court for the elementary schools.

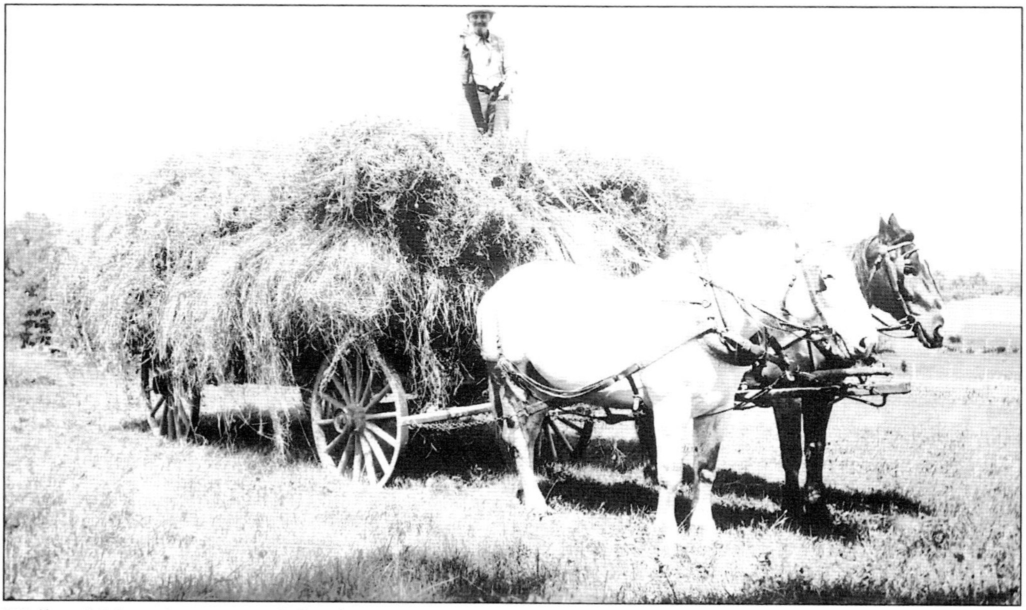

Wilbur Hilton haying with his horses, *c.* 1930.

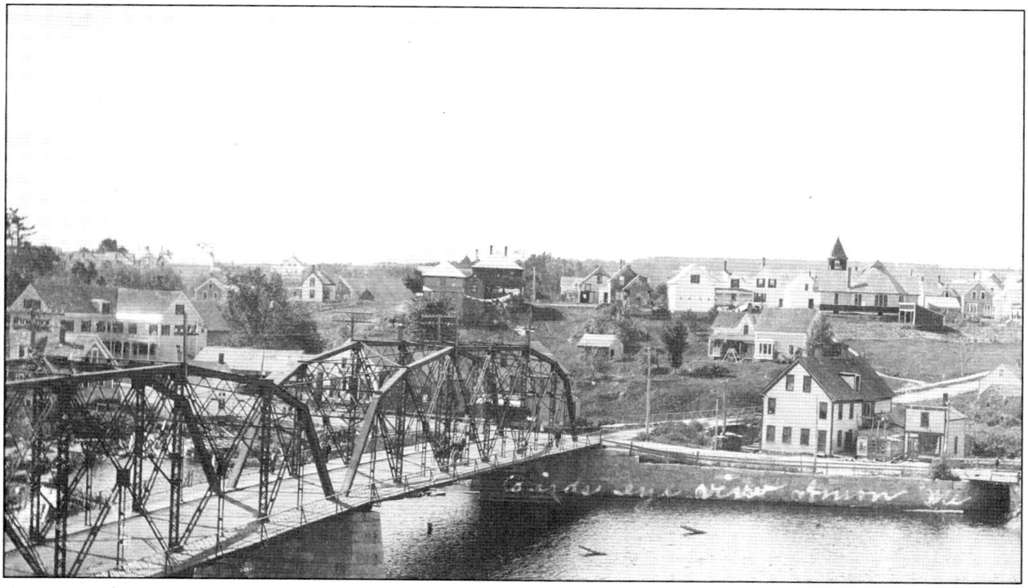

A view of Anson taken from Madison soon after the building of the iron bridge in 1903. A celebration on July 4, 1903, commemorated the new iron bridge across the Kennebec with a mile-long parade, three bands, 52 floats, and 99 horses, accompanied by 320 people. There was an estimated 8,000 to 10,000 people in the crowd.

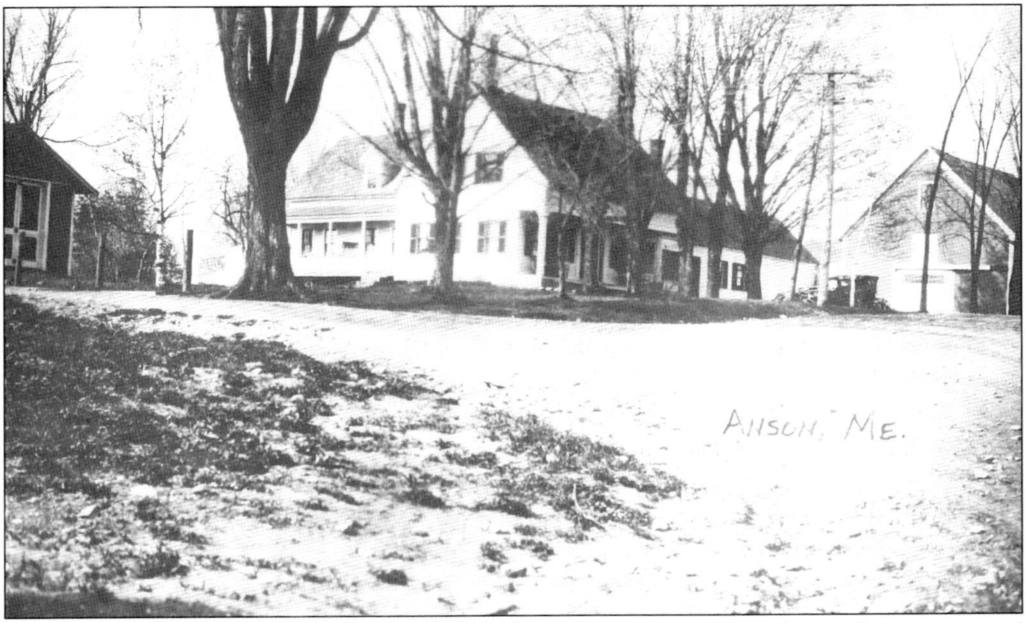

The former Tinkham house, built prior to 1885, later the Somerset Greenhouse. It is now owned by William and Jan Lynds. The Anson Post Office now stands in place of the barn.

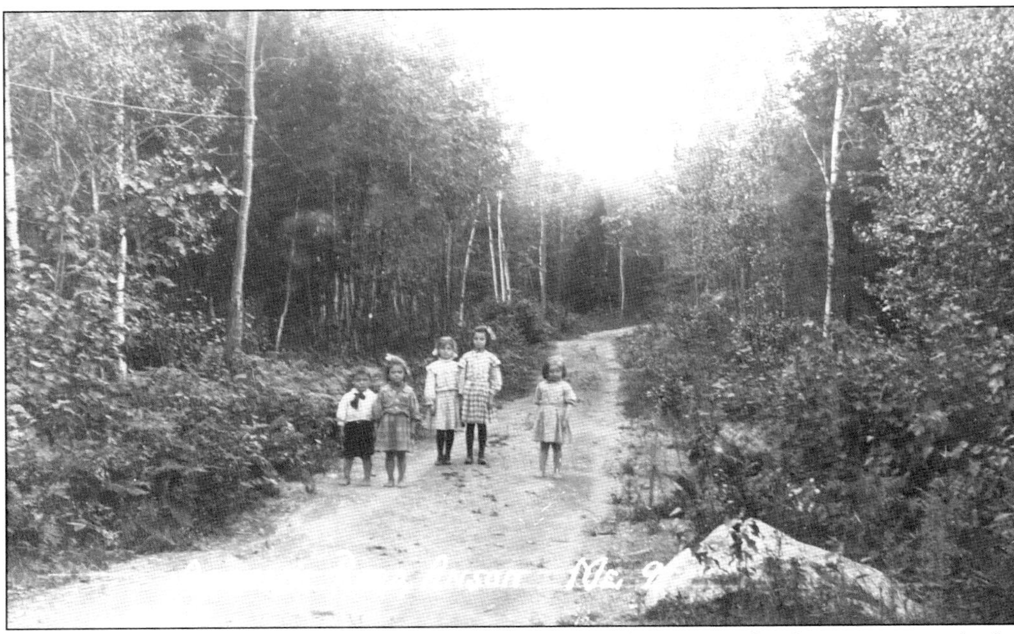

Arnolds Lane prior to the building of mill houses, c. early 1900s. This lane was named after Benedict Arnold. The rock in the picture is now labeled as a memorial to Arnold.

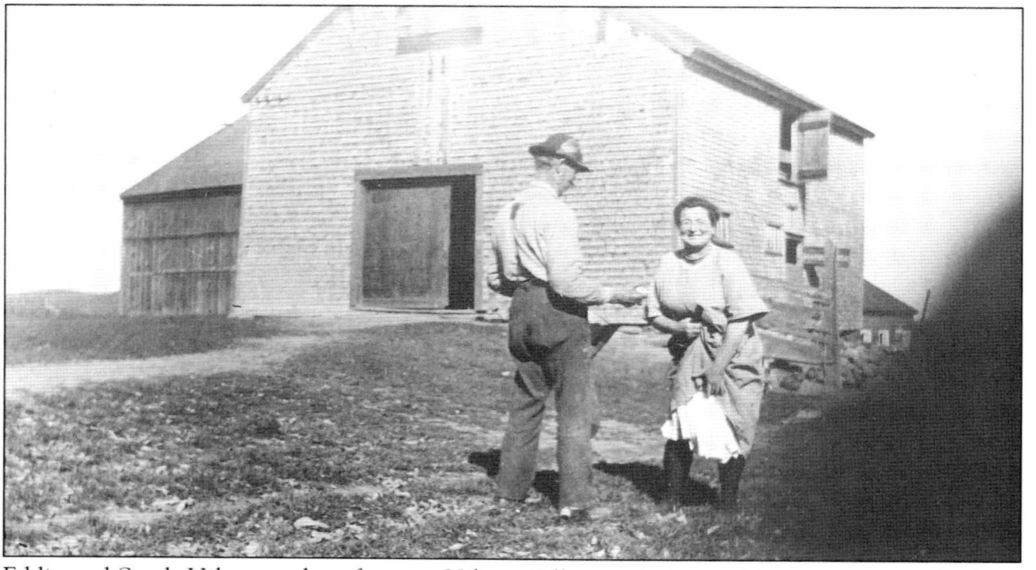

Eddie and Sarah Hilton at their farm on Hilton Hill, *c.* early 1900s. The notation on the back of the picture says, "Sarah has her dress full of eggs. Isn't this a cute picture?"

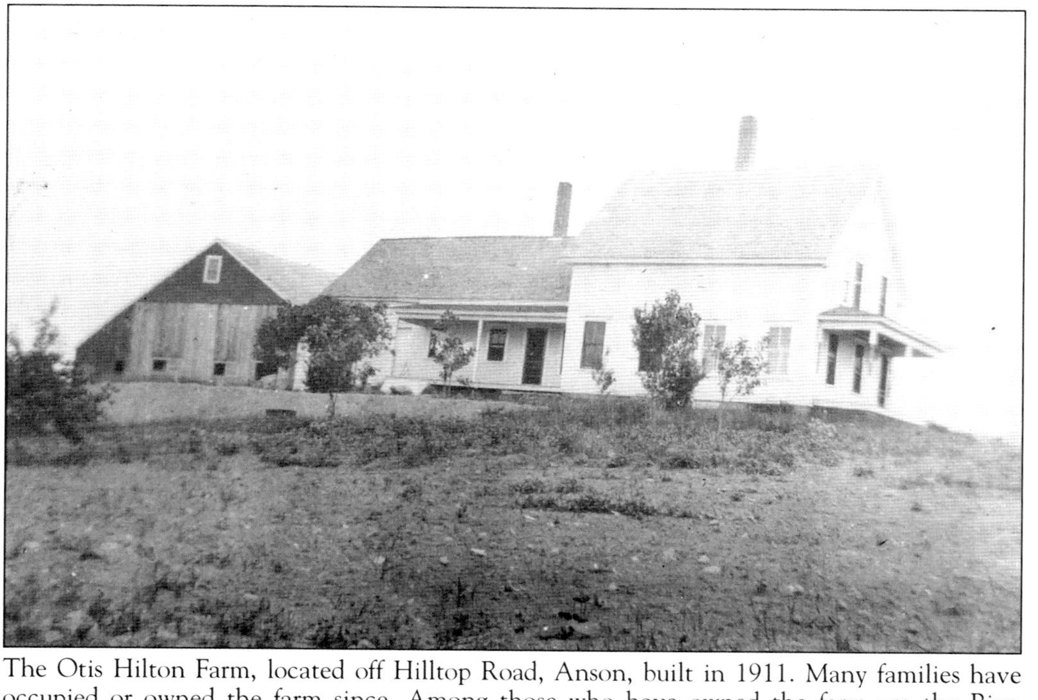

The Otis Hilton Farm, located off Hilltop Road, Anson, built in 1911. Many families have occupied or owned the farm since. Among those who have owned the farm are the Bion Pipers, George Johnson, and Dexter Higgins. It is currently owned by Eric and Mary Ann Berjeron-Fancy.

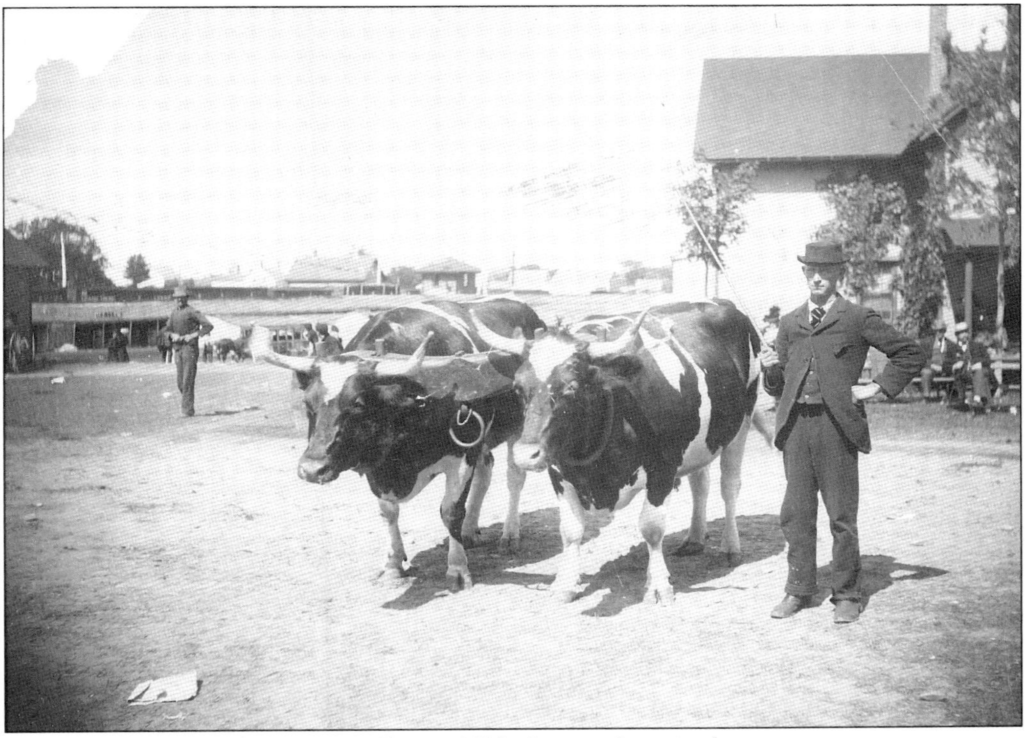

Edward A. Hilton at the Lewiston Fair in 1907, showing his prized steer.

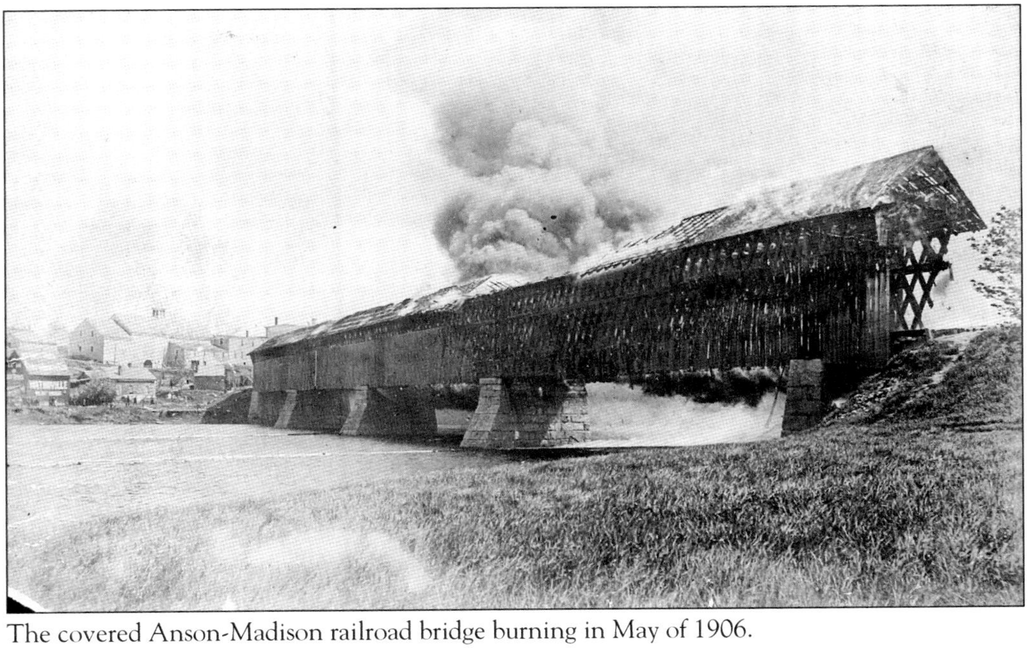

The covered Anson-Madison railroad bridge burning in May of 1906.

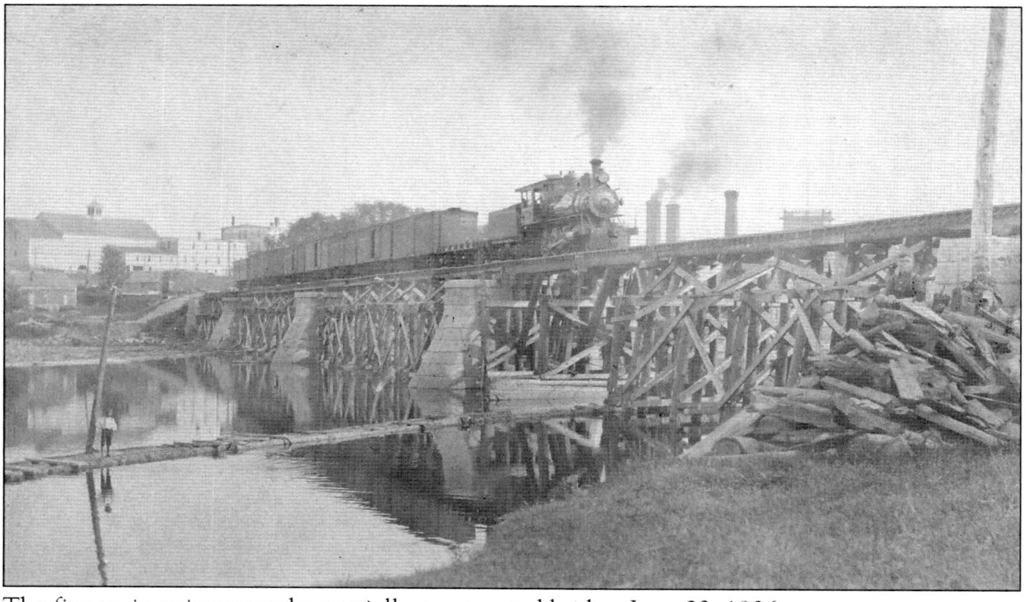

The first train going over the partially constructed bridge, June 23, 1906.

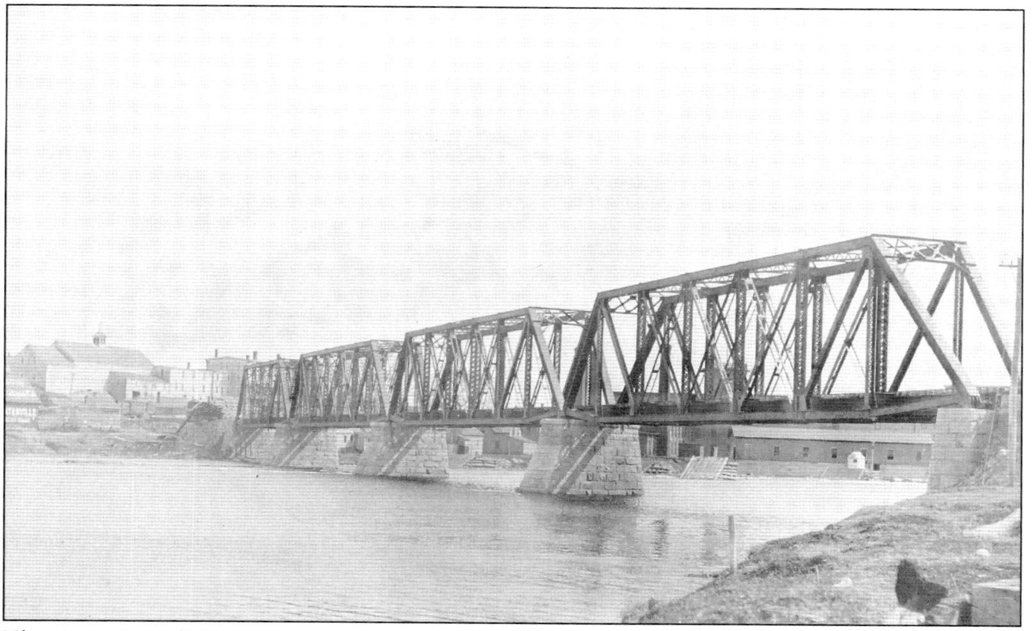

The Anson-Madison railroad bridge completed, c. 1906.

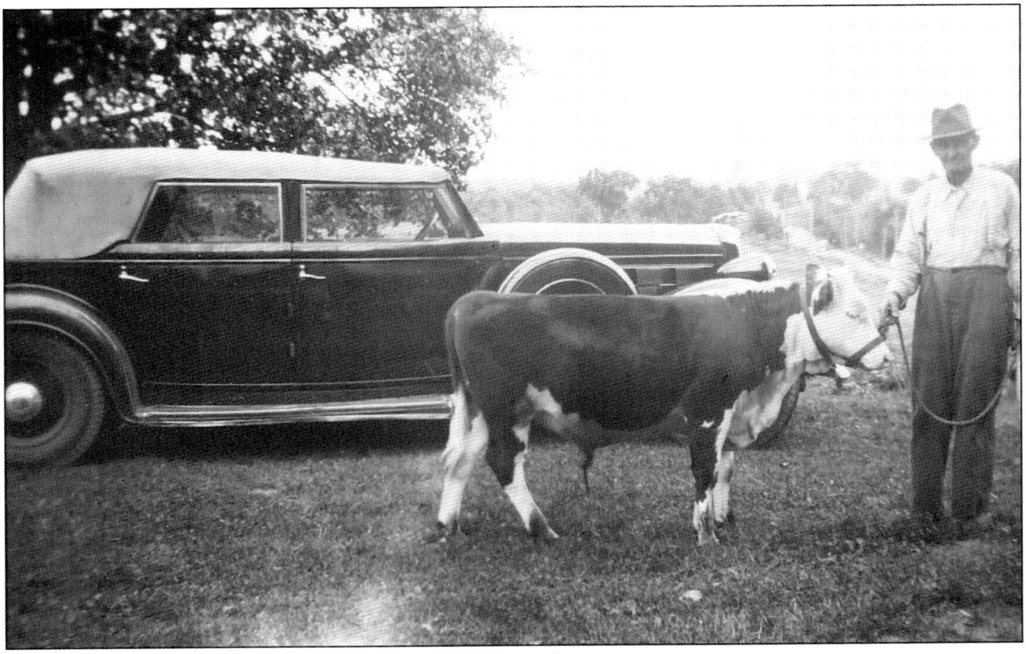

Wilbur Hilton, his prized steer, and his 1937 Lincoln car.

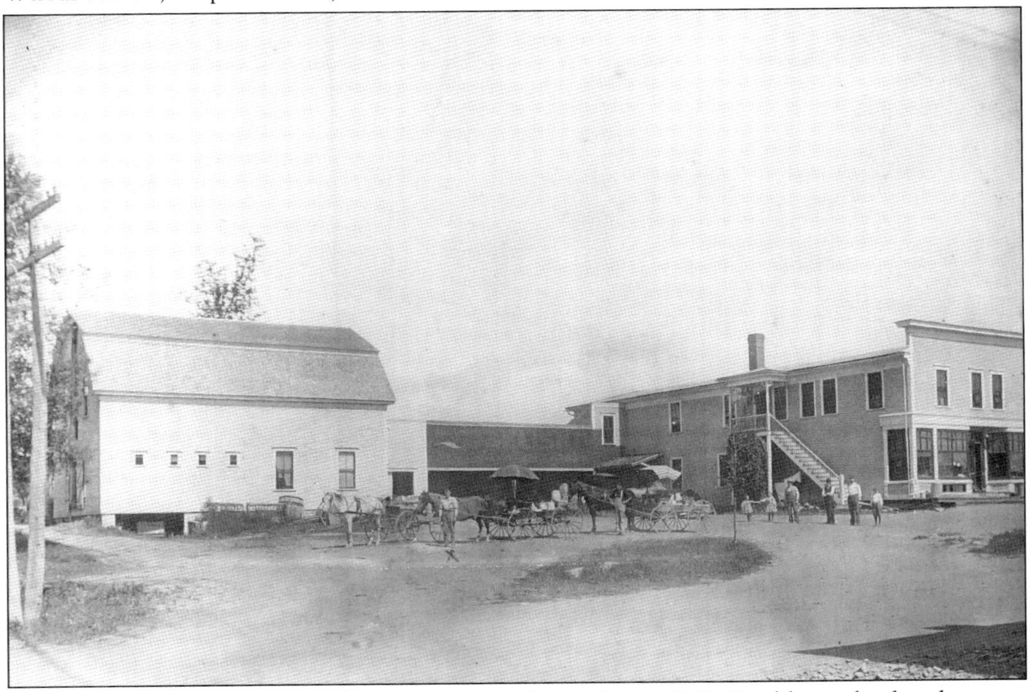

The R.E. Gould Store & Barn, located on upper Main Street. R.E. Gould was the fourth owner of the store, purchasing it in 1920 from A.B. Willis. The first owner, James Norton, built the store in 1900; the second owner was R.B. Norton. Shown here, from left to right, are: Percy (Bob) Norton, Arthur Oliver, J.M. Norton, R.B. Norton, Bertha Norton, Beryl ?, Gladys Norton, Frank Oliver, and Carl Baxter. The structure was destroyed by fire in 1945.

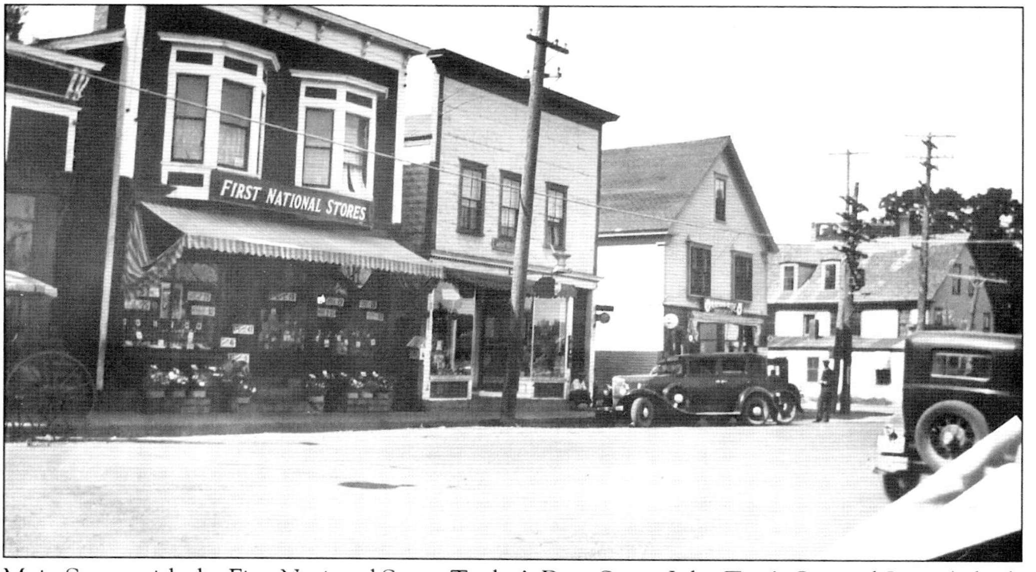

Main Street with the First National Store, Taylor's Drug Store, John Tarr's General Store (which housed the post office), Guy Fowke's Barbershop, and Scott Fletcher's Gas Station, *c.* 1936.

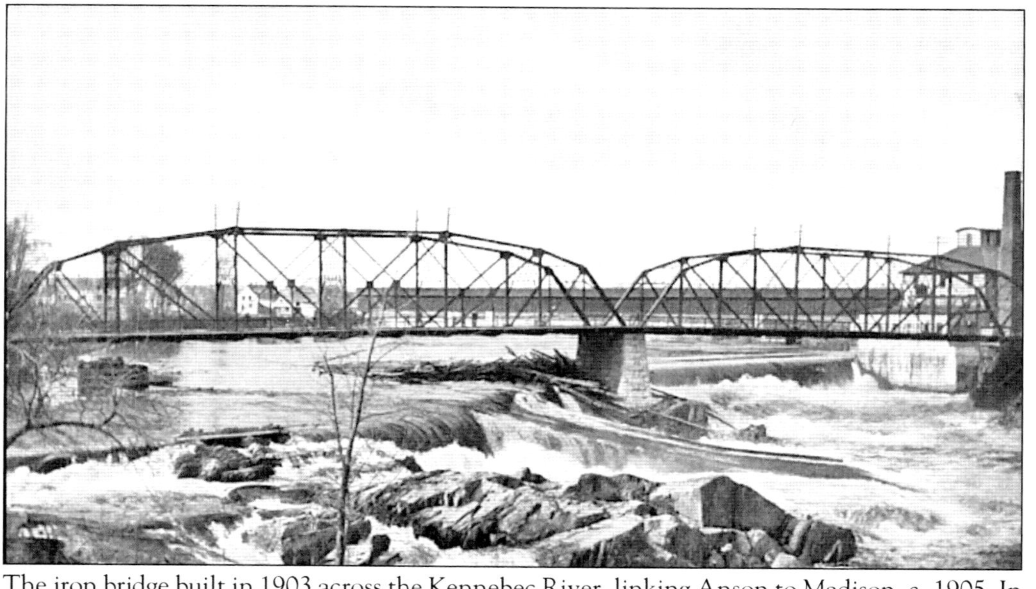

The iron bridge built in 1903 across the Kennebec River, linking Anson to Madison, *c.* 1905. In the background is the covered railroad bridge. To the right is the woolen mill.

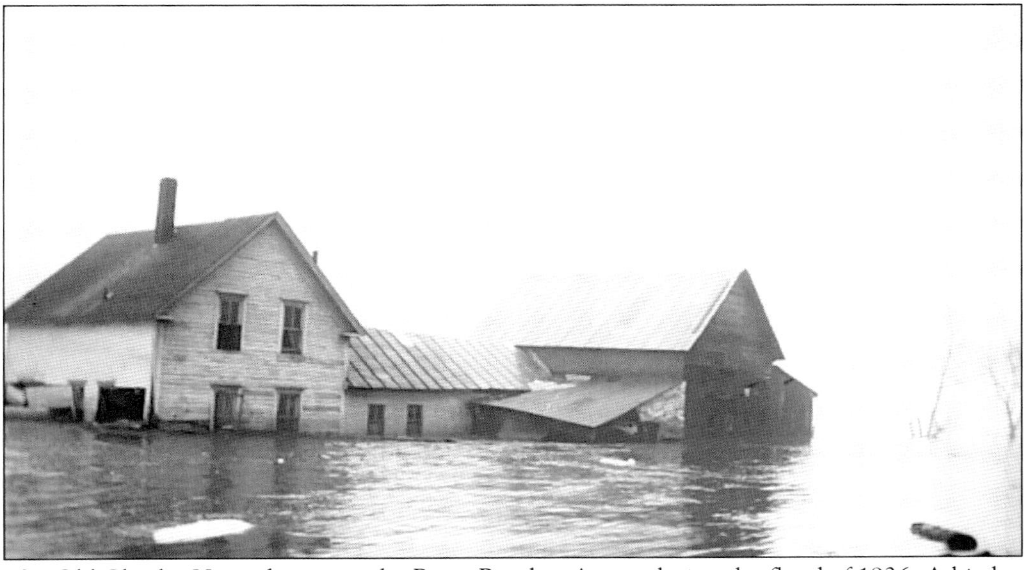

The Old Charles Henry house on the River Road in Anson during the flood of 1936. A big log and ice cakes went through the house.

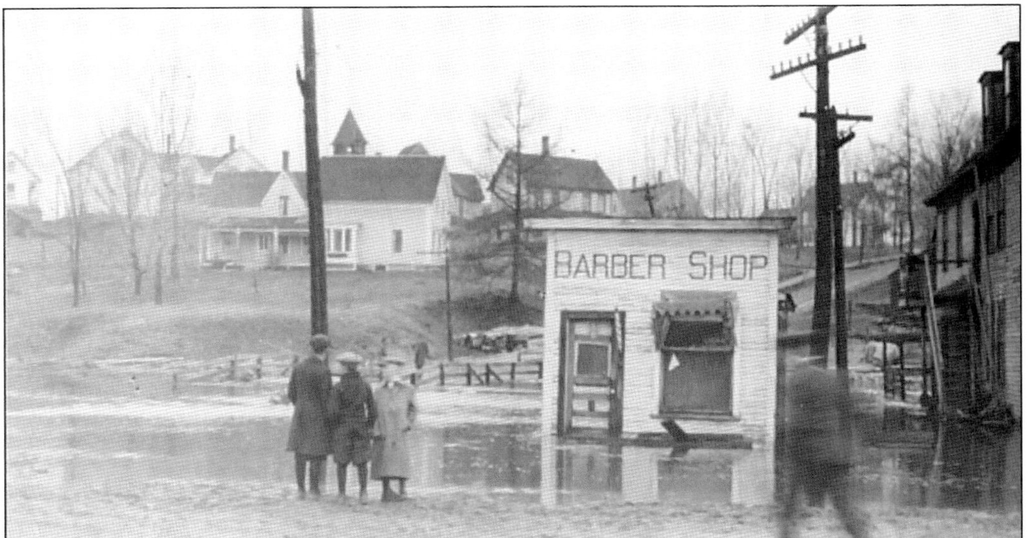

Guy Fowke's Barber Shop during 1936 flood. In the background to the left of the barber shop is the house built by Thomas H. Spear. The telegraph office was in the back room of the house.

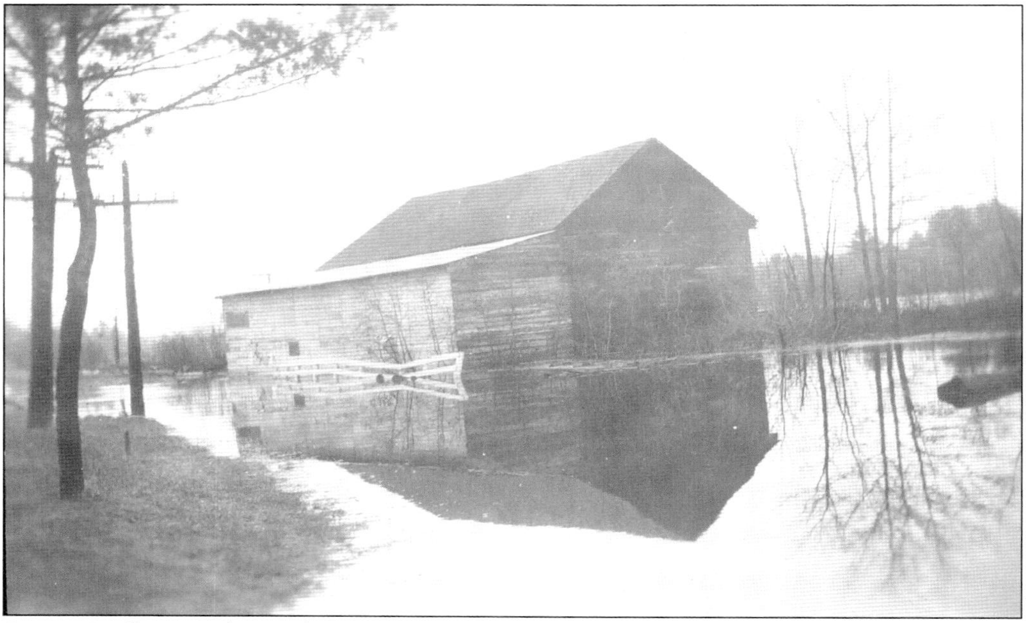

George Walker's ice house during the flood of 1936, located on Route 201, opposite the Camp Ground Road.

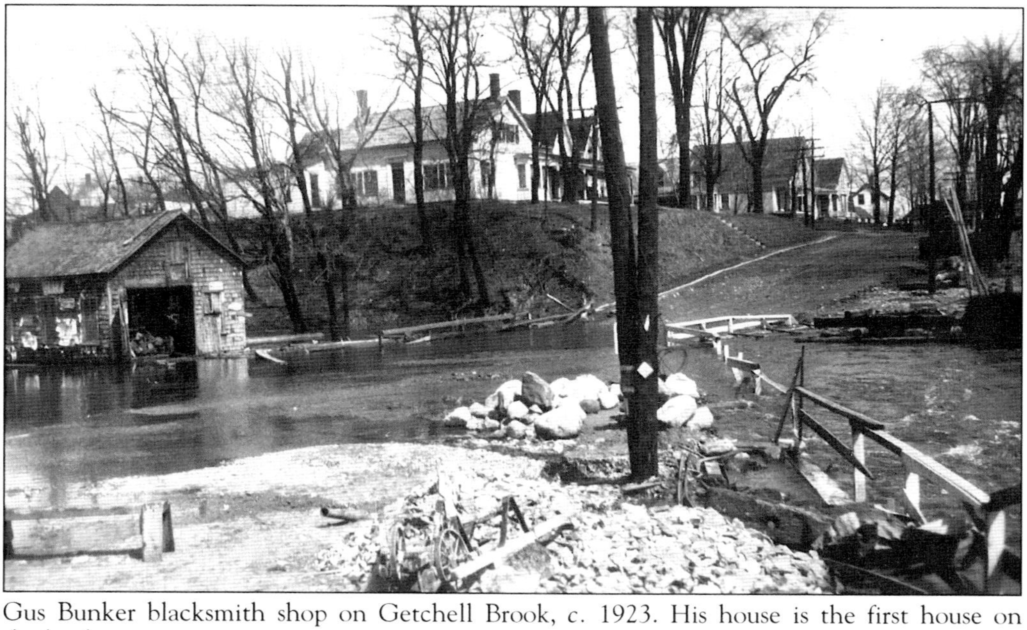

Gus Bunker blacksmith shop on Getchell Brook, *c.* 1923. His house is the first house on the bank.

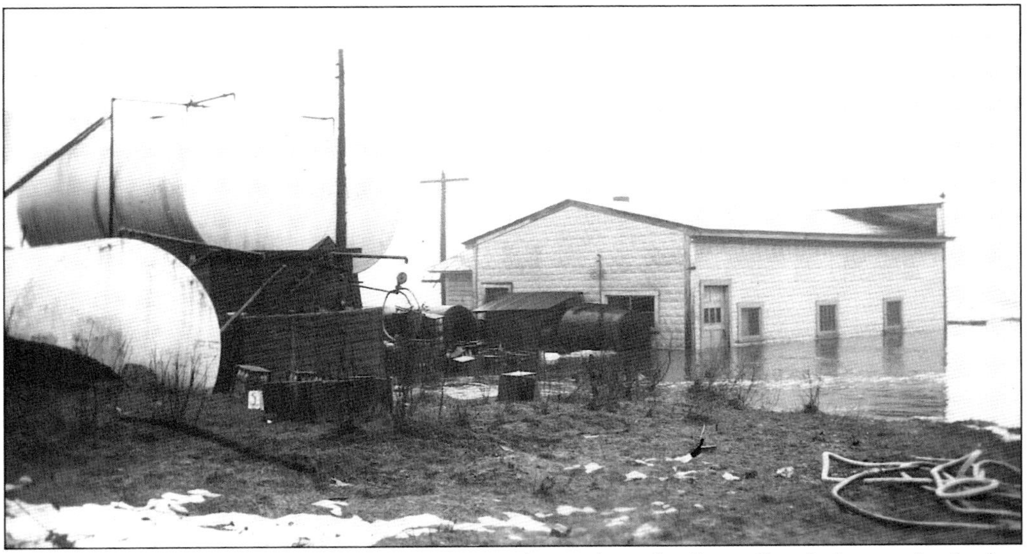
The Nevins and Goodwin Garage, at one time located on the River Road, during the freshet of 1936.

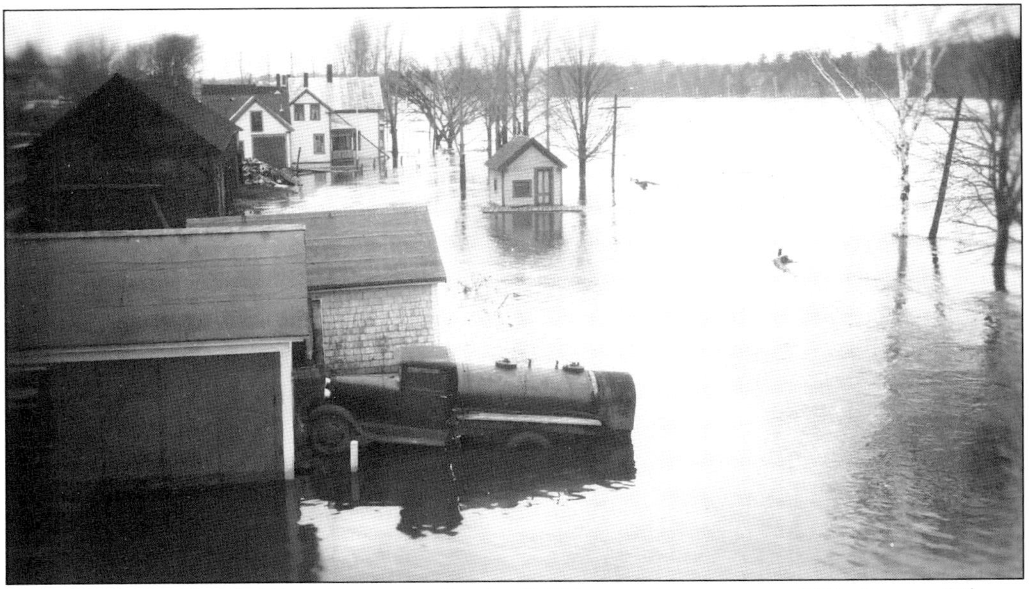
Hilton's Coal and Oil Office during the flood of 1936, now the property of J.R. Owens Oil.

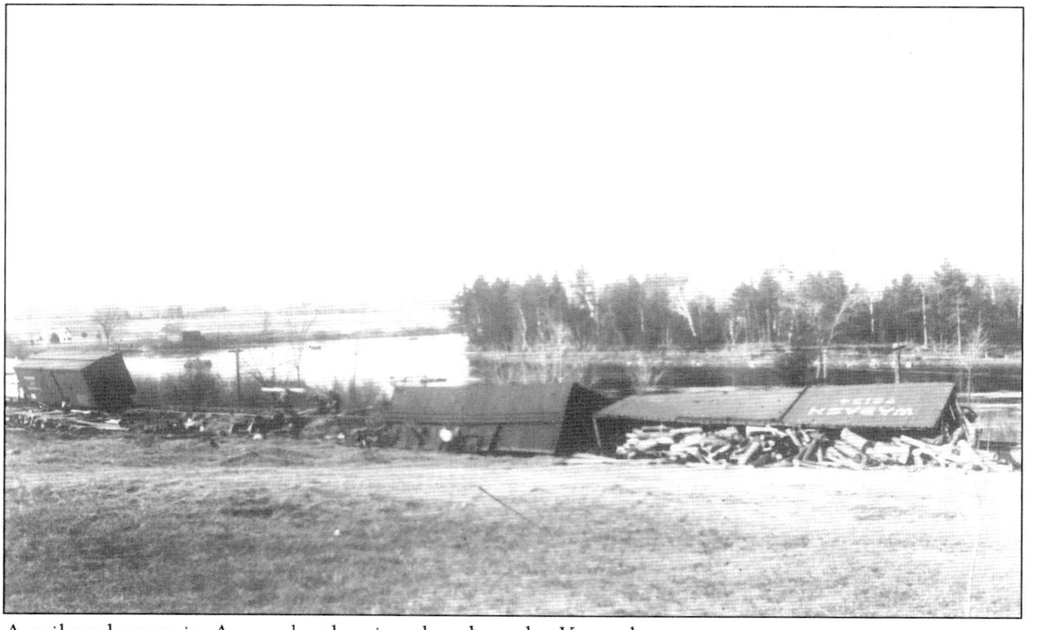

A railroad upset in Anson by the river bend on the Kennebec.

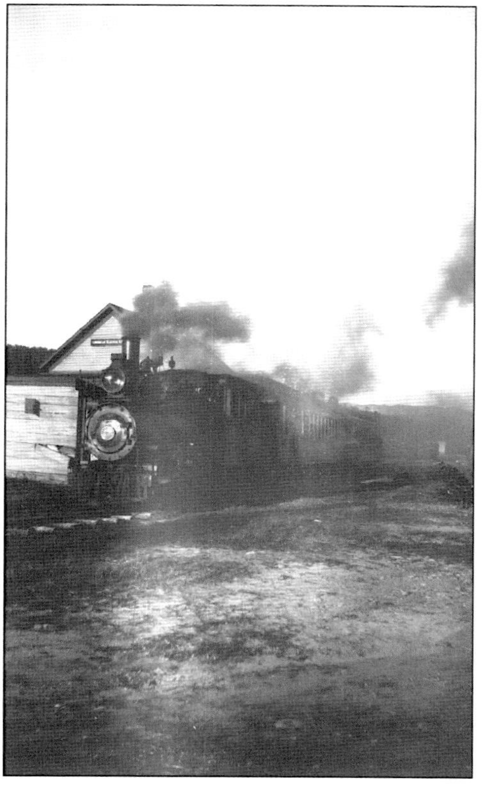

A Somerset Railroad steam locomotive in Anson, c. 1910.

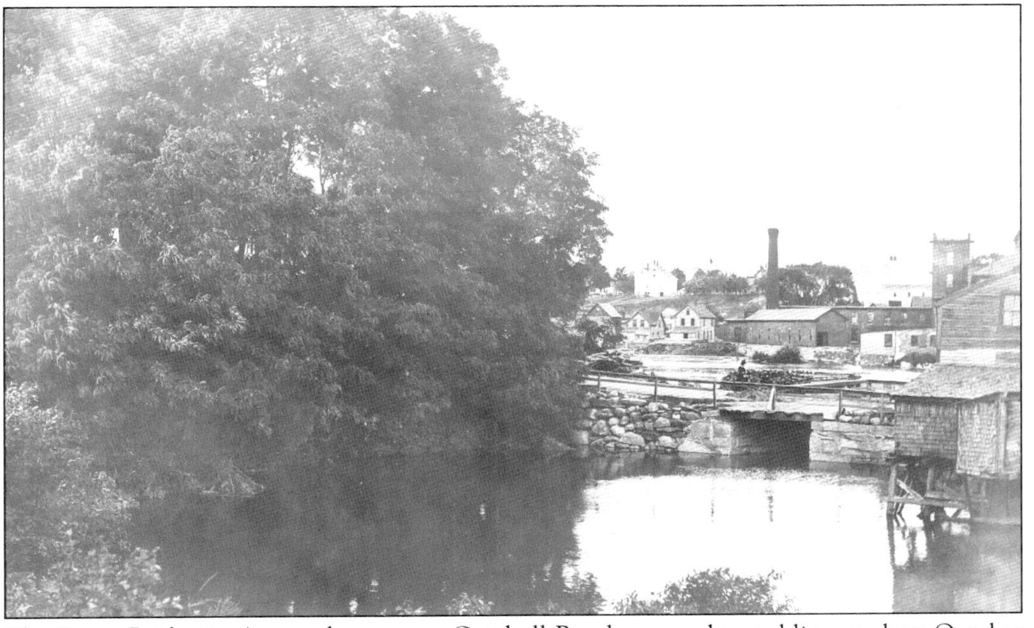

The Stone Bridge in Anson that crosses Getchell Brook, opened to public travel on October 16, 1900. It was also known as Metcalf Bridge.

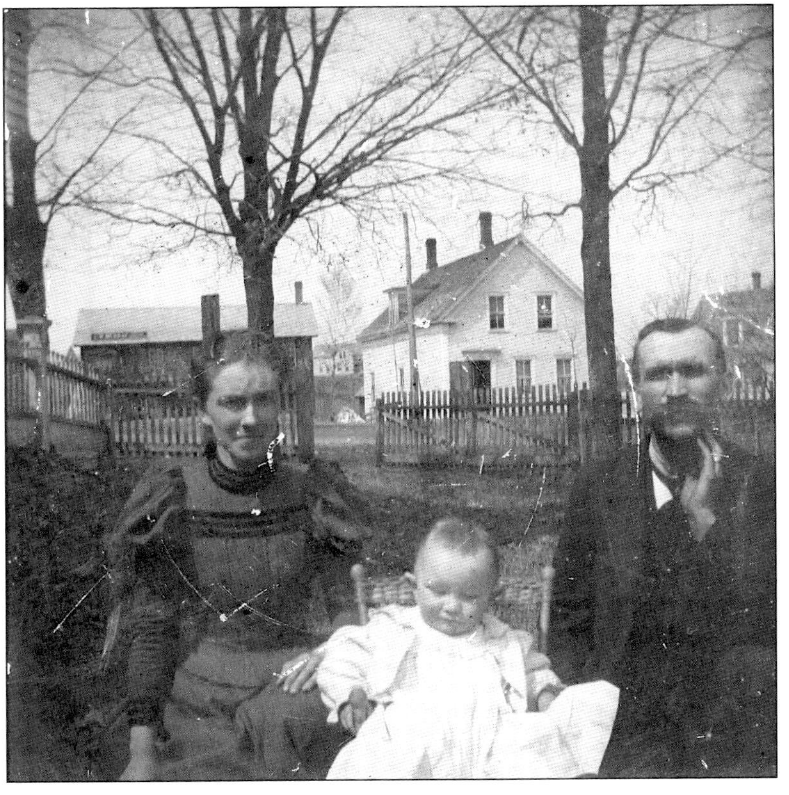

Fred Manter, his wife, Agustus Tinkham Manter, and their daughter Keturah, c. 1895. Fred was a well-known druggist, building a store on Main Street, Anson, in 1909. The store was later owned and operated by Keturah and her husband, Hazen Taylor. The house in the background was formerly Isaac Jeffers's house. Part of the Hotel Howard is visible.

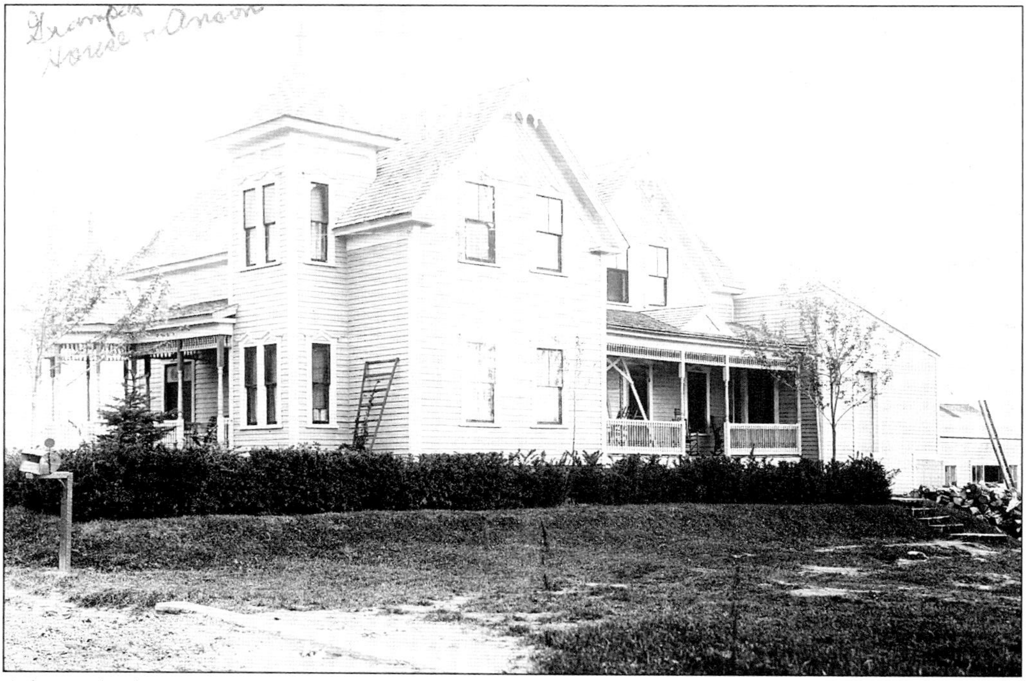

A house built in 1900 by Edward Chandler, grandfather of Wesley Preble. In 1914–17 he ran a garage on the property. In later years the place was known as Rocky Acres Greenhouse, operated by Beatrice and Wallace Brooks and located on Preble Avenue.

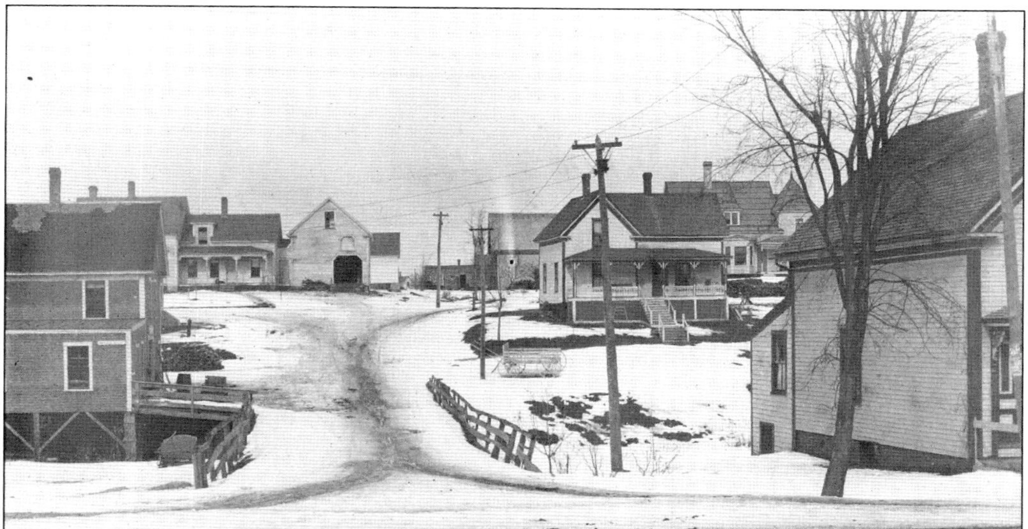

Brook Street (formerly Bridge Street) in the early 1900s. On the far right is a portion of the Wm. Washburn house with the Senko house in the background. On the left is the sawmill with the Drottar house at the top of the hill.

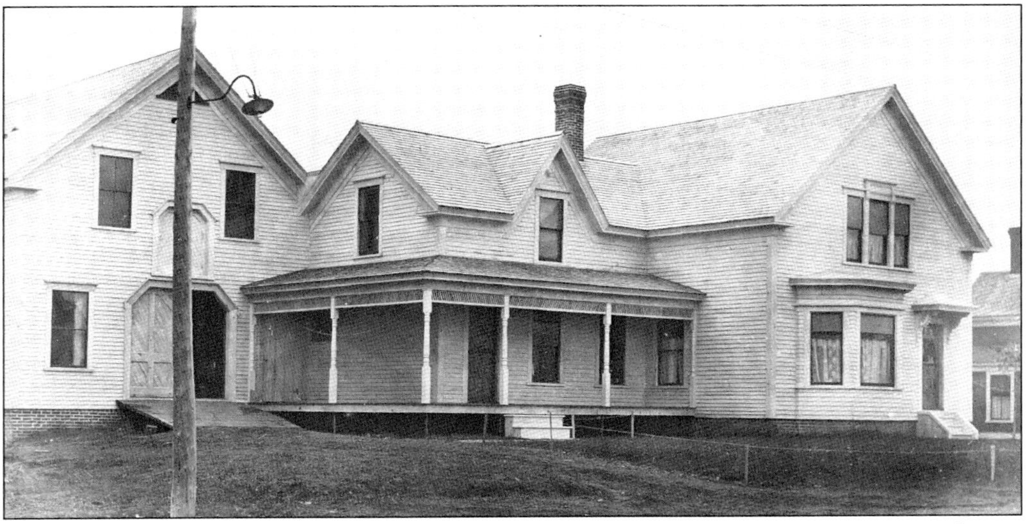

On December 18, 1907, 110 friends and relatives of Mr. and Mrs. Lysander Berry gave them a house warming in their newly built home. Mr. Berry was an R.F.D. mail carrier for many years. The house, located on Church Street, was later owned by Harry Harris, another longtime mail carrier. It is now owned by John and Sylvia Corson.

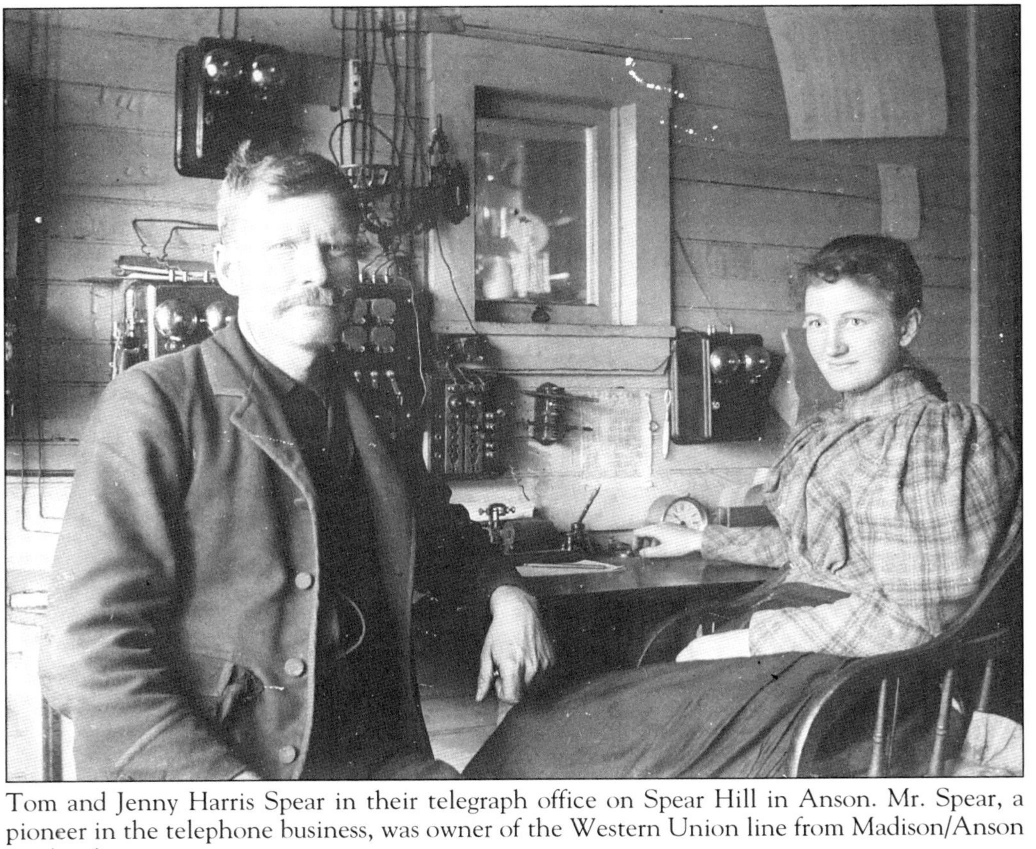

Tom and Jenny Harris Spear in their telegraph office on Spear Hill in Anson. Mr. Spear, a pioneer in the telephone business, was owner of the Western Union line from Madison/Anson to Skowhegan.

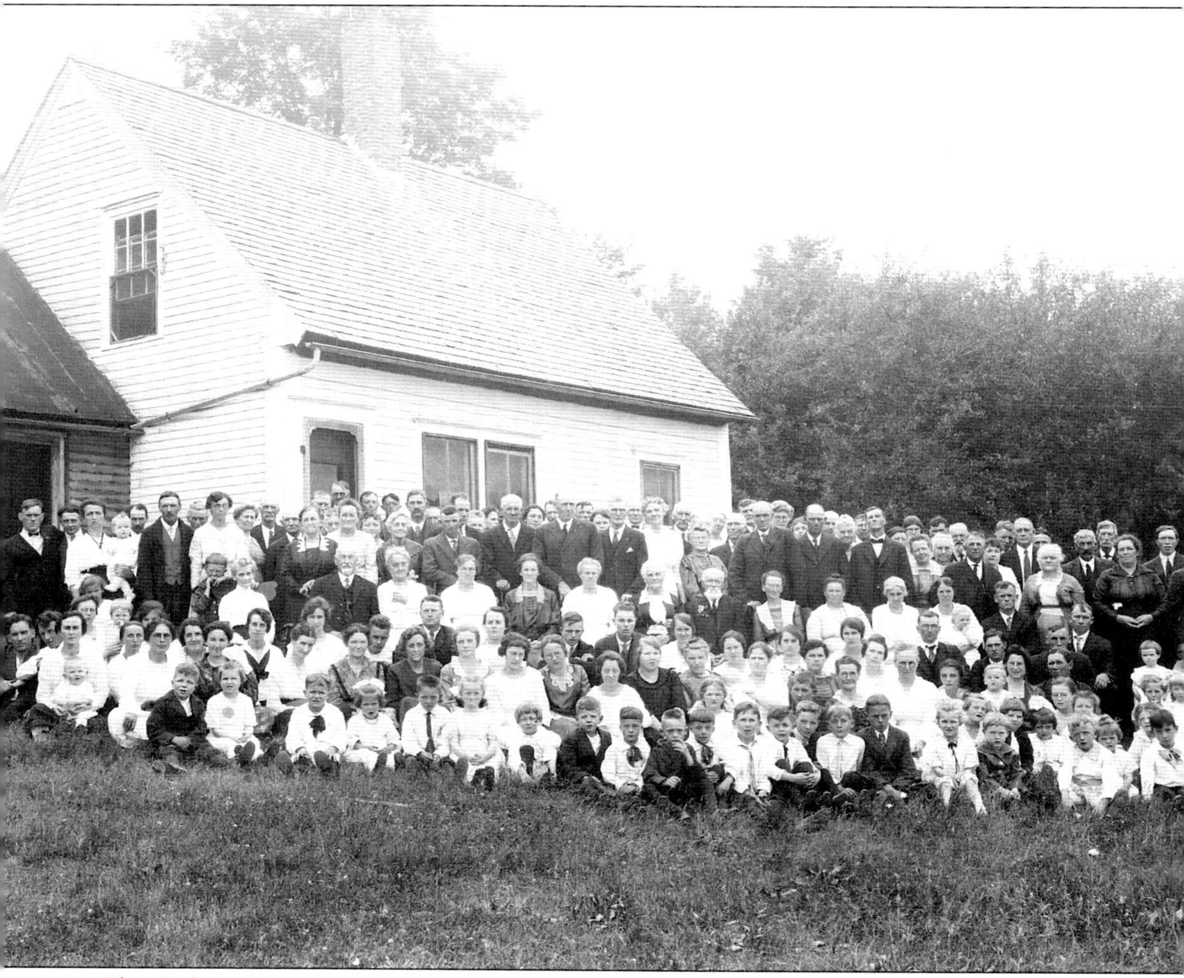

The 50th wedding anniversary of Mr. and Mrs. Joel K. Fletcher, June 29, 1921. Mr. Fletcher (the bearded gentleman seated in the center with the boutonniere) is a descendant of Joel K. Fletcher, who came to Anson in 1804 at the age of 18 and built the house shown here. The house still stands today. Families represented here include the Fletchers, Luces, Bracketts, Fishes, Fowkes, Rands, Gates, Frazers, Kennedys, Robinsons, Spencers, Browns, Houghtons, and Plazes. Children in the picture living today include Euleta Rand, Jenny Fish, Grover Luce, Blendon Brown, Betty Kennedy, and Edna Brackett, possibly among others.

Fred Barron and crew sawing wood on Main Street in Anson, c. 1889.

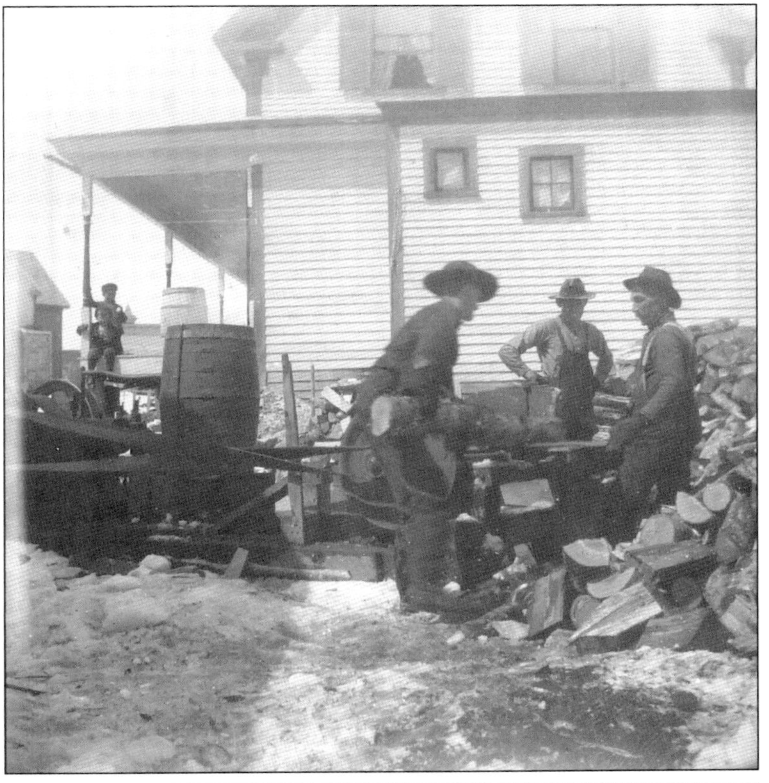

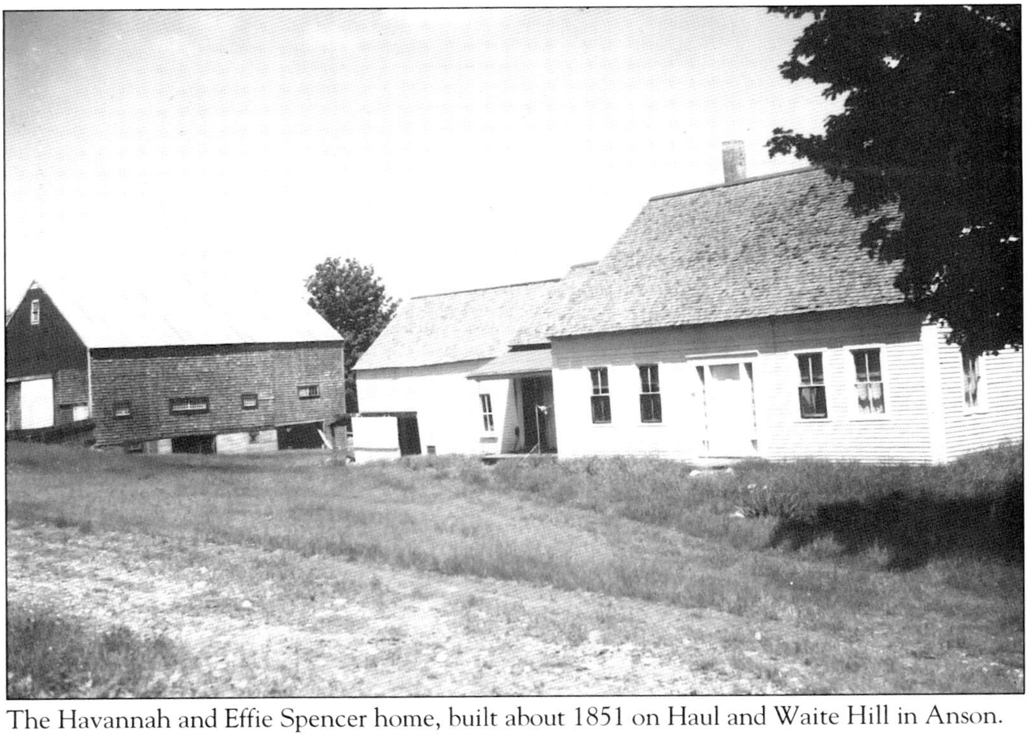

The Havannah and Effie Spencer home, built about 1851 on Haul and Waite Hill in Anson.

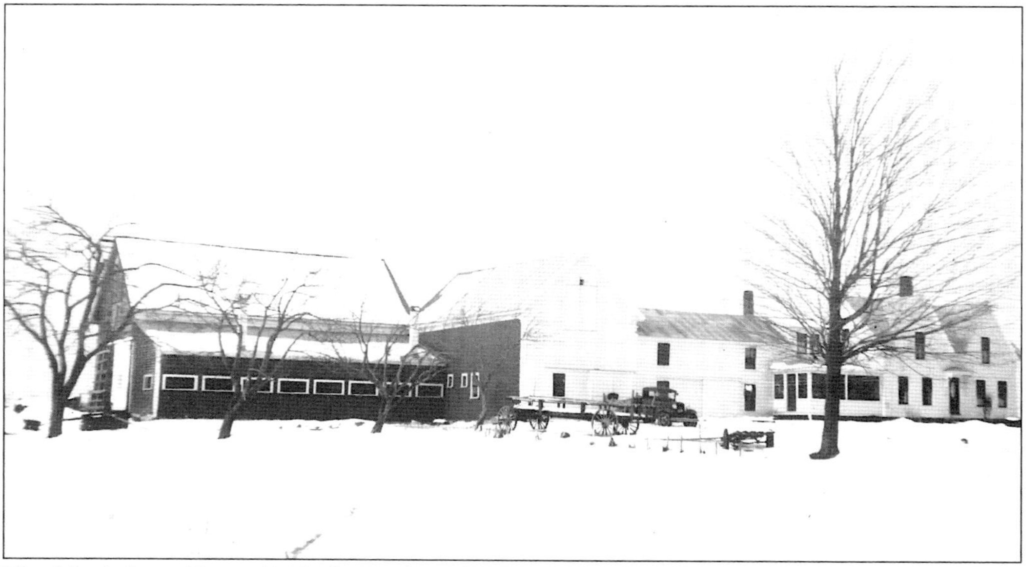

The Maple Lane Farm, 1920s, located on the Horseback Road.

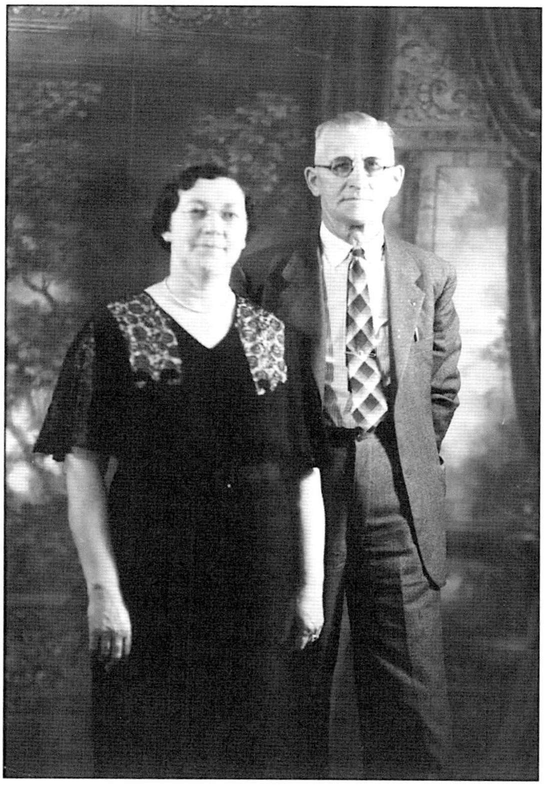

Frank and Elsie Oliver Smith, owners and operators of the Maple Lane Farm, 1919–1943. Mr. Smith was a representative for Eastern States Farmers Exchange during this time. The farm was sold to the Albert Ouellette family and operated by them for several years. It is now the home of Doug and Cathy Sears and their daughter Holly.

The late 1930s truck used for delivering Maple Lane Farm milk. Milk was 6¢ per quart in the summer and 2¢ more in the winter.

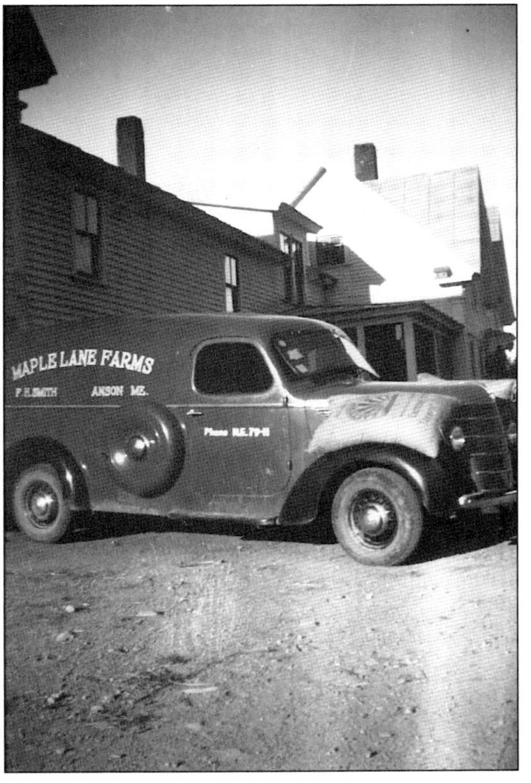

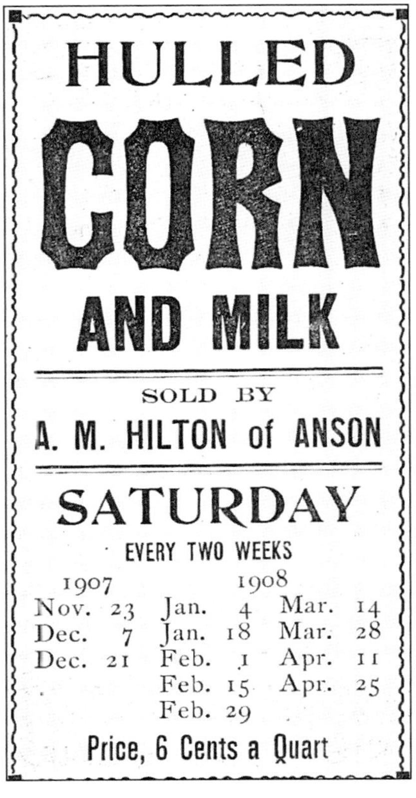

An early advertisement of an all-but-forgotten basic food.

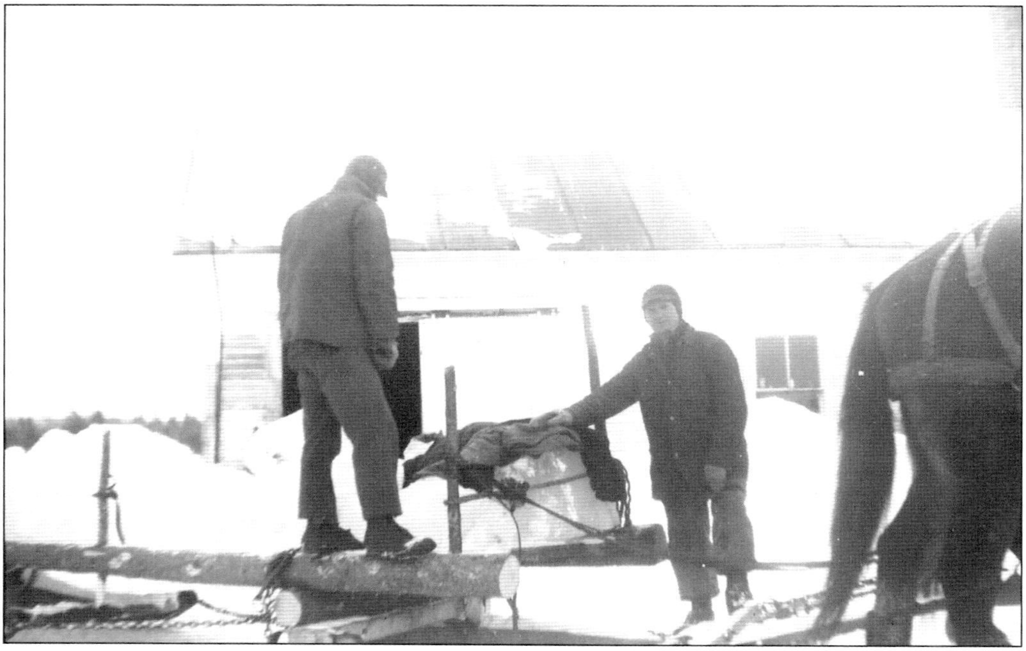

Bernard Fletcher facing camera with his son Hurley, with ice cut on a little pond near the Fletcher Farm, *c.* 1940.

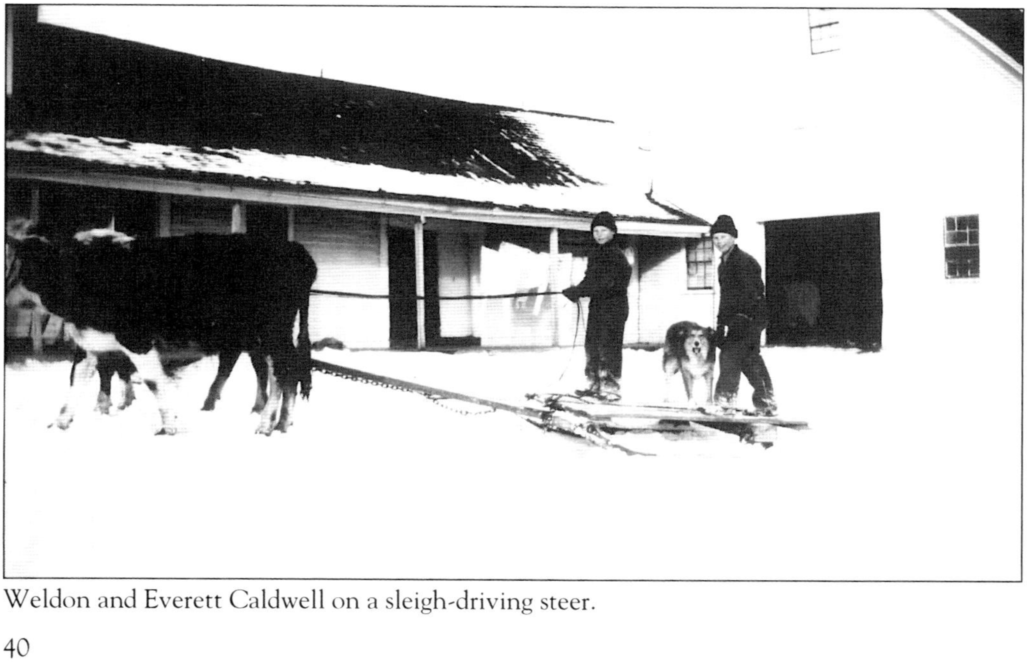

Weldon and Everett Caldwell on a sleigh-driving steer.

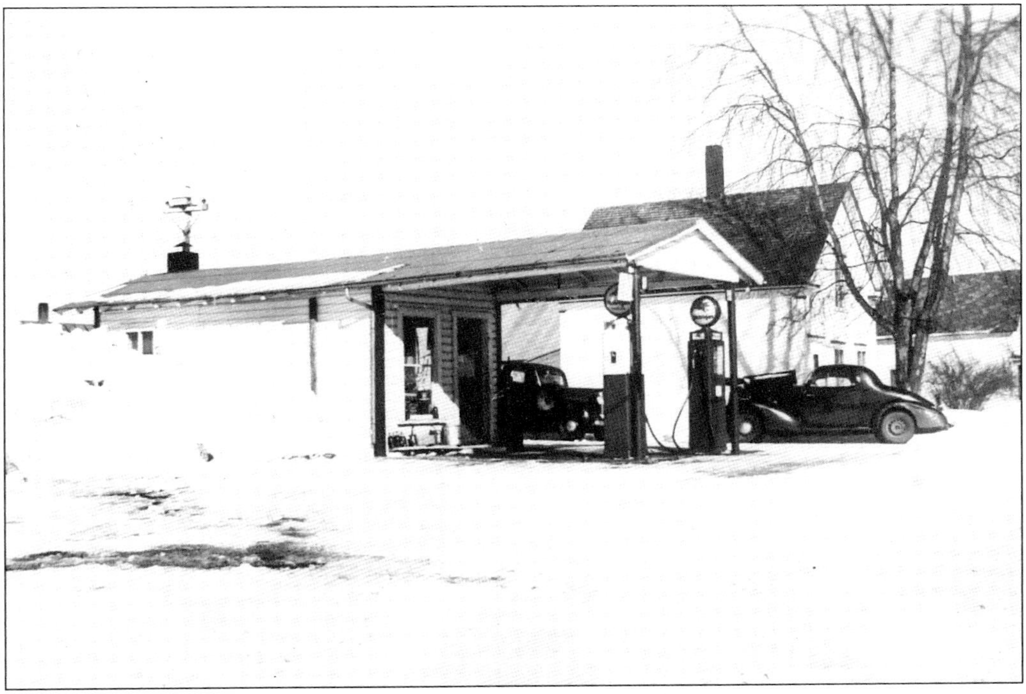

Archie Spencer's gas pumps and store (1922–1979), the first "gas" pumps.

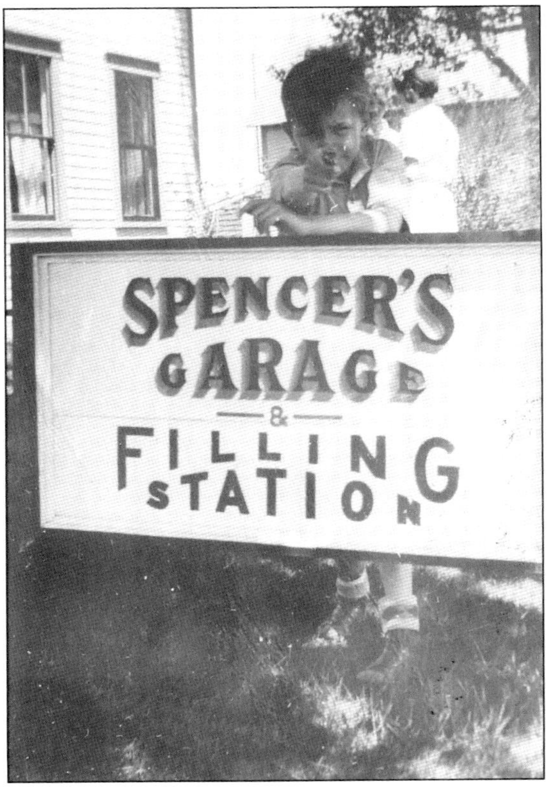

The sign for "Archie's filling station." Ralph Conners is leaning on it.

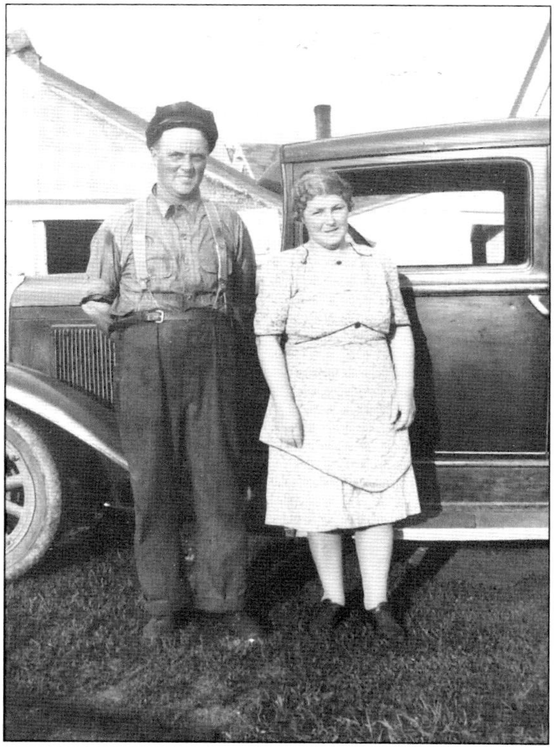

Archie and Aurelia Spencer, in a photograph taken June 1944 with their 1931 Pontiac in the background.

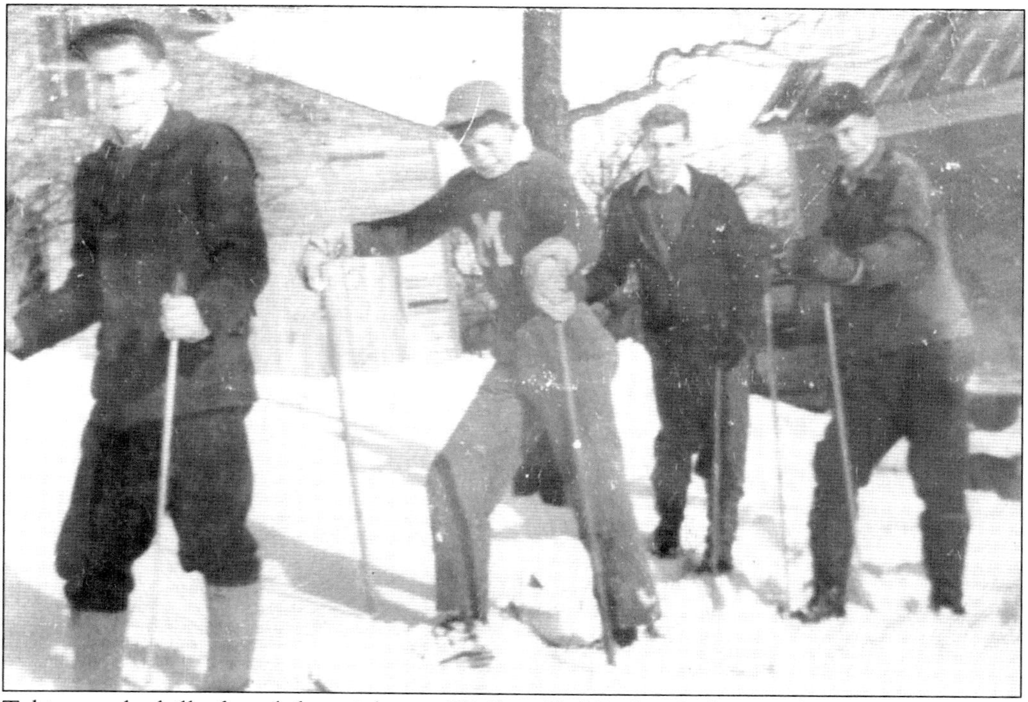

Taking to the hills, from left to right are: Wallace "Jr." Petley, Robert "Bobby" Dunlap, Robert "Hitler" Ray, and Ernest Dawes *c.* 1940.

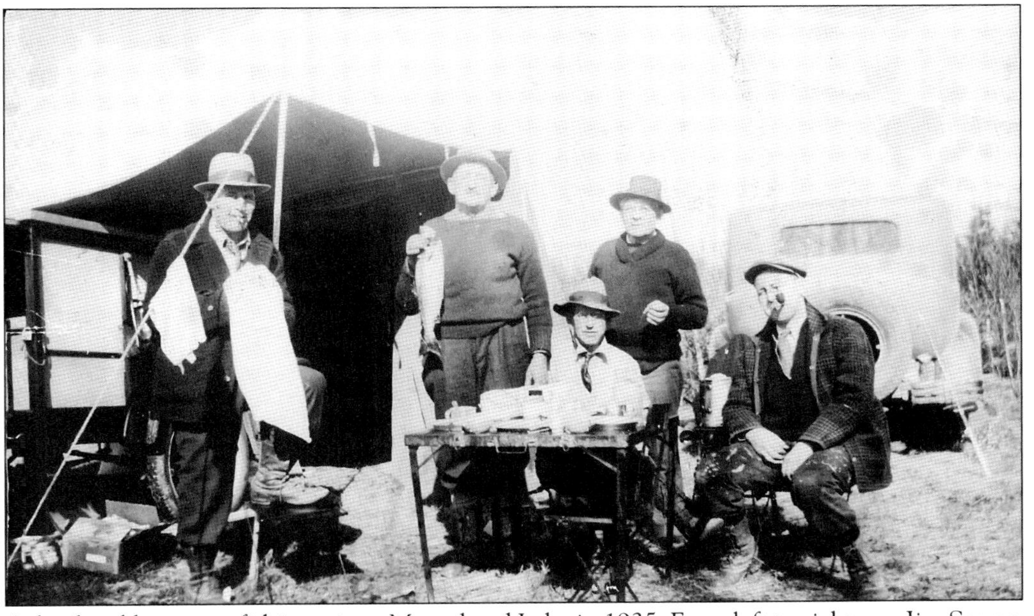

A few local boys on a fishing trip at Moosehead Lake in 1935. From left to right are: Jim Seams, Charlie Hastings, Pearly Bowren, and two unidentified men.

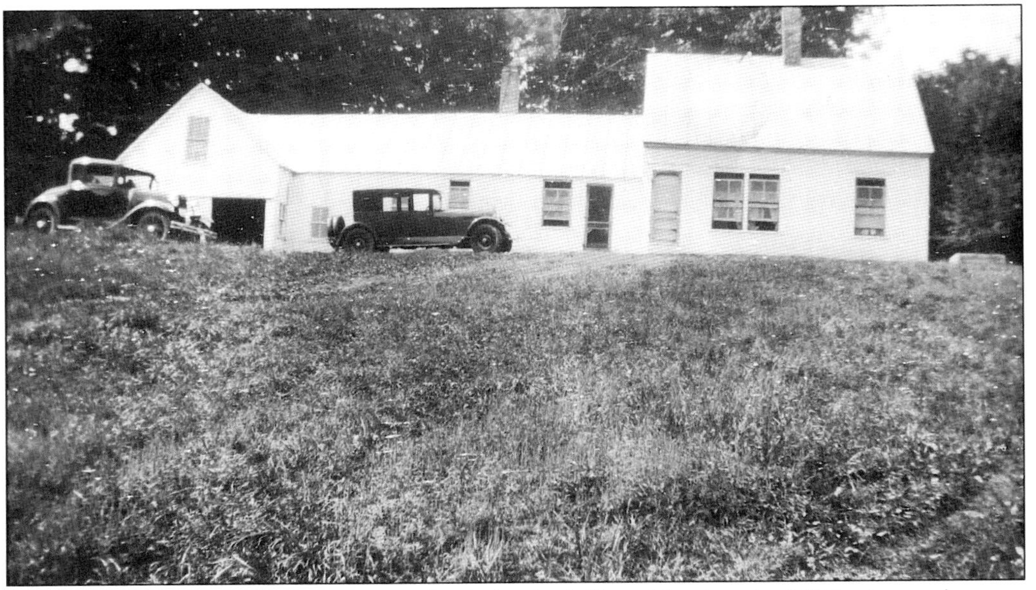

The Fletcher Farm in West Anson, built by Joel Kyes Fletcher in 1804, shown here in 1931. It was occupied by Fletchers until the 1970s and is now owned by Jeffrey Pelletier of New Hampshire.

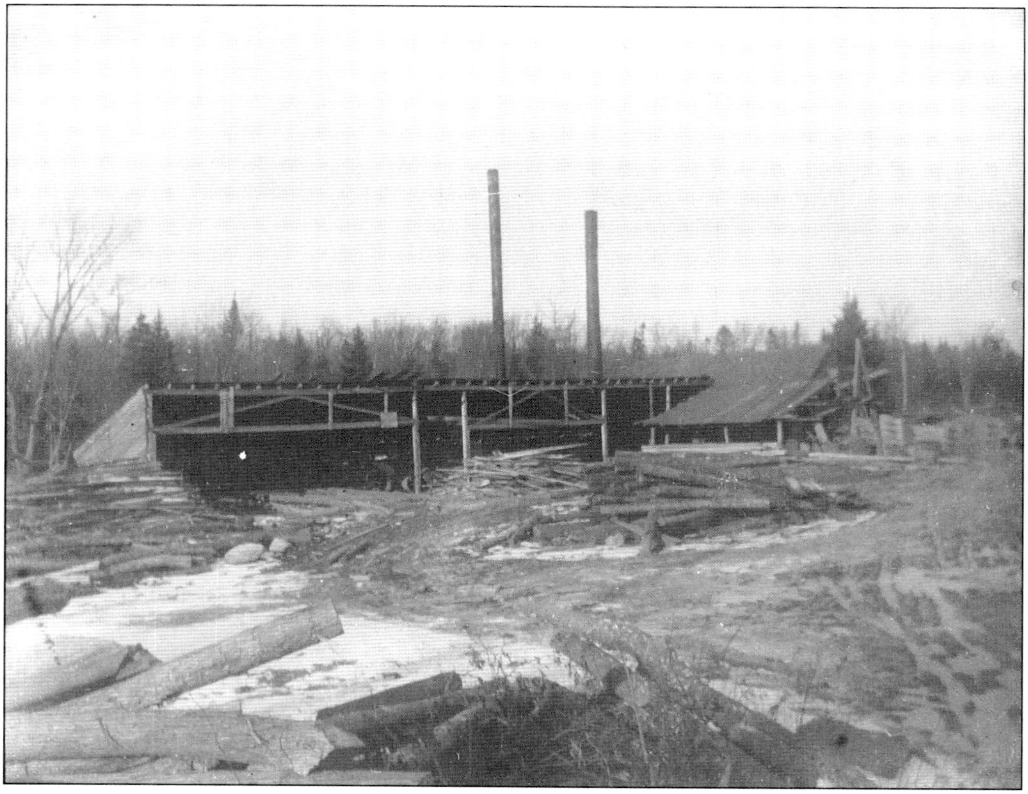

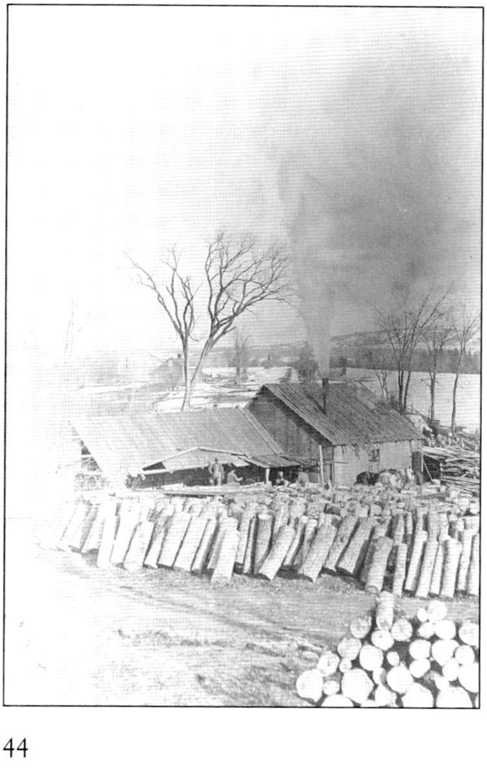

The Hoyt Brothers' steam-powered sawmill, purchased from Olin Gordon *c.* 1910, located in Anson Valley on Route 234. This early source of power was used when mills could not be located on a stream and before electricity. The steam was generated by burning the slabs and sawdust.

W.S. Oliver's steam-powered mill, located at 4 mile square, Anson Valley, on Route 234. This mill sawed hardwood squares which were made into handles, doorknobs, dowels, etc.

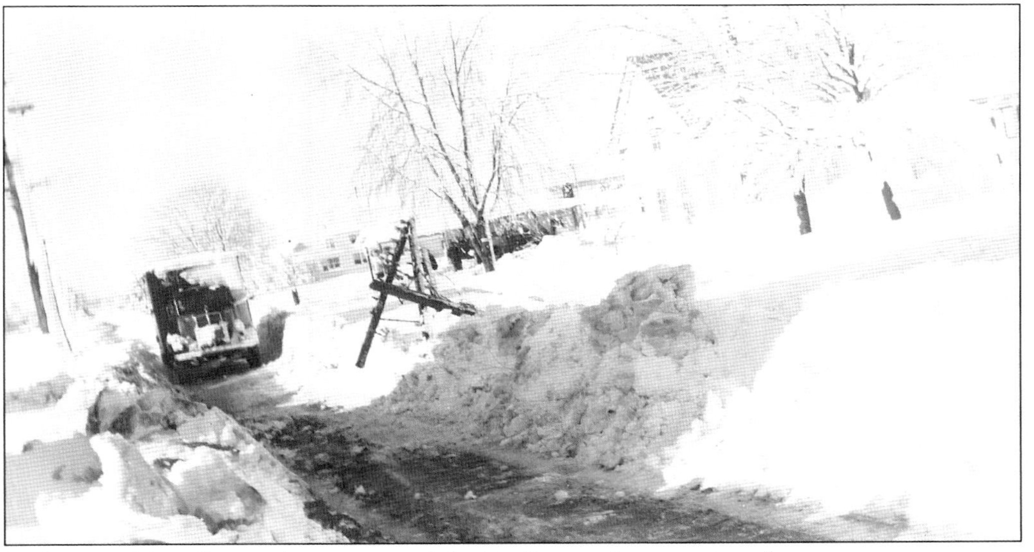

Looking up Main Street, Anson, toward Archie Spencer's gas station after a snow storm.

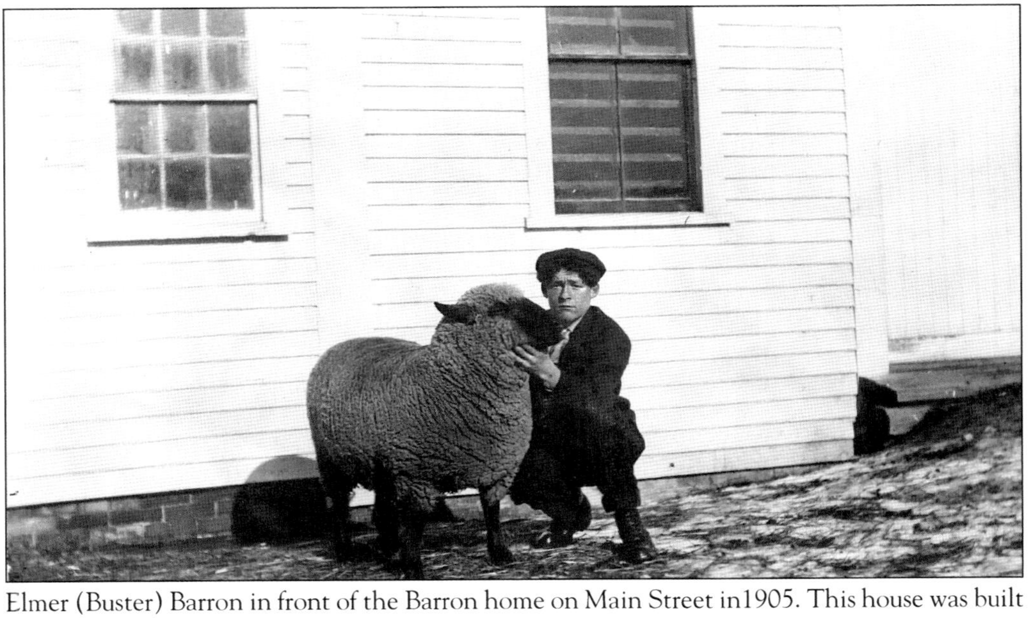

Elmer (Buster) Barron in front of the Barron home on Main Street in1905. This house was built by Buster's father.

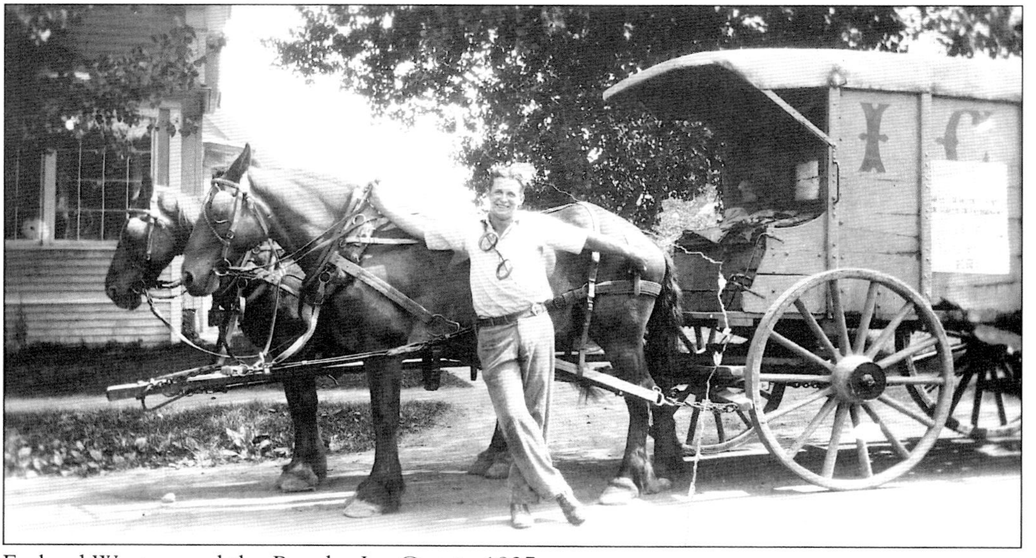

Earland Weston and the Peoples Ice Cart in 1927.

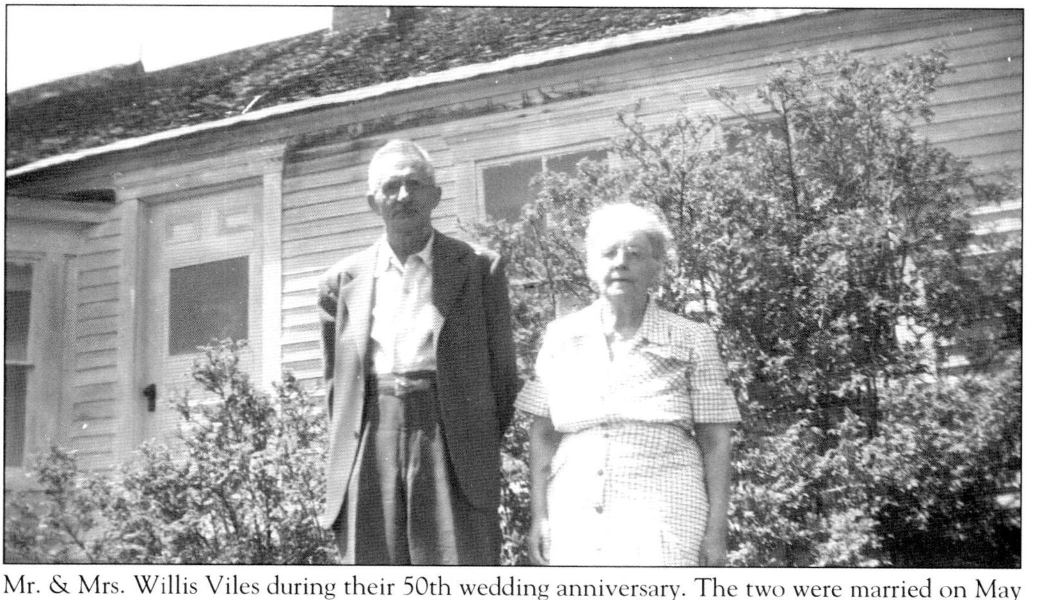

Mr. & Mrs. Willis Viles during their 50th wedding anniversary. The two were married on May 27, 1908, by the Reverend George Paine. They are the parents of five children. For 33 years he was employed at the Weston Gristmill in Madison. He was superintendent of Sunday school for many years.

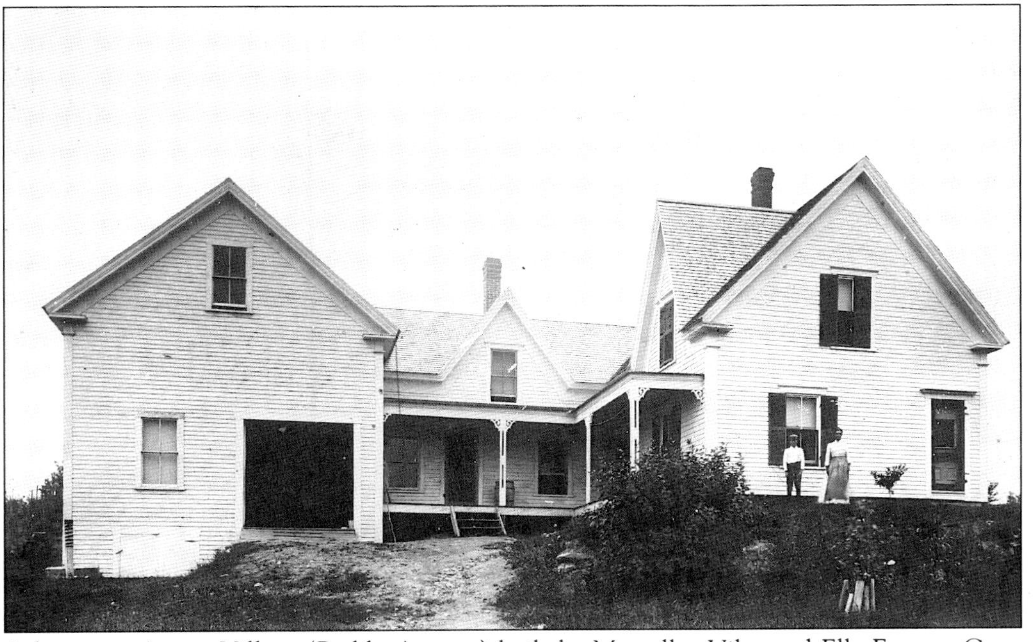

A house in Anson Village (Preble Avenue) built by Marcellus Viles and Ella Frances Copp Viles, c. 1901–1903. Later this became the residence of Erland Weston. It is now owned by Jamie Doiron.

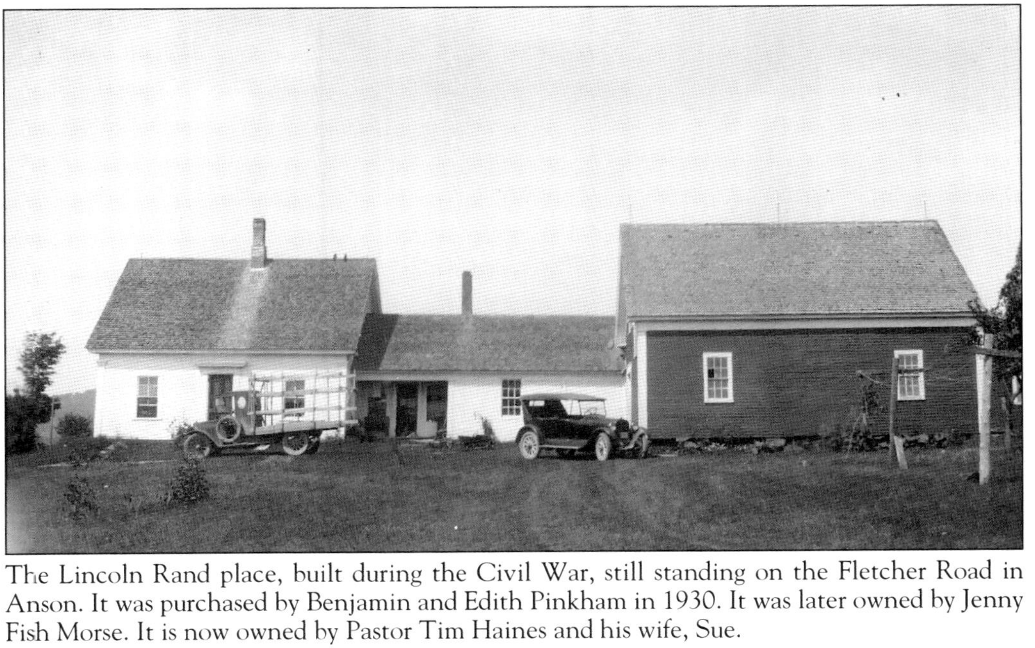

The Lincoln Rand place, built during the Civil War, still standing on the Fletcher Road in Anson. It was purchased by Benjamin and Edith Pinkham in 1930. It was later owned by Jenny Fish Morse. It is now owned by Pastor Tim Haines and his wife, Sue.

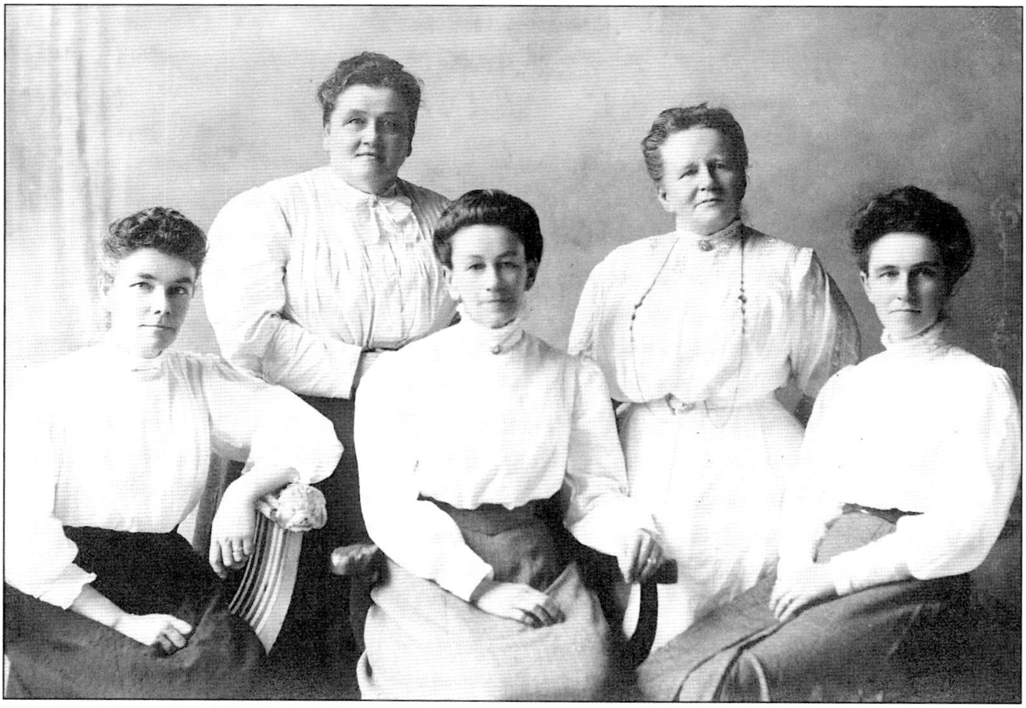

The Tinkham "girls"—Marinda, Fannie, Gusta, Susie, and Maria Briggs (a cousin). Susie married Bryce Edwards (not B.K.). He was a minister, and she also preached. Gusta married druggist Fred Manter.

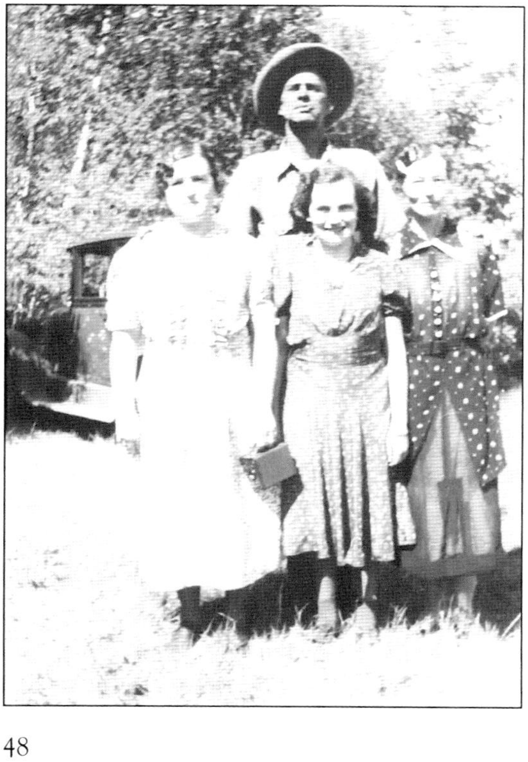

Leon Hewey, Amy Campbell Fletcher, Augusta Pulsifer, and Alice Hewey in 1938.

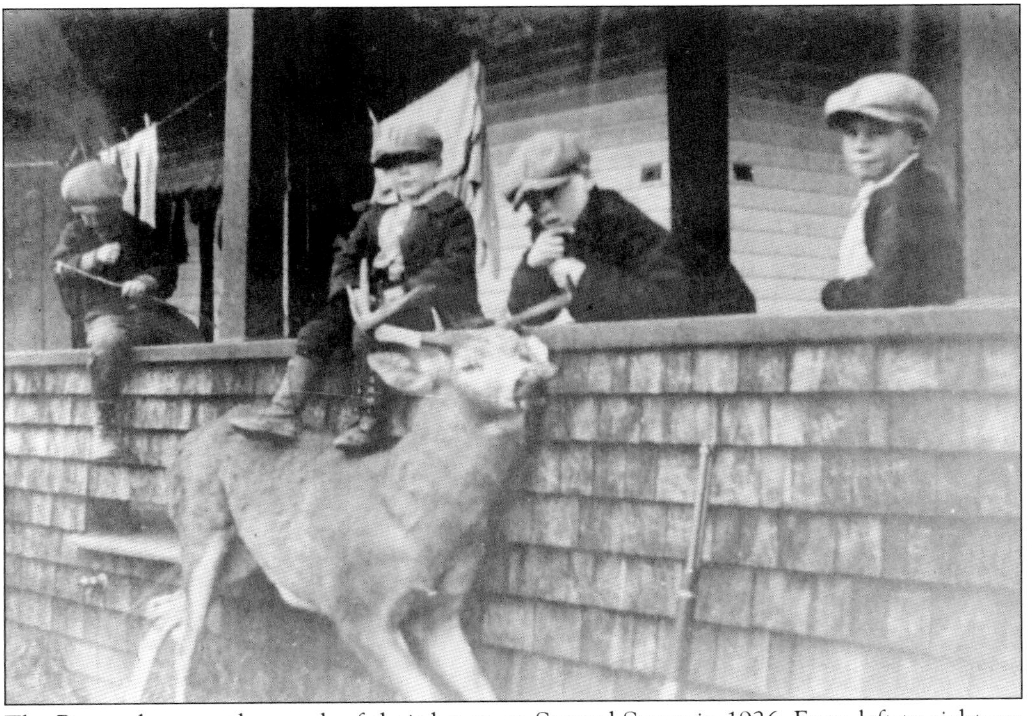

The Barron boys on the porch of their home on Second Street in 1926. From left to right are Raymond, Erlon, Wallace, and cousin Robert.

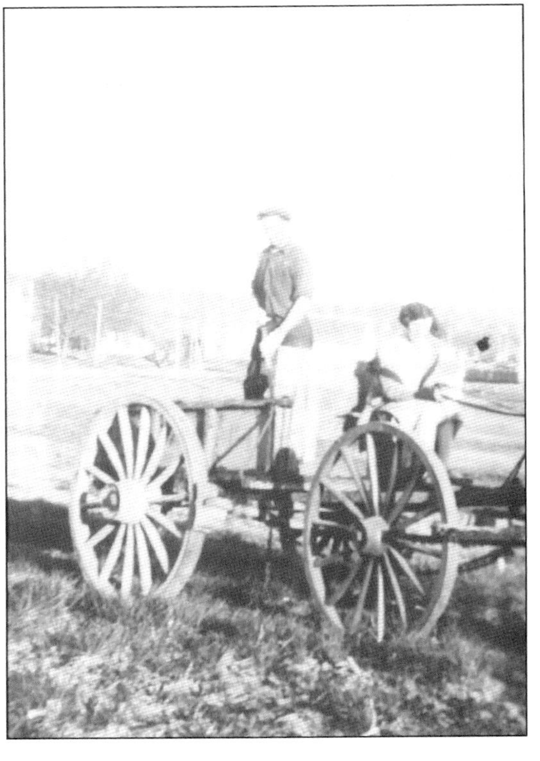

Guy and Leona Dunlap, 1930, probably fertilizing the fields. The background is looking toward Anson Village. The building barely visible at the far right is the Garfield School.

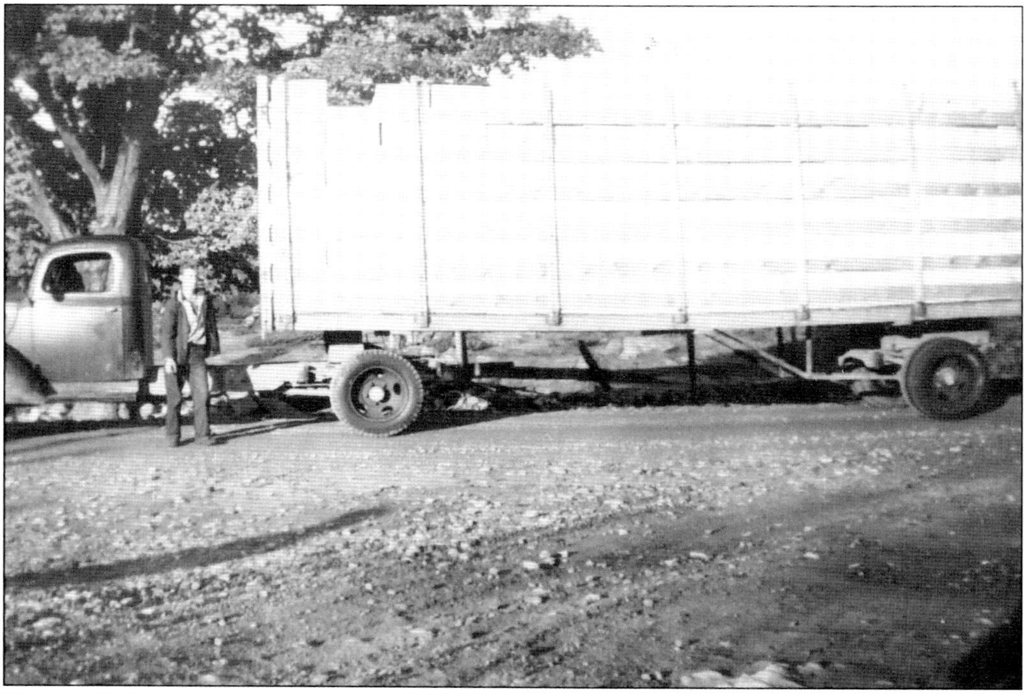

Howard Jackson driving a trailer truck, the first of its kind in the area, 1930–1940s. The truck was built by Elbridge Rand, and was used to haul fish and apple boxes, hauling 2,250 boxes per load.

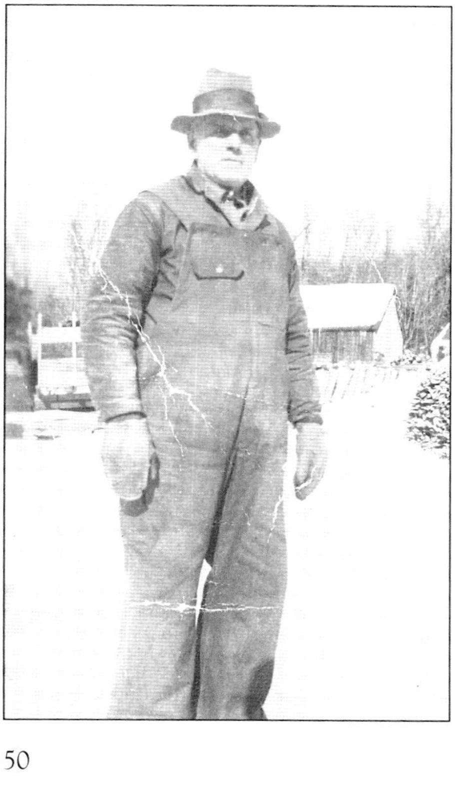

Rand's Mill, 1942. Elbridge Rand operated Rand's Mill, which was built from a mill his father hauled with a team of oxen from Lexington Plantation to the Greenleaf Road. They sawed squares for novelty mills and made fish and apple boxes. The mill site contained a horse hovel (in picture), a cook's camp, and a bunk house. The heirs sold the mill following his death to the Goodwins of North Anson, who took the box machinery and sold the mill to Almon Watson, now of Industry.

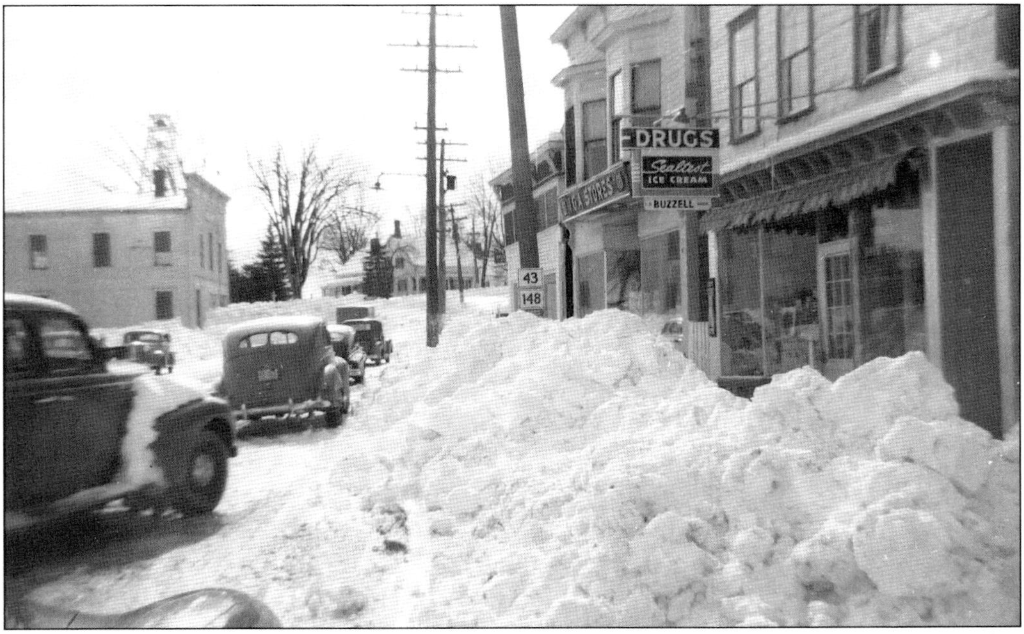

Winter in Anson, c. 1940. Snow was plowed on both sides with a strip in the middle, so that there was a left and right lane.

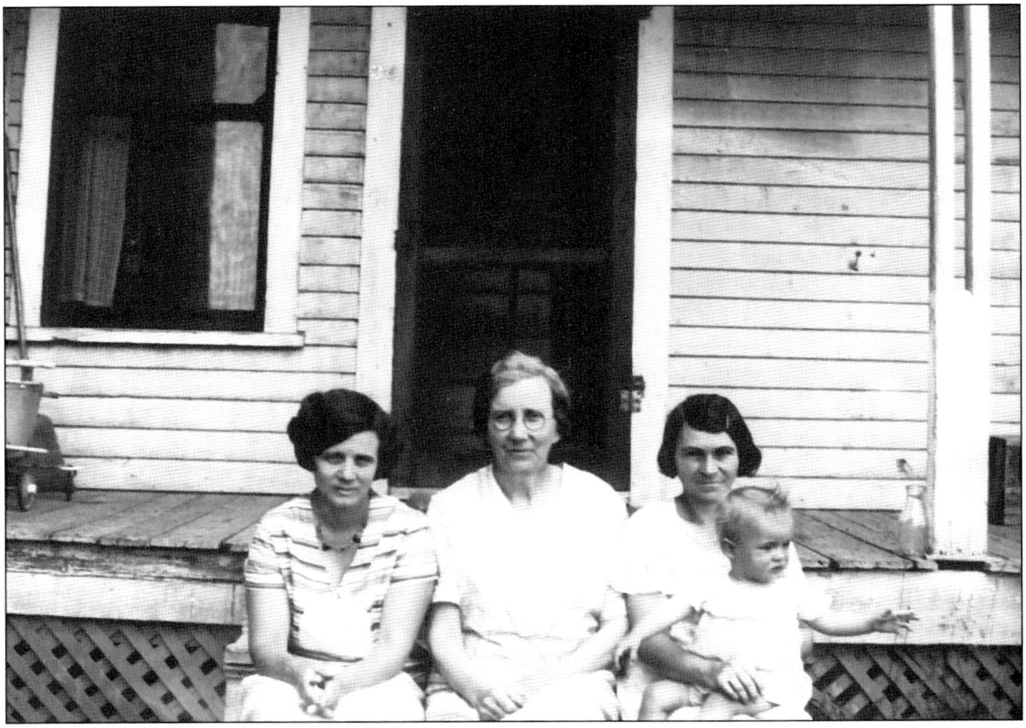

A neighborhood gathering, c. 1930s. From left to right are Grace Redmond, Kate Garland, and Jenny Bearor. The child remains unidentified.

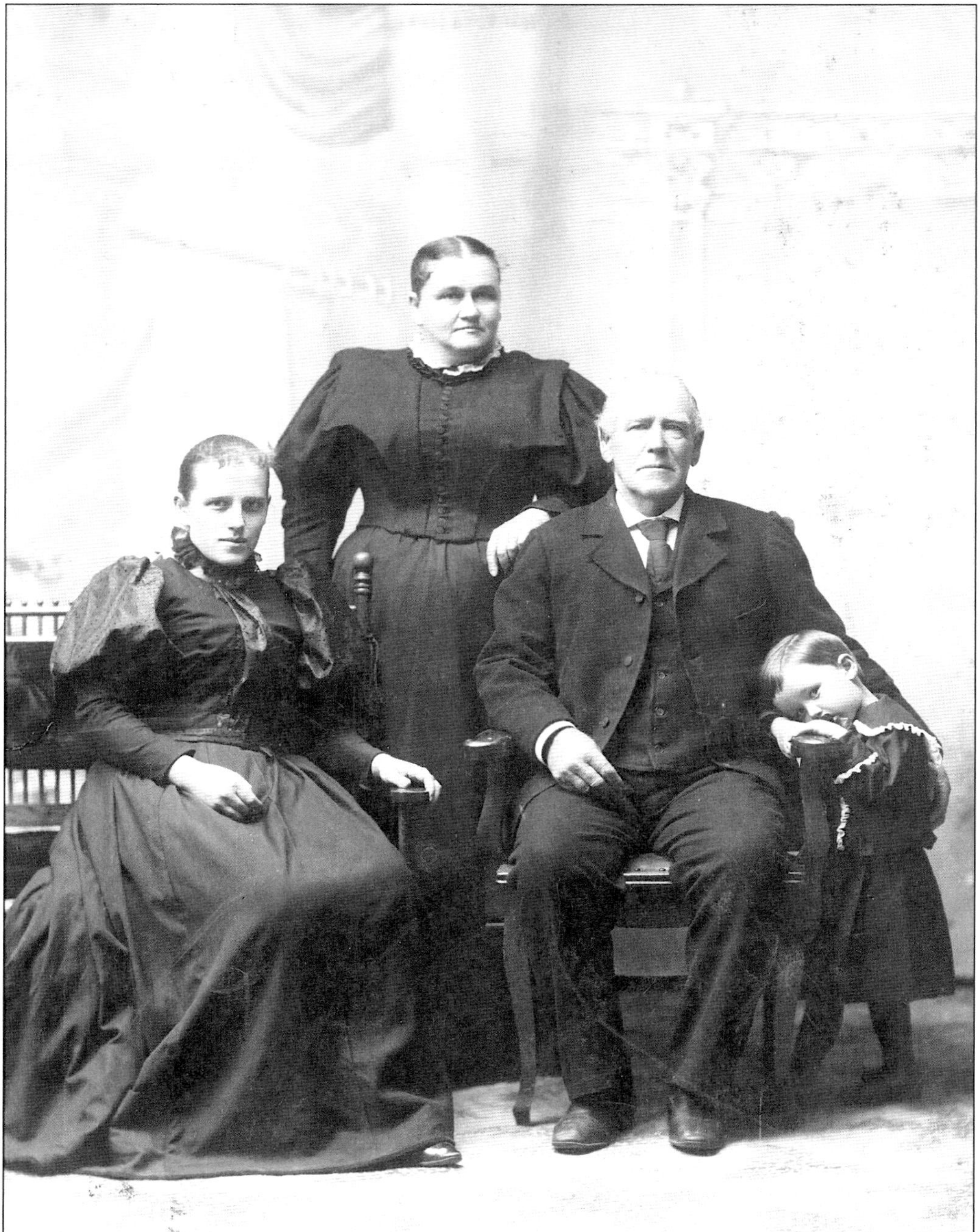

Four generations. John Tinkham, his daughter Susie Edwards, her daughter Crissie, and Crissie's son Samuel are shown here *c.* 1896. John Tinkham owned the Tinkham and Tinkham Store, where he sold meats, groceries, provisions, flour, grain, and feed.

Two

North Anson

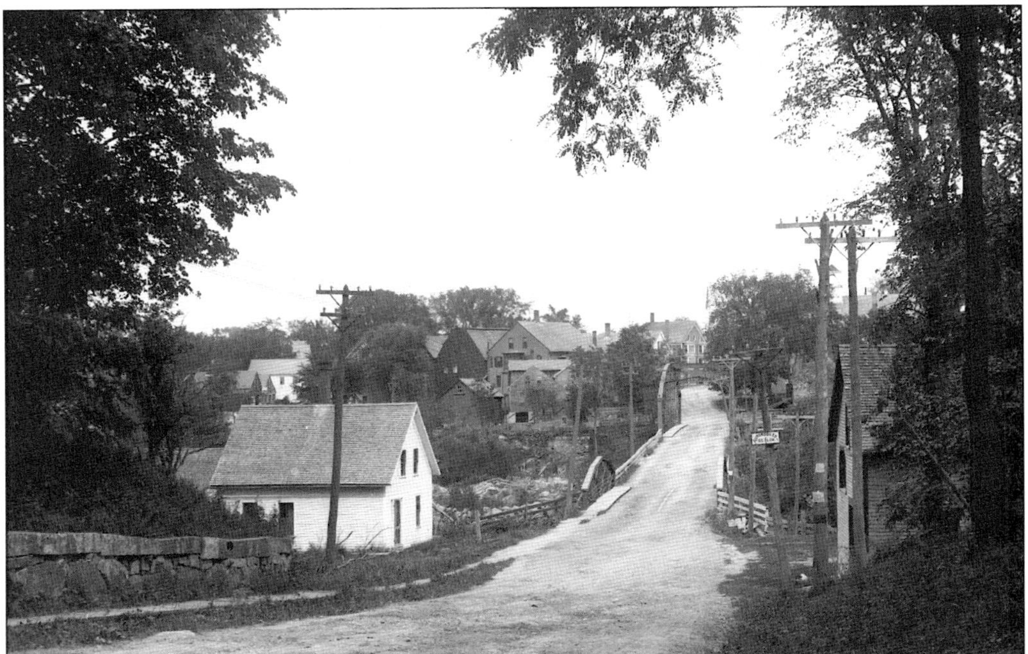

Main Street, entering from the south over the Carrabassett River, taken about 1908.

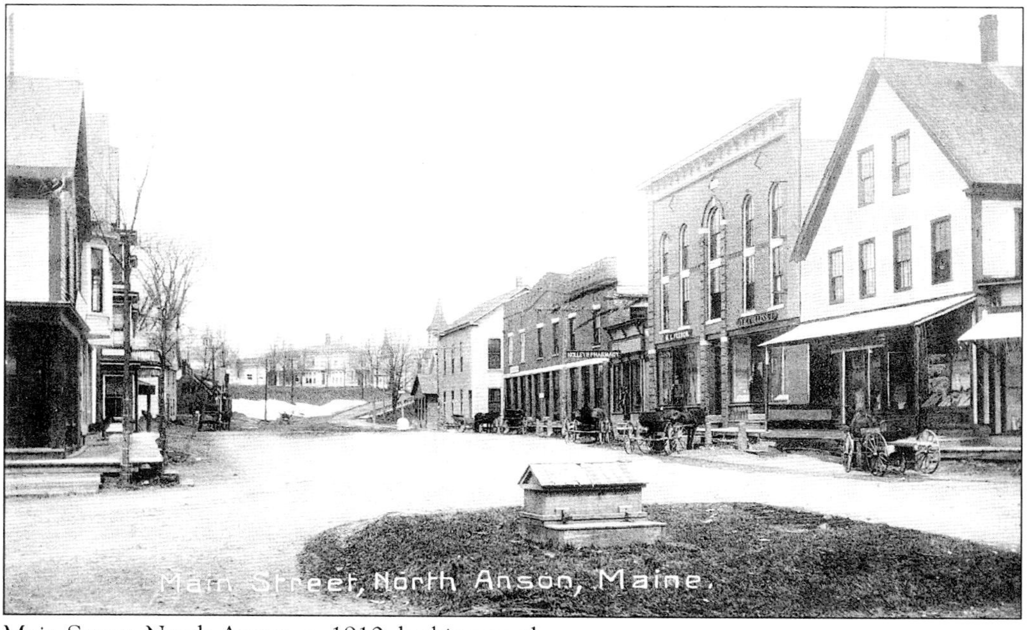

Main Street, North Anson, c. 1910, looking north.

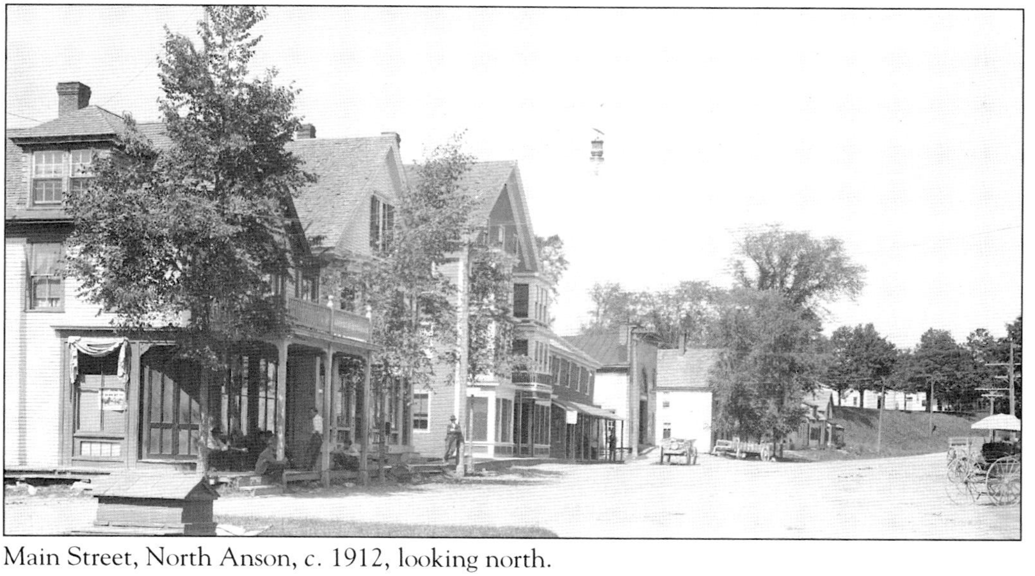
Main Street, North Anson, c. 1912, looking north.

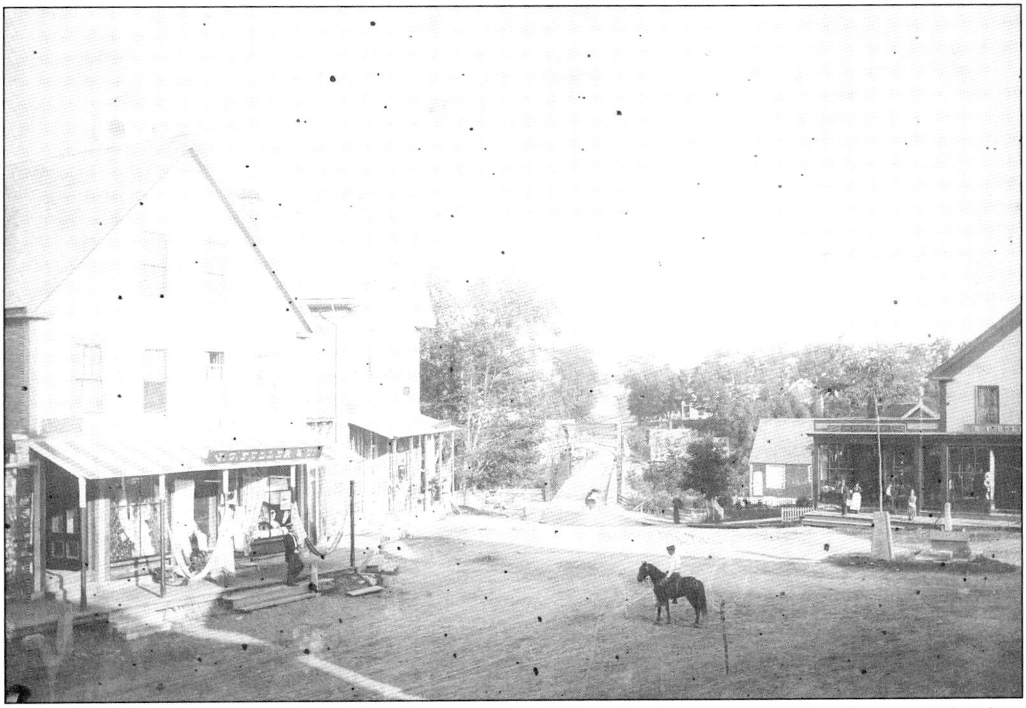

Looking south on Main Street, North Anson, c. 1888. In the center is the first steel bridge. Harry B. Hilton is on the pony.

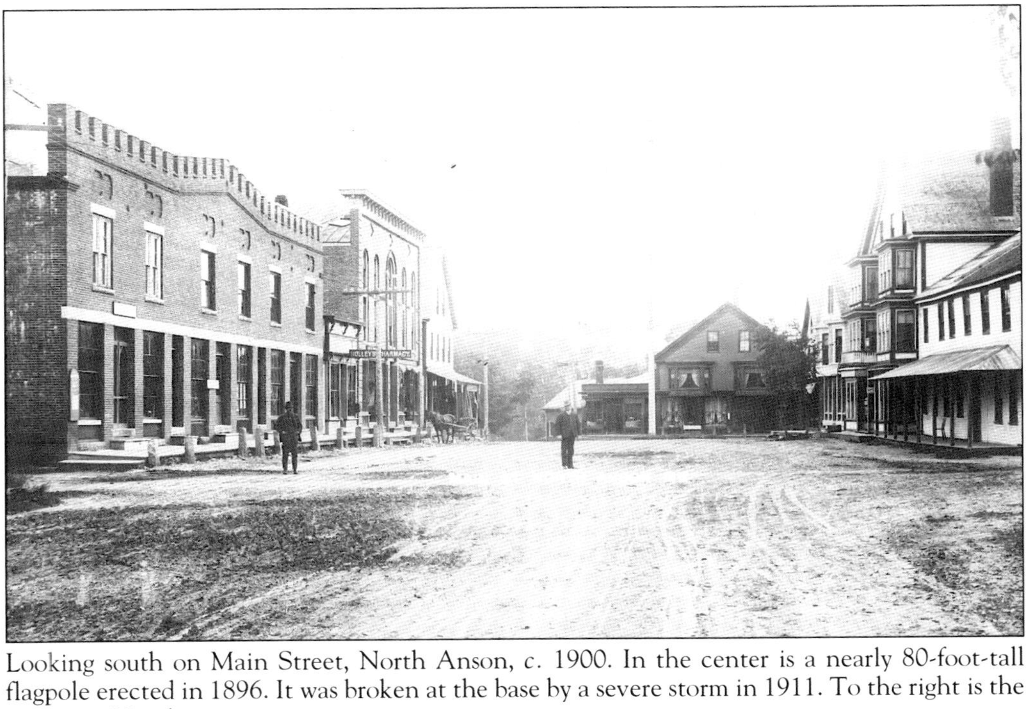

Looking south on Main Street, North Anson, c. 1900. In the center is a nearly 80-foot-tall flagpole erected in 1896. It was broken at the base by a severe storm in 1911. To the right is the Somerset Hotel.

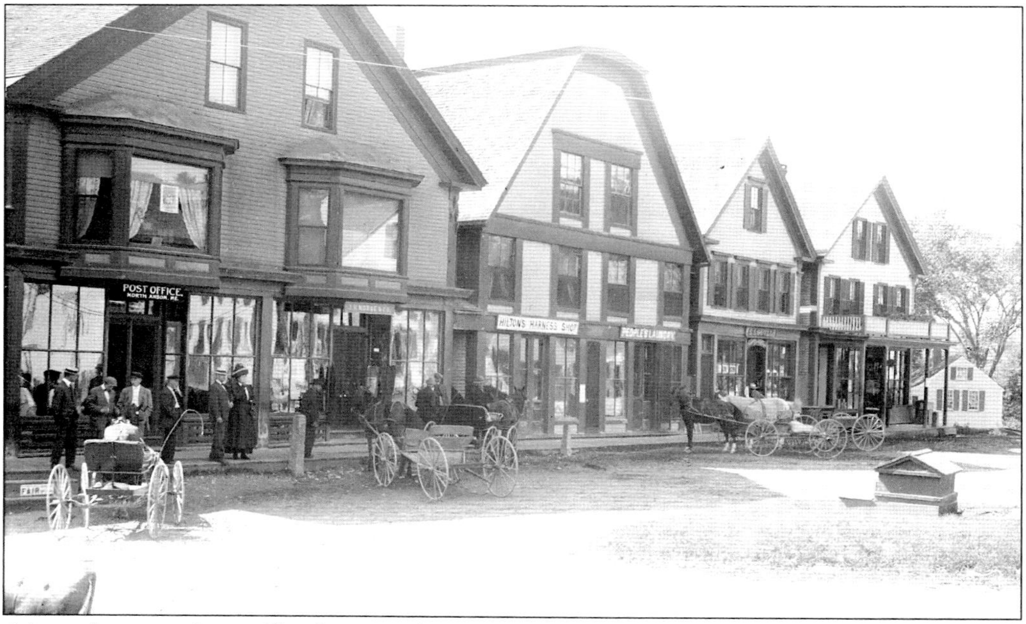

A busy shopping day on Elm Street at the square in North Anson, *c.* 1890. From left to right are the post office, the J.W. Morse Co., the Hilton Harness Shop, People's Laundry, and S.S. Gould (on the site of the present telephone company building).

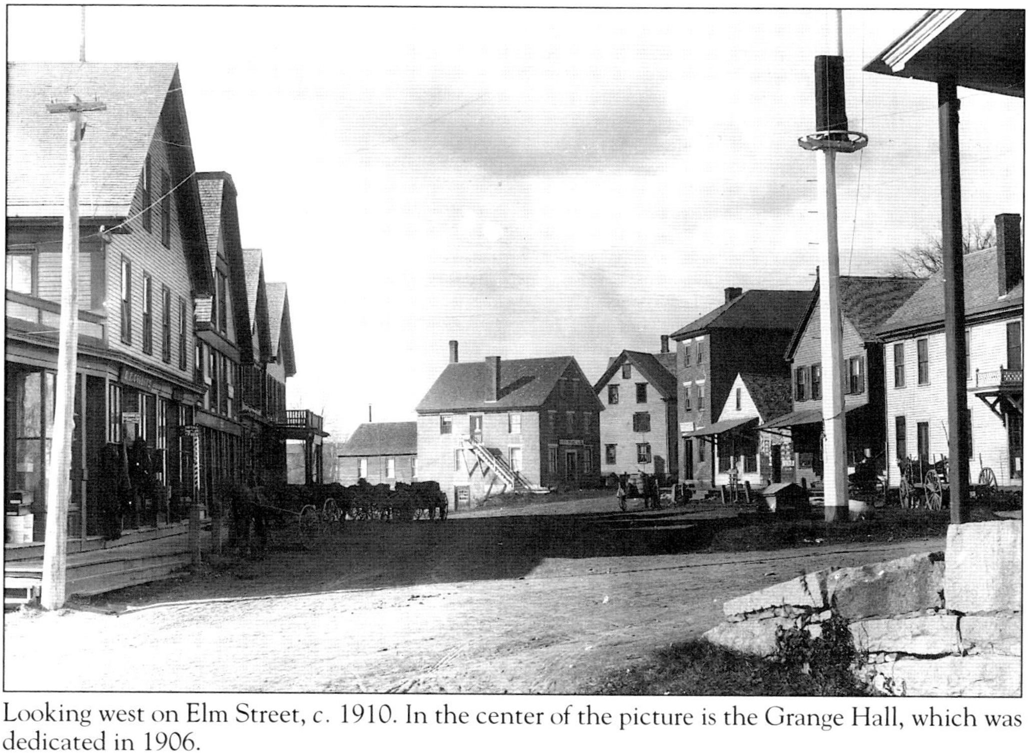

Looking west on Elm Street, *c.* 1910. In the center of the picture is the Grange Hall, which was dedicated in 1906.

A store on Elm Street, North Anson, c. 1900.

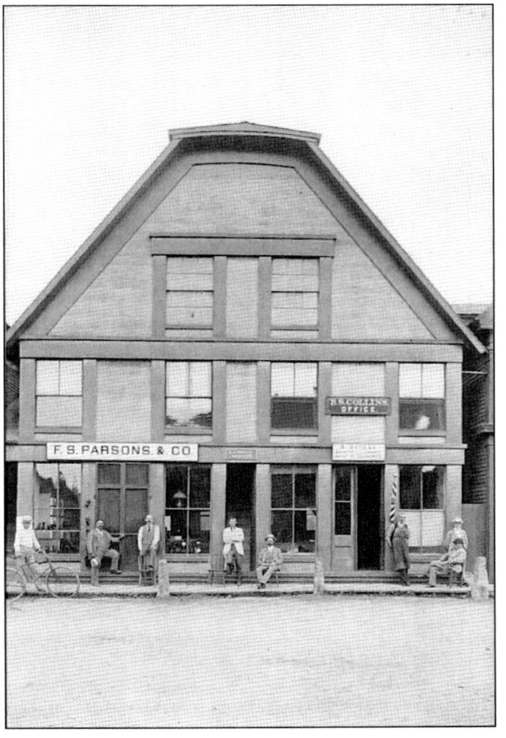

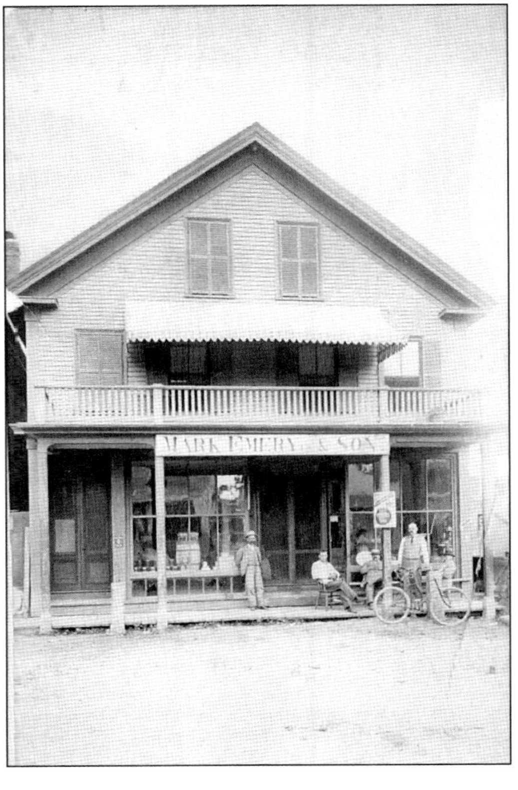

The Mark Emery & Son Grocery Store, located on Elm Street, North Anson, c. 1900. Pictured are Willis Emery, Gene Mitchell, Fred Parson, and Wallace Emery. This store was later owned by Porter and Marston.

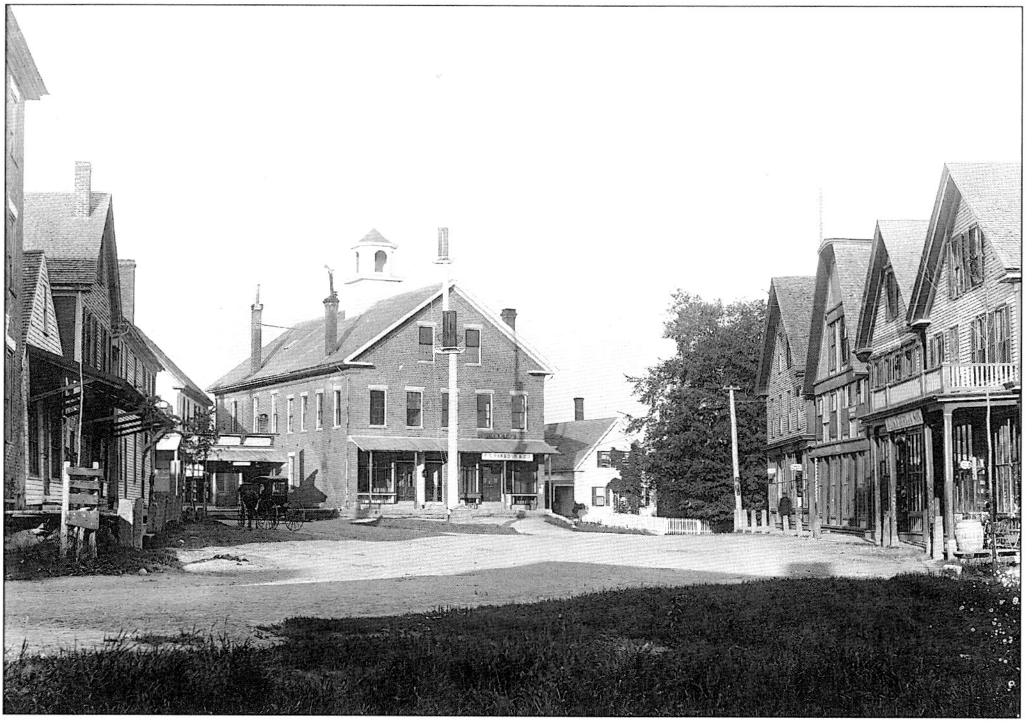

A view from Elm Street looking east at the square, *c.* 1910. In the center is the Bunker Block.

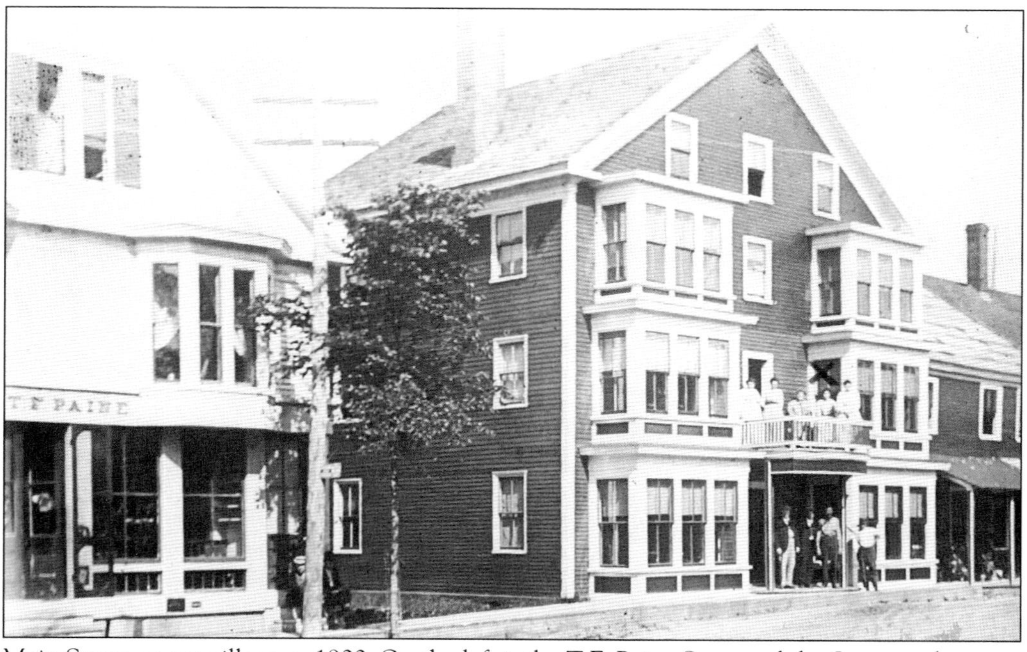

Main Street, upper village, *c.* 1900. On the left is the T.F. Paine Store and the Somerset house.

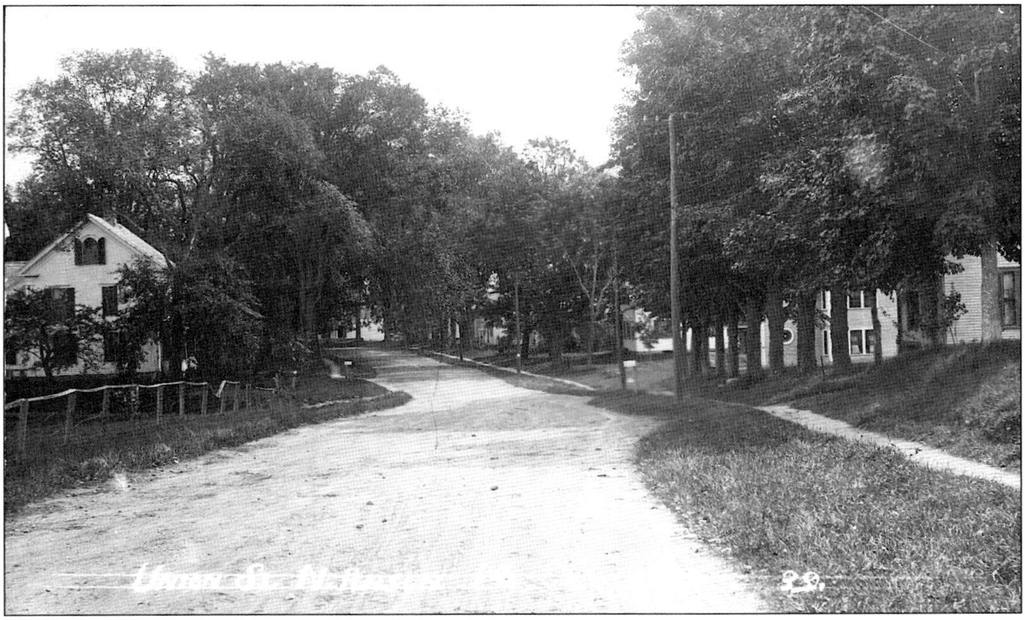

Union Street, North Anson, *c.* 1910, looking east.

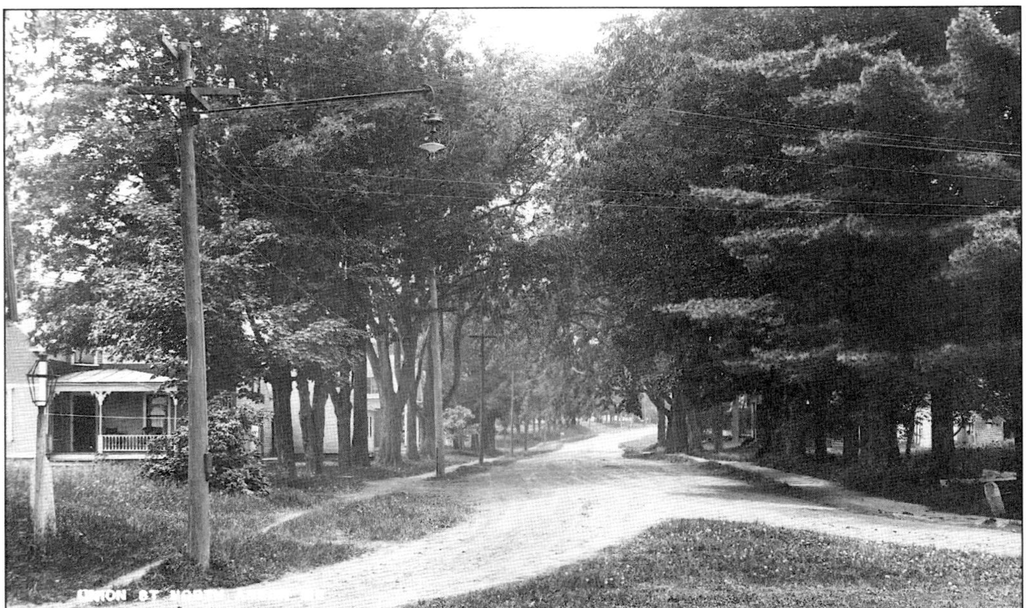

Union Street, North Anson, *c.* 1910, looking west.

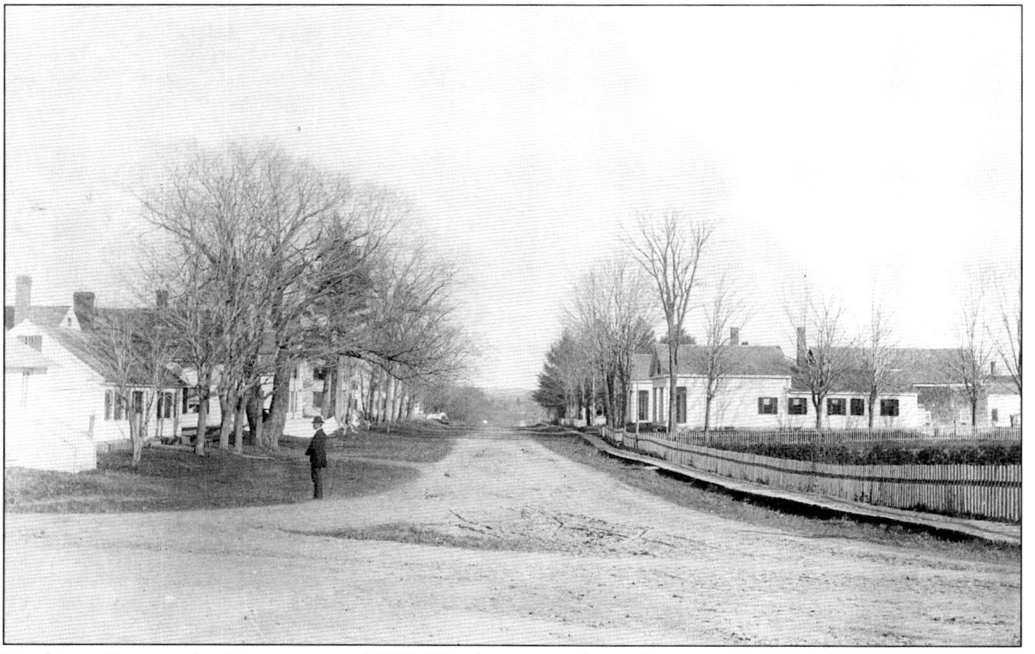

Madison Avenue looking east, *c.* 1875. The house to the right is a rare example of a single-story three-columned Greek Revival house. Three houses of this type were built on this street and are in use today.

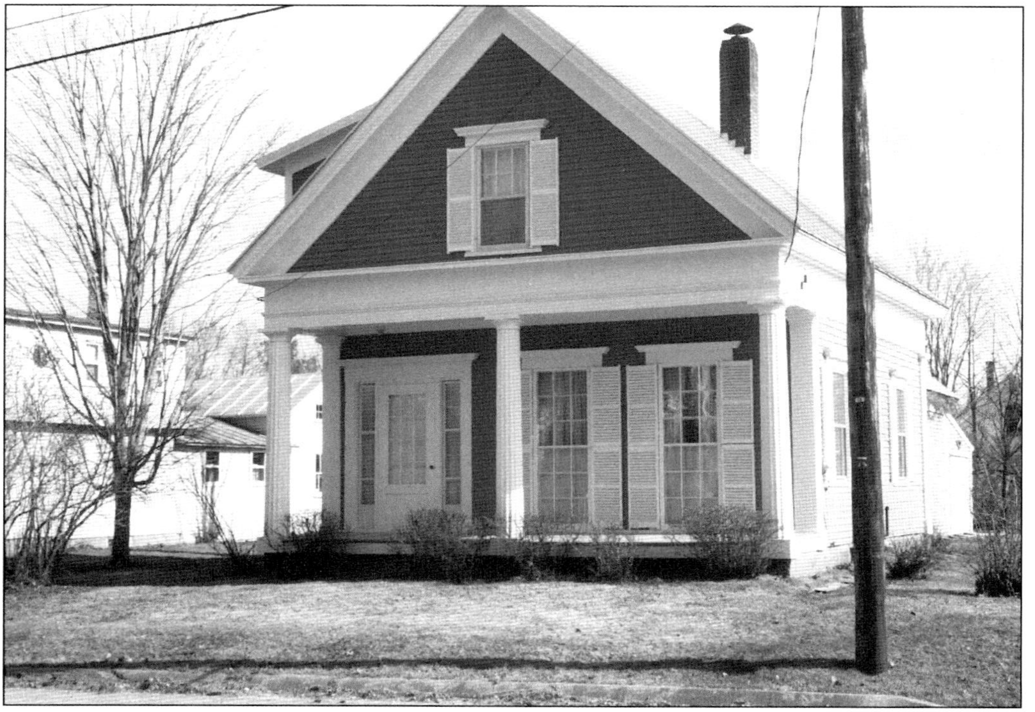

A closer view of the Greek Revival architecture.

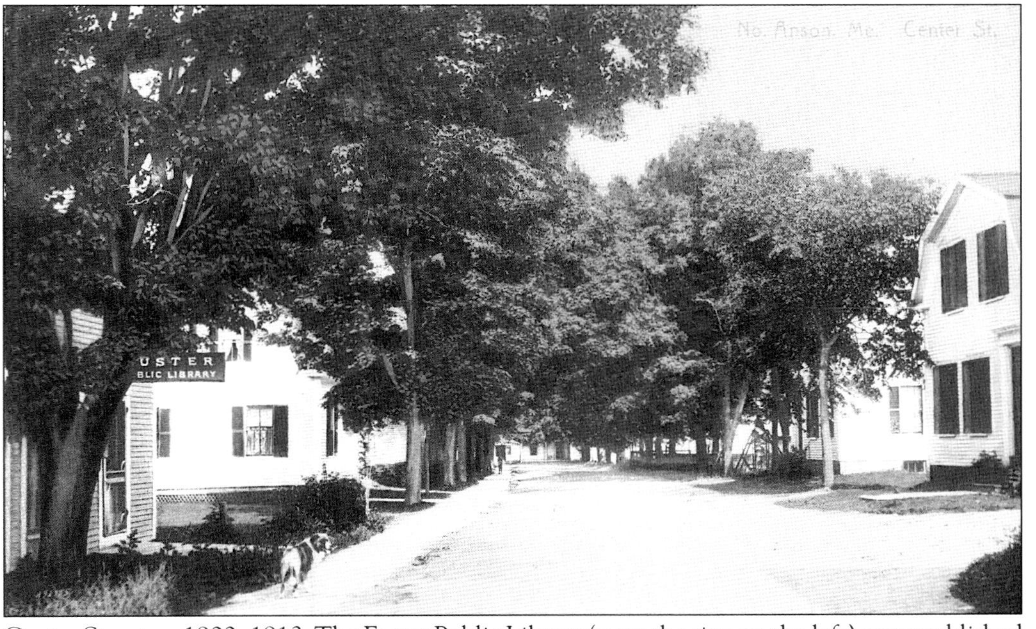

Center Street, *c*. 1900–1913. The Foster Public Library (note the sign on the left) was established in 1899. It was first known as the Anson Public Library and was housed in a building on Center Street belonging to the Masons.

The new public library and building. After the 1913 fire, the name was changed to the Stewart Public Library, and the present Elm Street building was purchased from the Carrabassett Stock Farms.

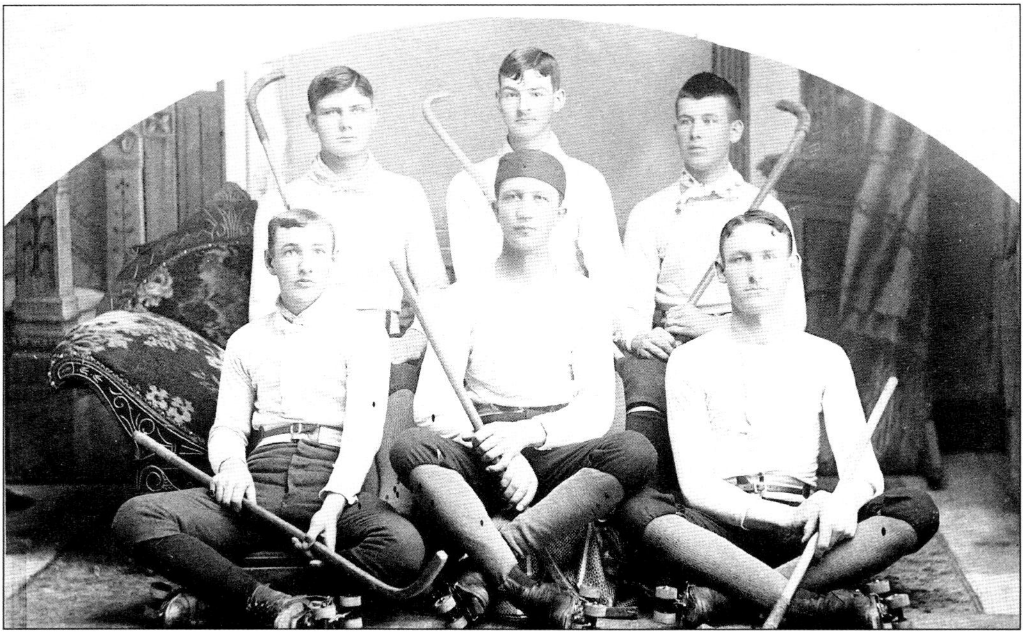

A *c.* 1900 photograph featuring a roller hockey team from North Anson. From left to right, they are as follows: (front row) Clarence "Stub" Penny, Ben Mantor, and Dan McLaughlin; (back row) Frank Jones, ? Russell, and Pearly B. Thompson.

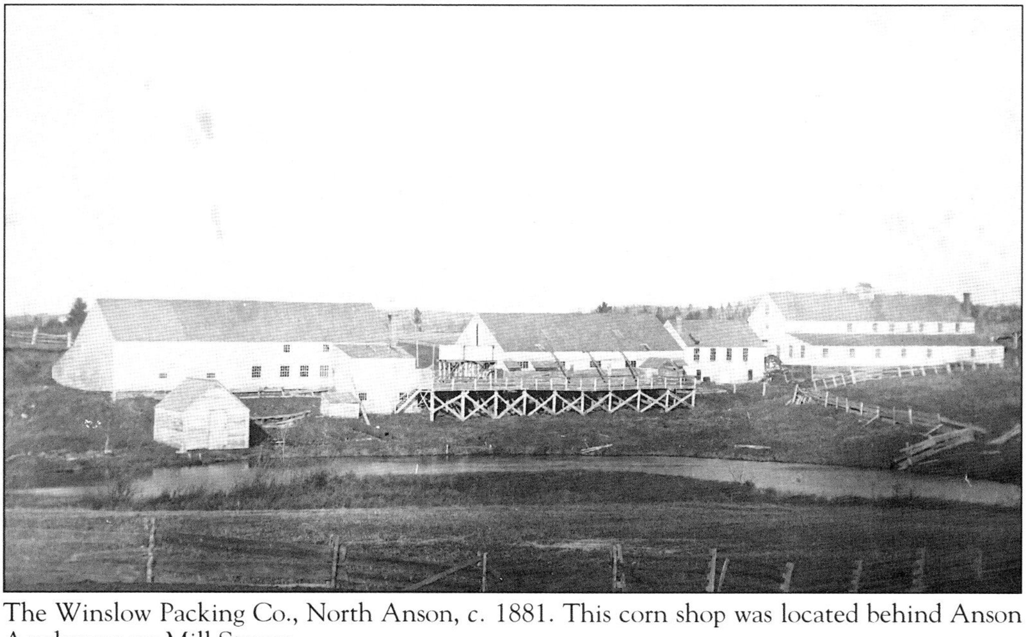

The Winslow Packing Co., North Anson, *c.* 1881. This corn shop was located behind Anson Academy near Mill Stream.

The old wooden bridge spanning the Carrabassett River at North Anson, built in 1851. Though earlier bridges were washed away, this bridge continued in service until 1886, when it was replaced with the first iron bridge. The building to the left is shown before the fire of 1863, which consumed most of the stores on the east side of Main Street from the bridge to Center Street.

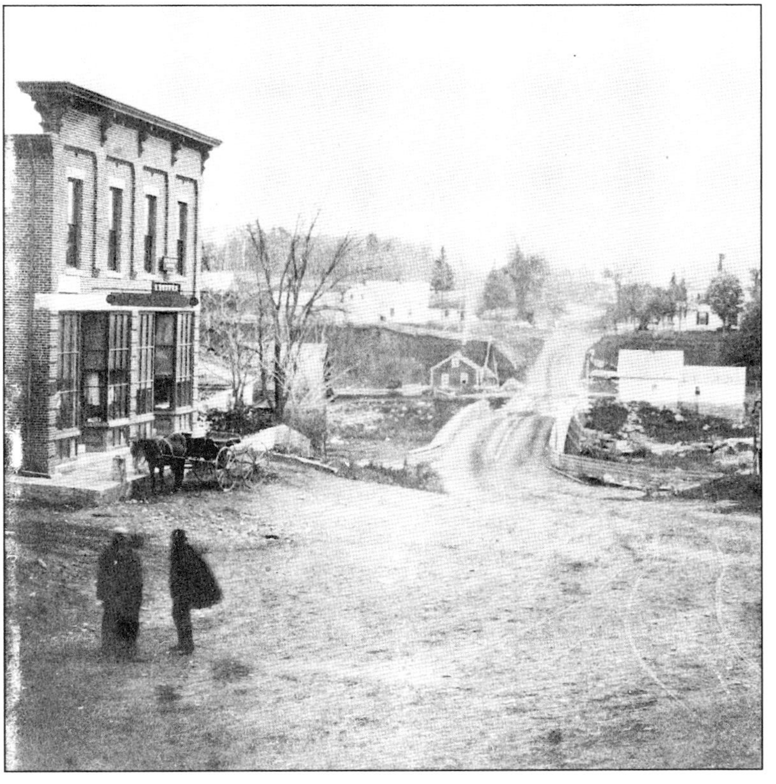

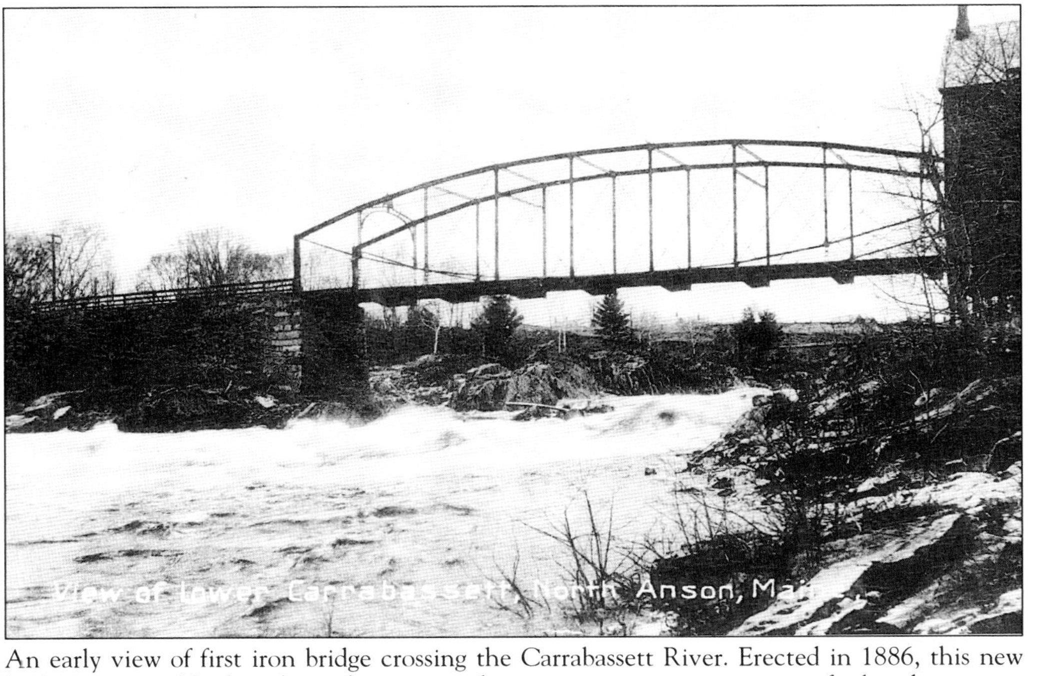

An early view of first iron bridge crossing the Carrabassett River. Erected in 1886, this new bridge was raised higher above the water with no center supports to prevent freshet damage.

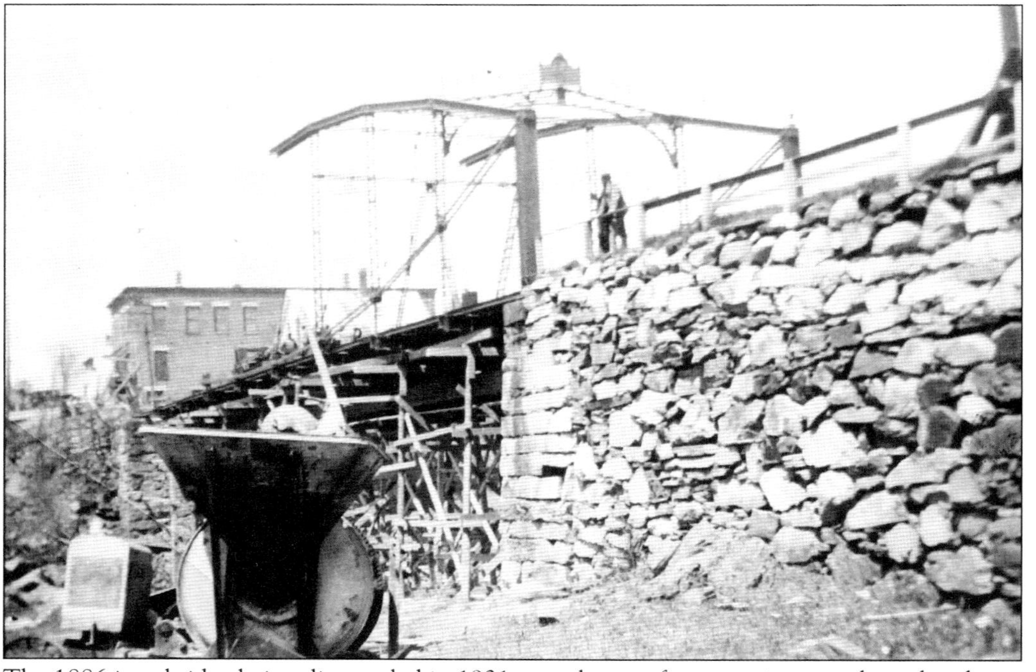

The 1886 iron bridge being dismantled in 1931 to make way for a new improved overhead iron bridge, the so-called "green bridge."

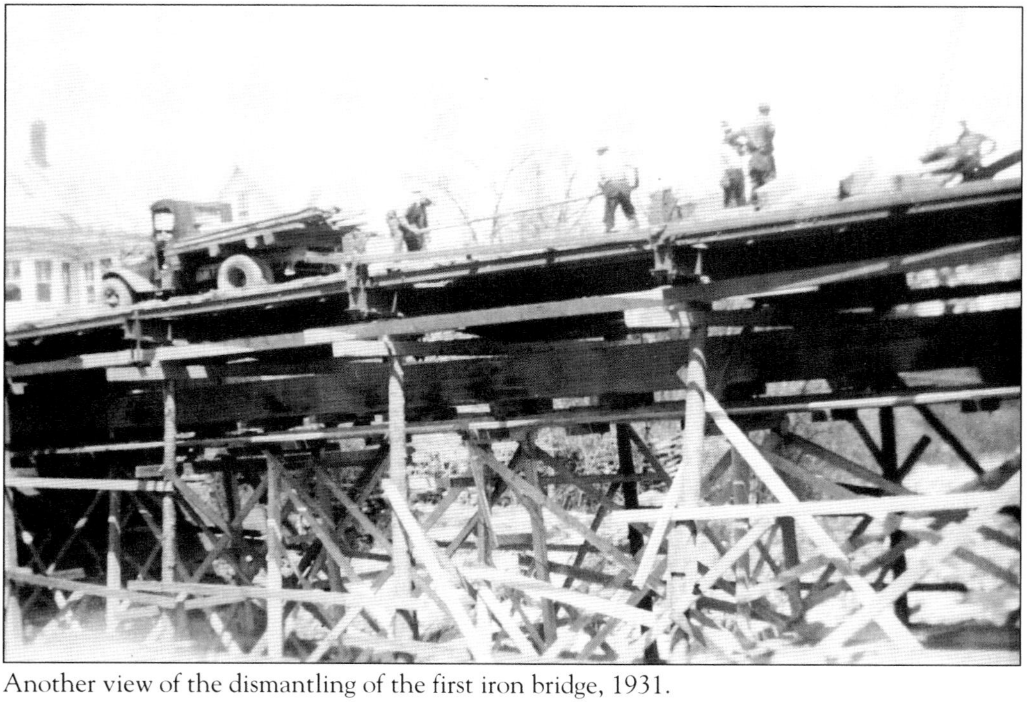

Another view of the dismantling of the first iron bridge, 1931.

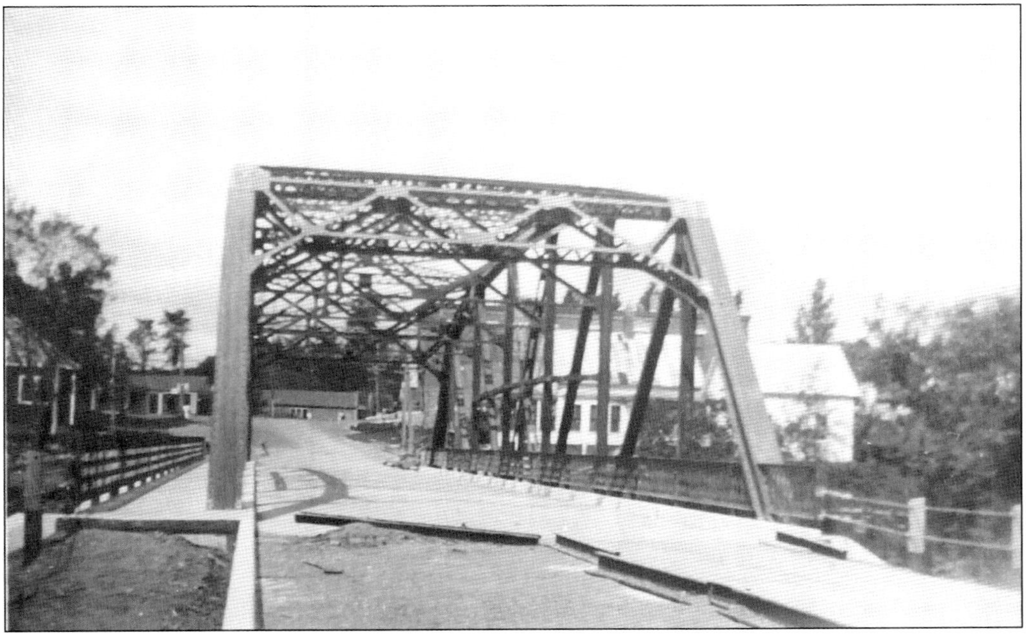

A view of completed second iron bridge in 1931.

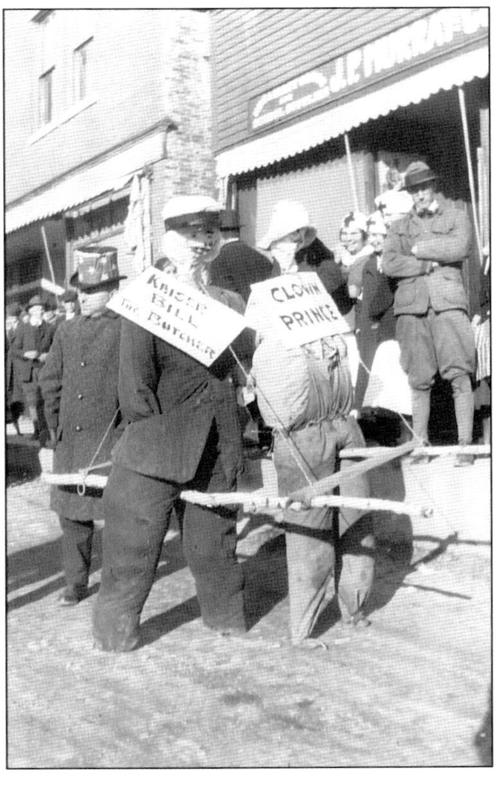

A WW I rally on Main Street, North Anson, *c.* 1914–1918. George Allen is shown here in knickers.

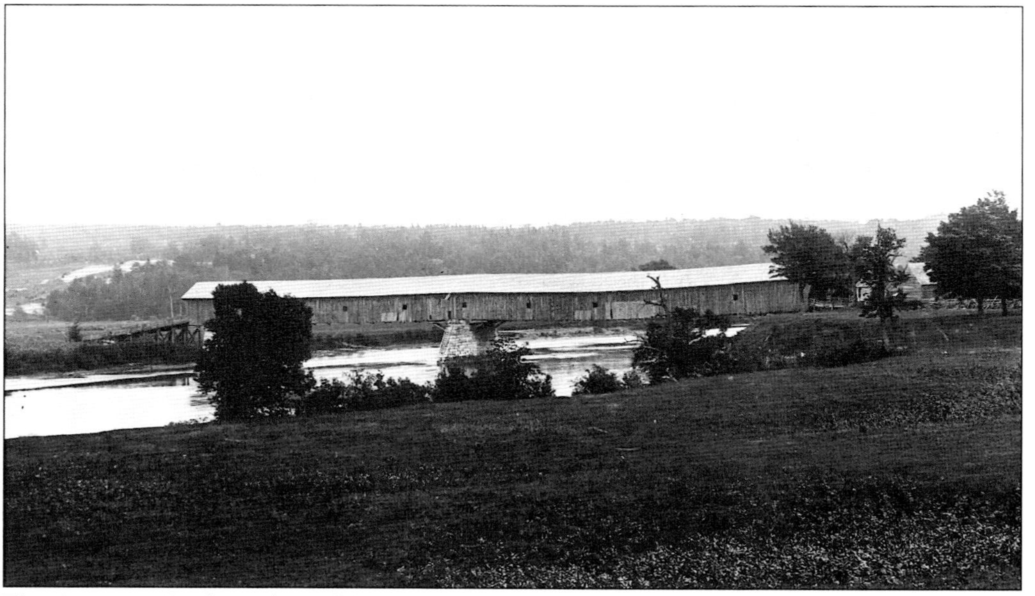

The Patterson Bridge. This toll bridge was built across the Kennebec River in 1840, and was first known as the Madison and Anson Bridge. It consisted of two spans, 160 and 170 feet long, on granite abutments and one center pier. The roof was supported by three trusses. The two lanes of the bridge were separated by lattice work. The sides were enclosed but had window-like openings. The bridge was destroyed by fire in July 1926.

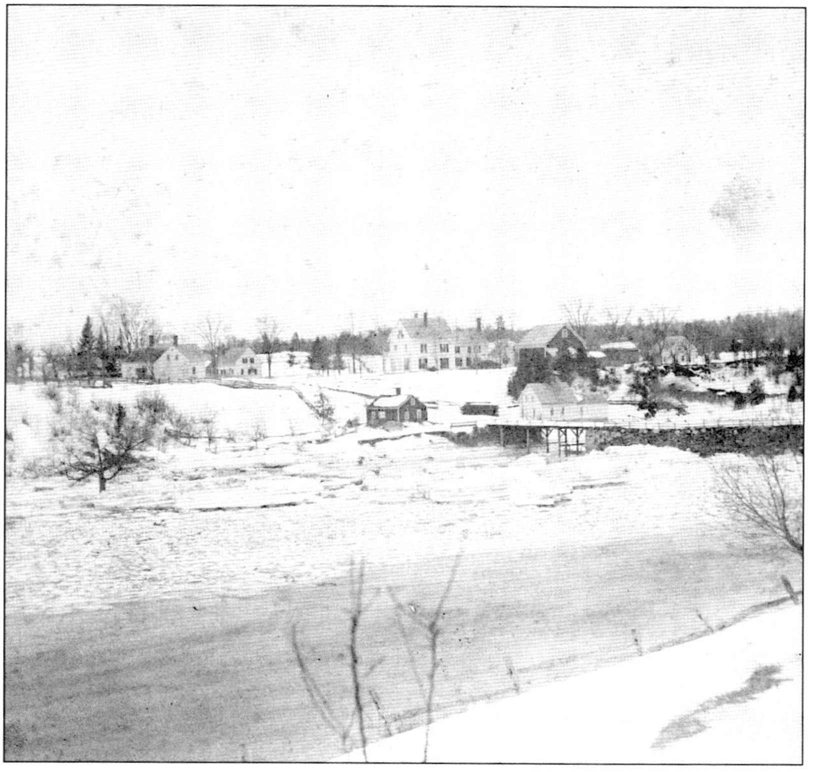

A stereoptic view looking across the Carrabassett River, c. 1875. The house in the center is now known as the Carrabassett Inn.

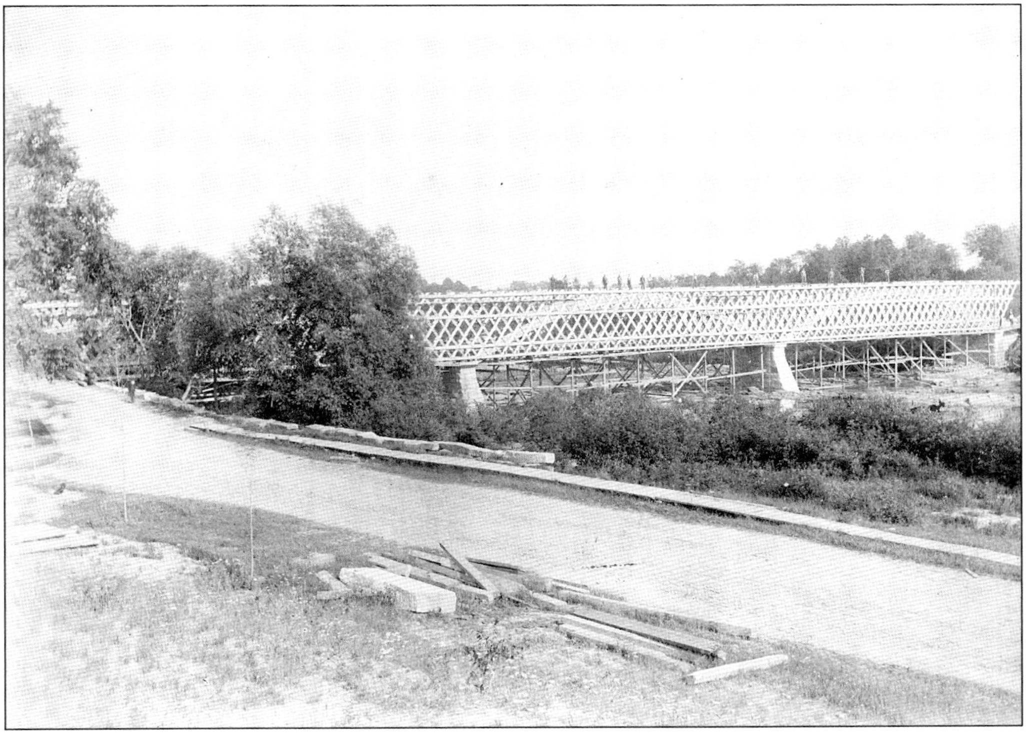

The first Somerset Railroad Bridge under construction over the Carrabassett River, 1888, looking downriver.

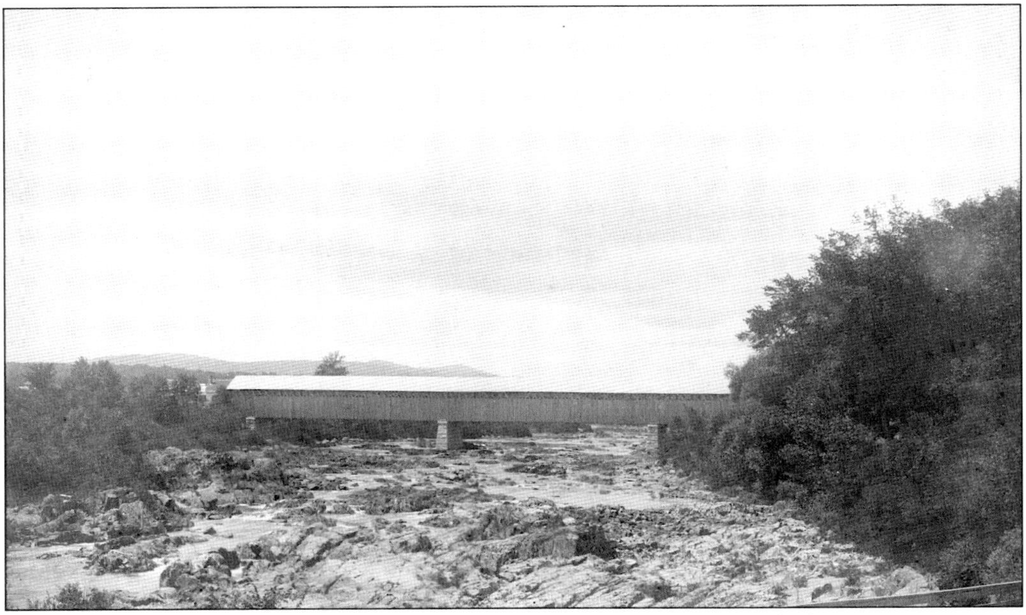

The completed covered railroad bridge crossing the Carrabassett River, looking upriver.

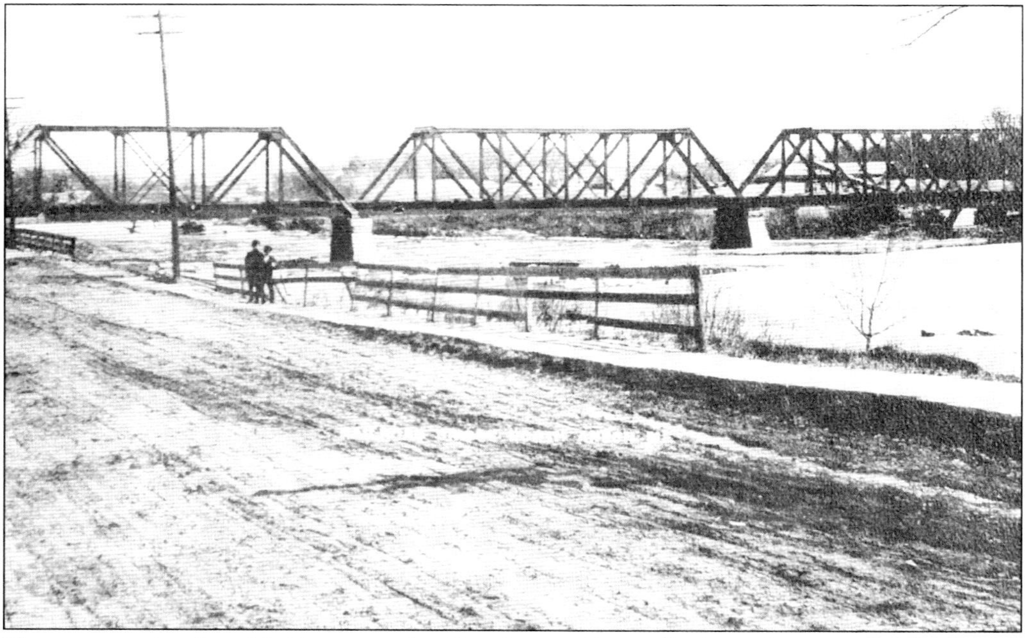

The new steel railroad bridge over the Carrabassett River (looking downriver). This bridge replaced the covered wood bridge in 1907.

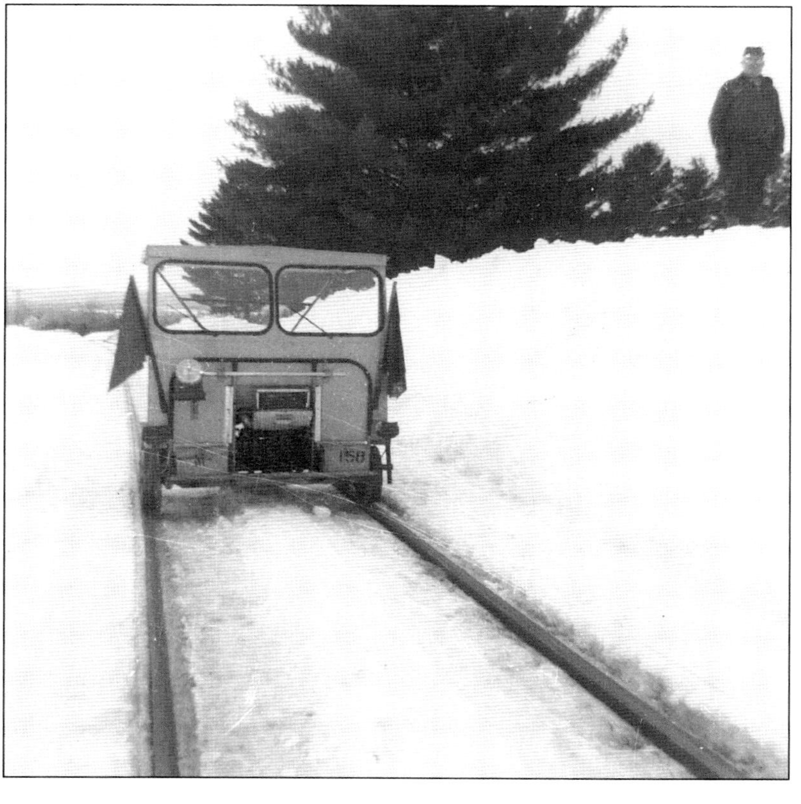

A motor car used by the section crew to inspect and repair the tracks. The man on the snowbank is Guy Rolfe, a member of the crew.

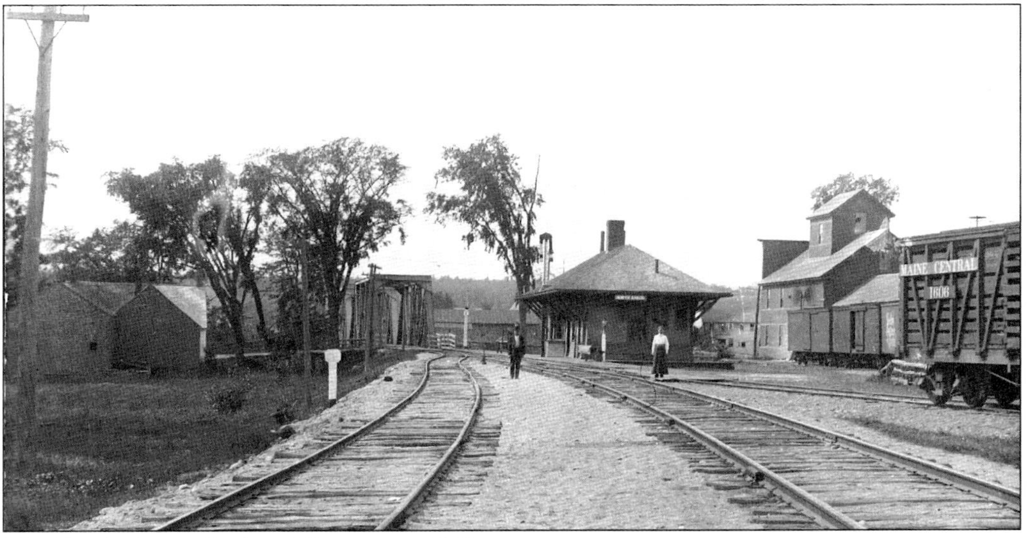

The North Anson Railroad Station, c. 1920.

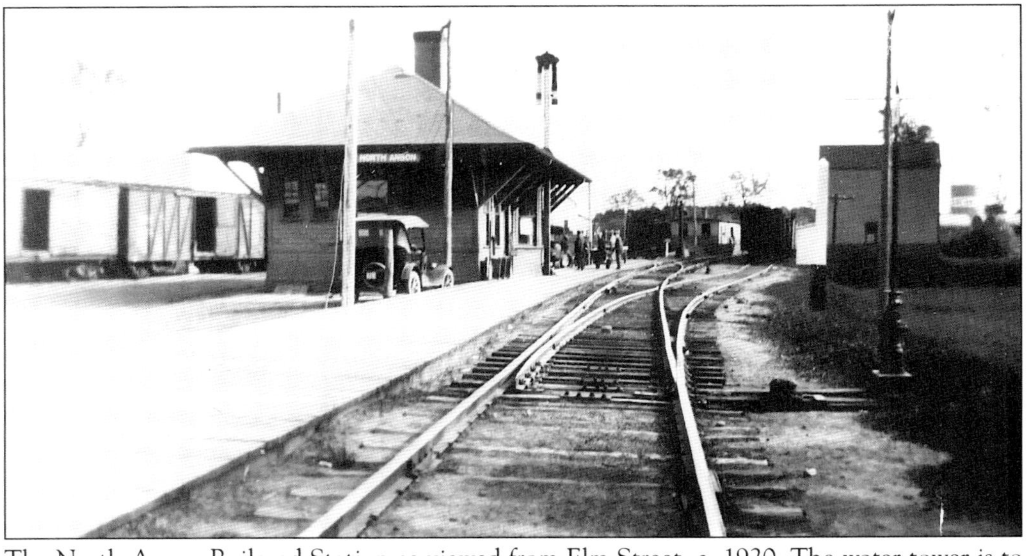

The North Anson Railroad Station as viewed from Elm Street, c. 1920. The water tower is to the right, while the freight station is to the rear.

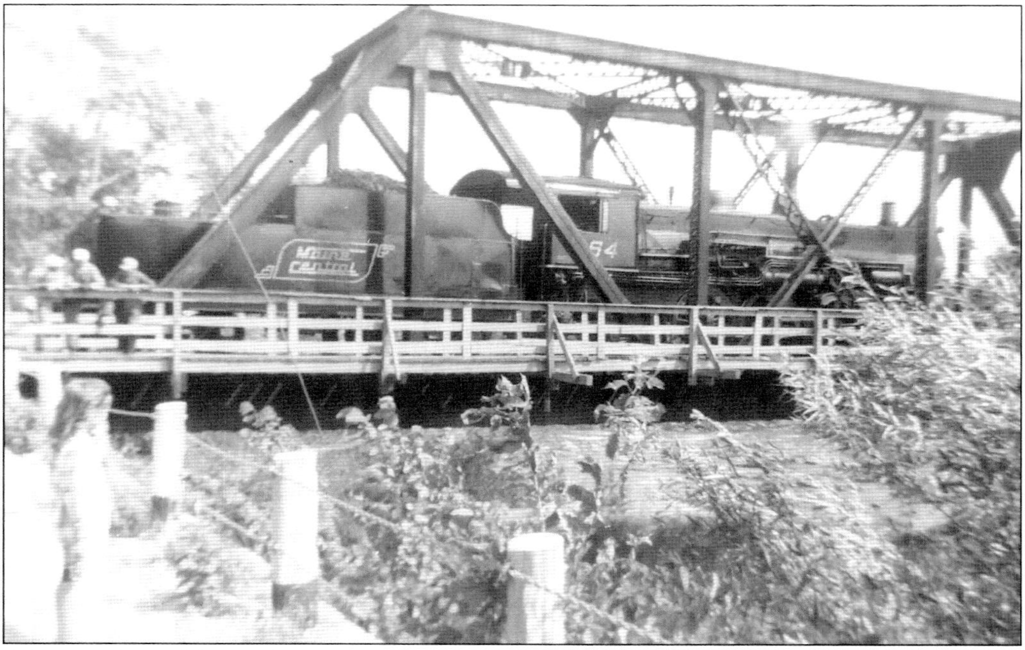

A Maine Central Steam Locomotive passing over the Carrabassett.

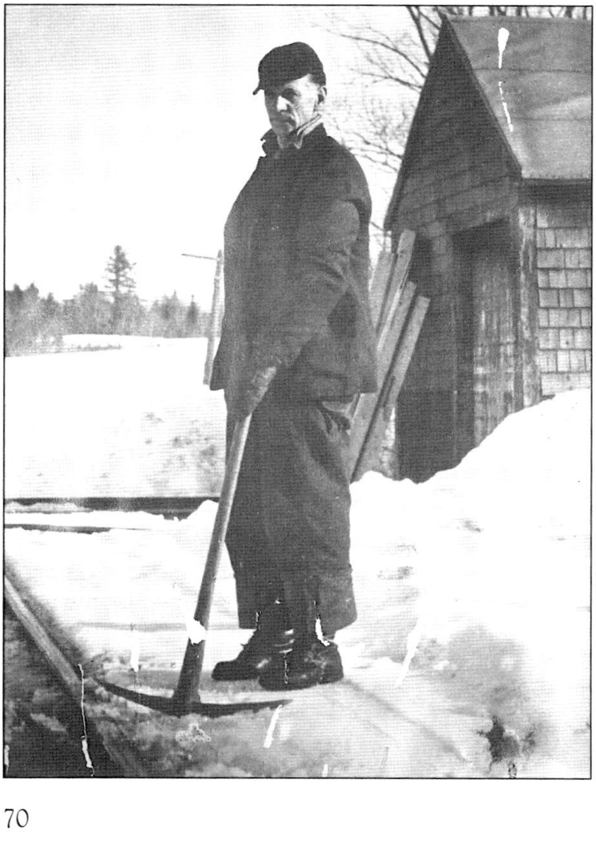

Warren Bessey, section foreman for the Maine Central Railroad in North Anson for 33 years. This photograph was taken in front of the carhouse before his retirement in 1969.

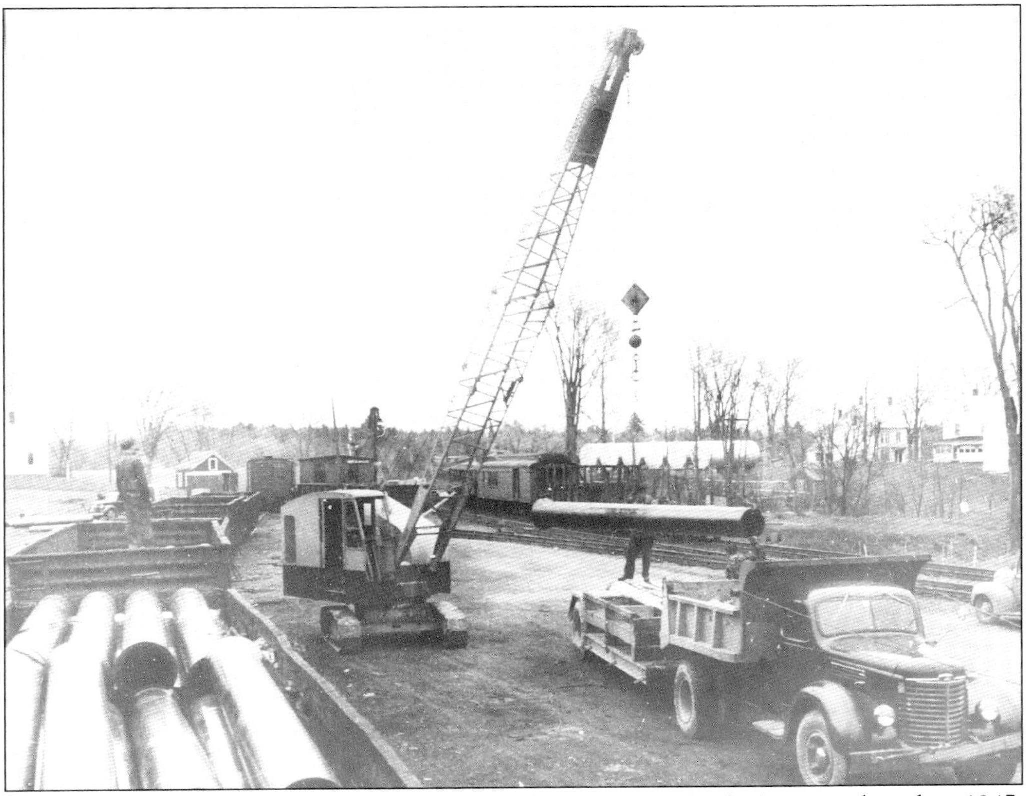

Anson Water District unloading 16-inch main line pipes at North Anson rail yard in 1947. This pipe was used to replace wooden pipes to Hancock Pond.

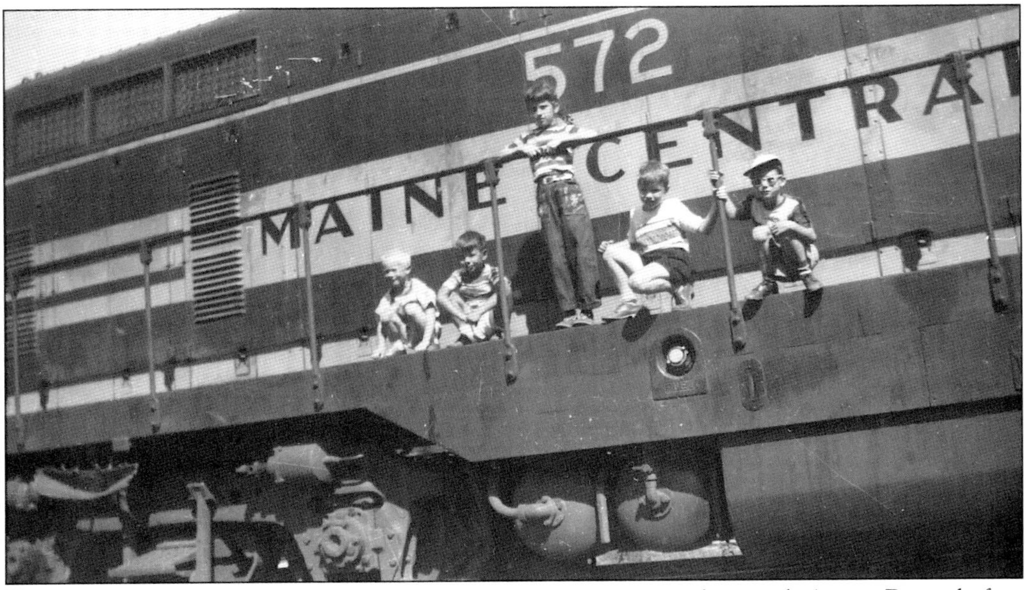

Devereux children checking out a Maine Central locomotive at the North Anson Depot before their trip home to Pennsylvania.

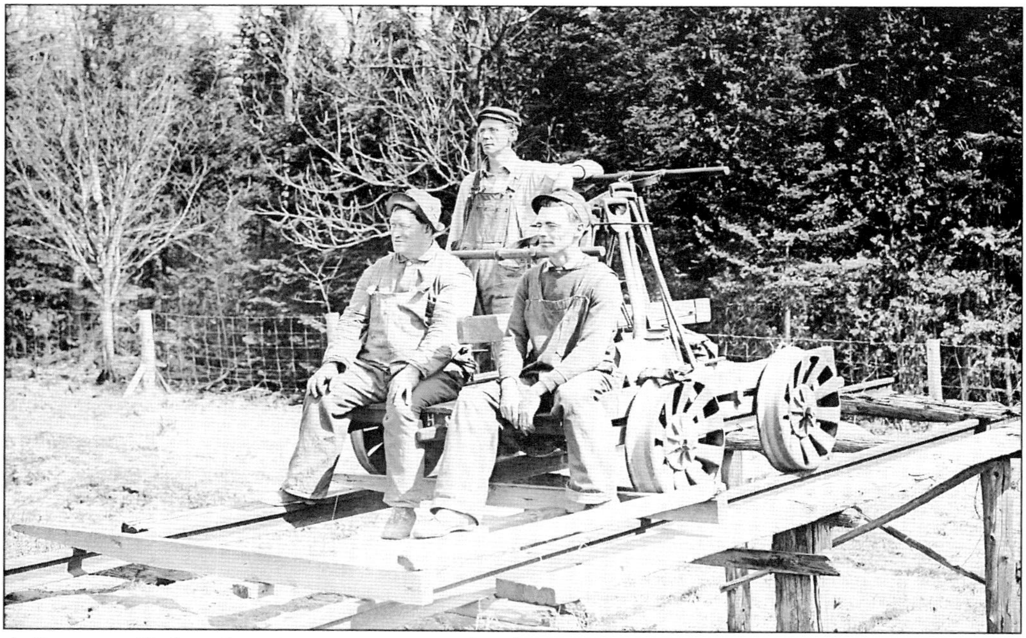

A Somerset Railroad section crew waiting for the train to pass, *c.* 1910. They are, from left to right: Lonnie Otis, Fred Viles, and Raymond Gordon.

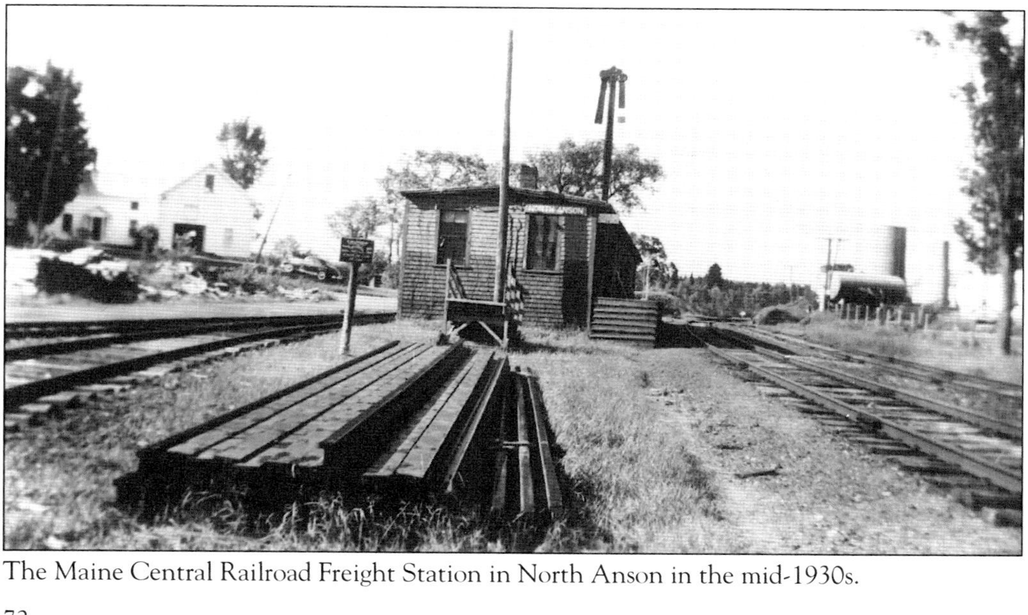

The Maine Central Railroad Freight Station in North Anson in the mid-1930s.

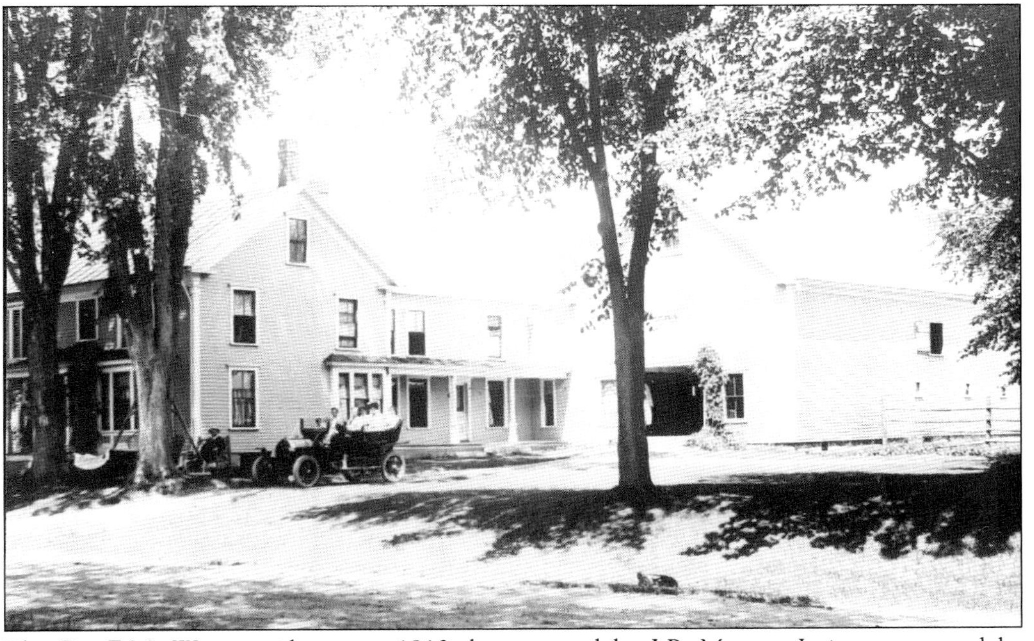

The Dr. E.M. Wing residence, c. 1910, later owned by J.P. Murray. It is now owned by Gary Agren.

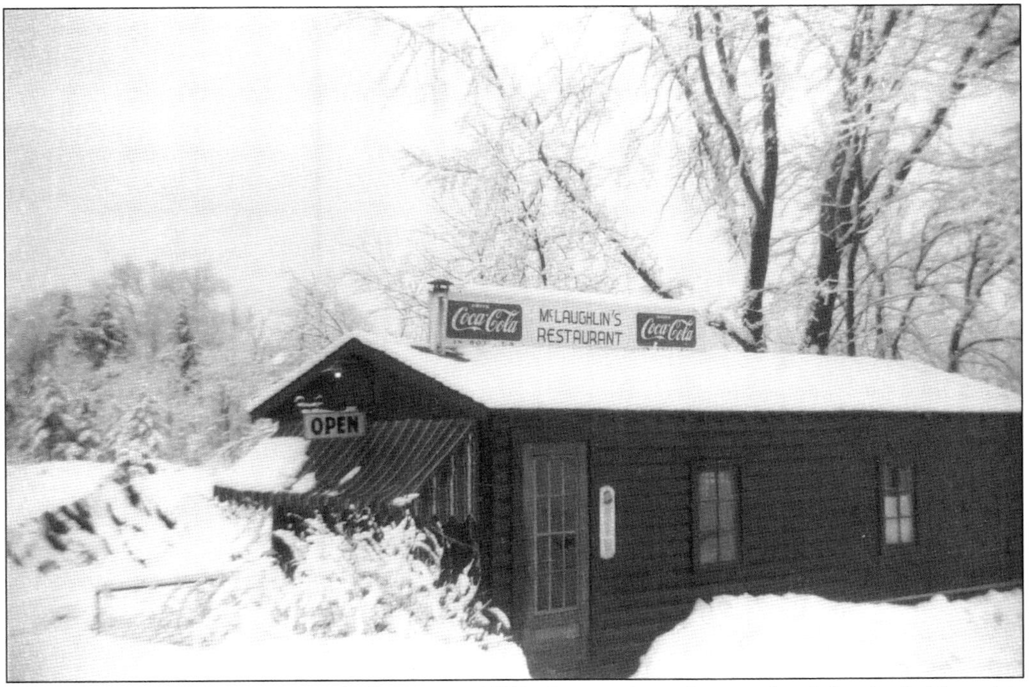

McLaughlin's Restaurant, North Anson, c. 1950s. Located on the riverbank by the bridge, this little restaurant, run by Mel McLaughlin, was known for its great food.

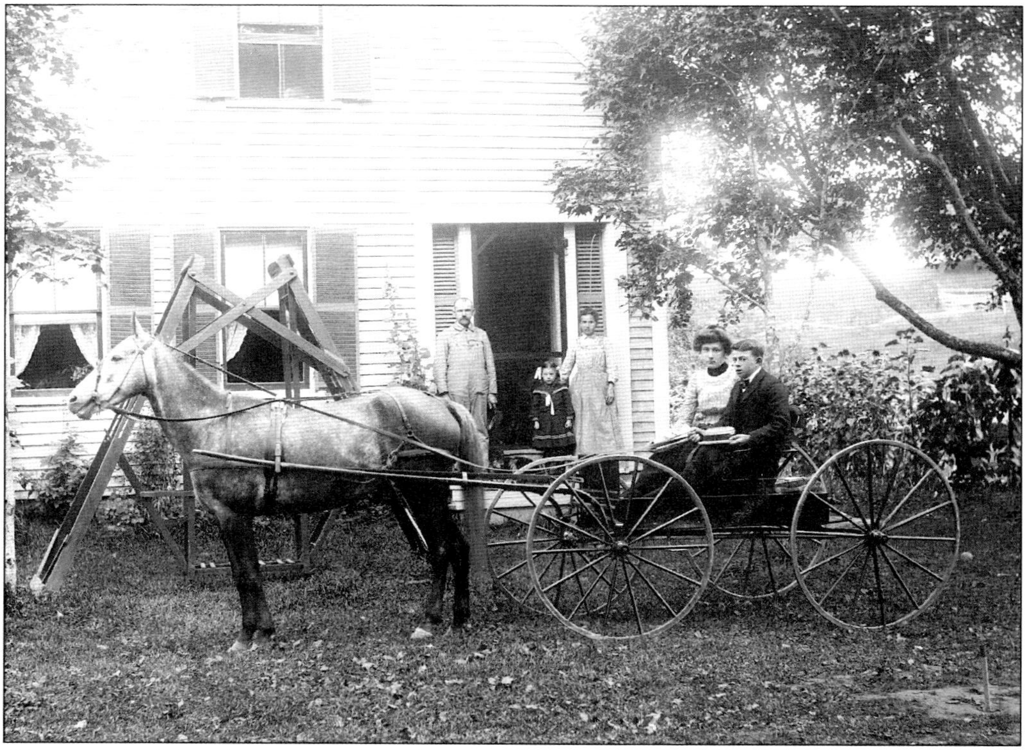

Olistin and Althea Savage and their family, c. 1915. Olistin and Althea are standing in the doorway. They are the owners of O.W. Savage Livery Service.

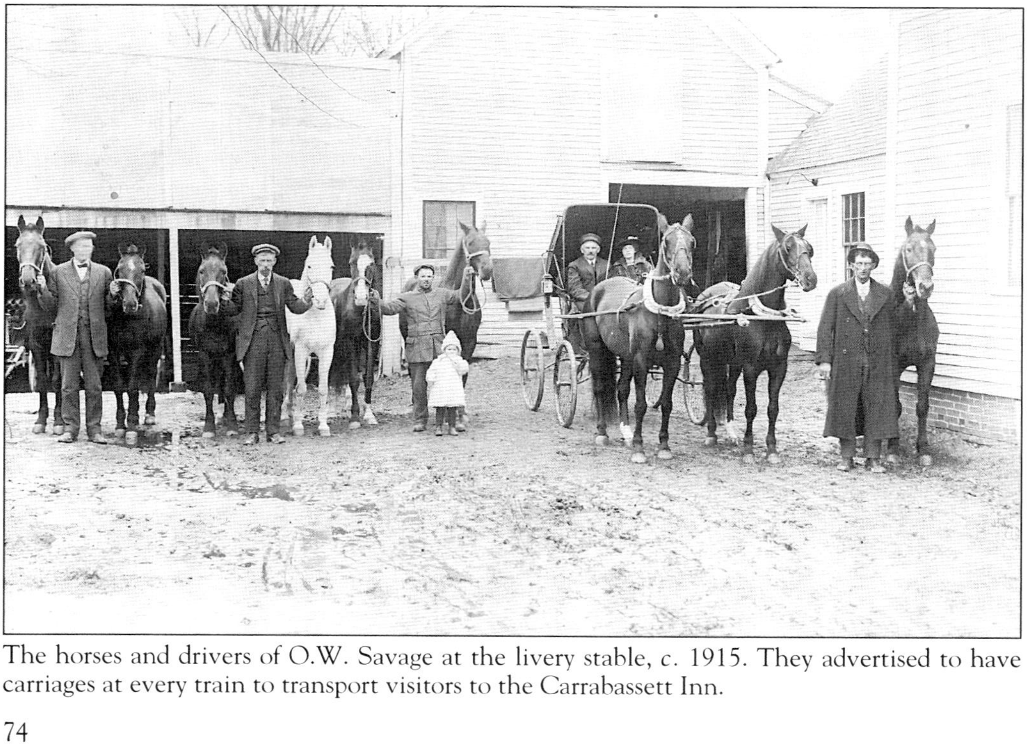

The horses and drivers of O.W. Savage at the livery stable, c. 1915. They advertised to have carriages at every train to transport visitors to the Carrabassett Inn.

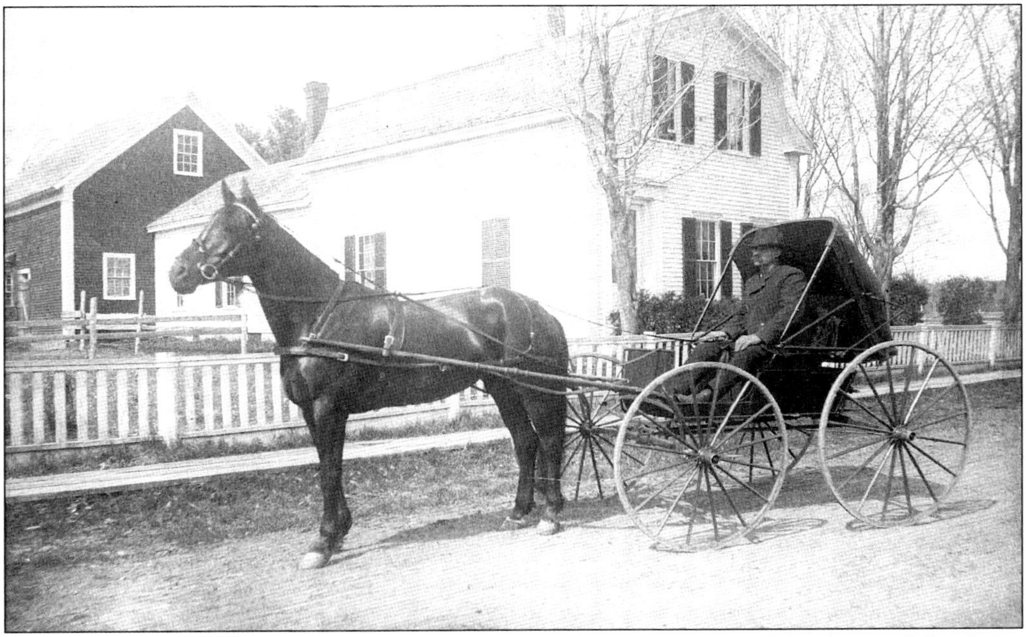

A view of the horse-drawn buggy days on Center Street, North Anson. The date and the driver are unknown. The house is the William Hartwell house.

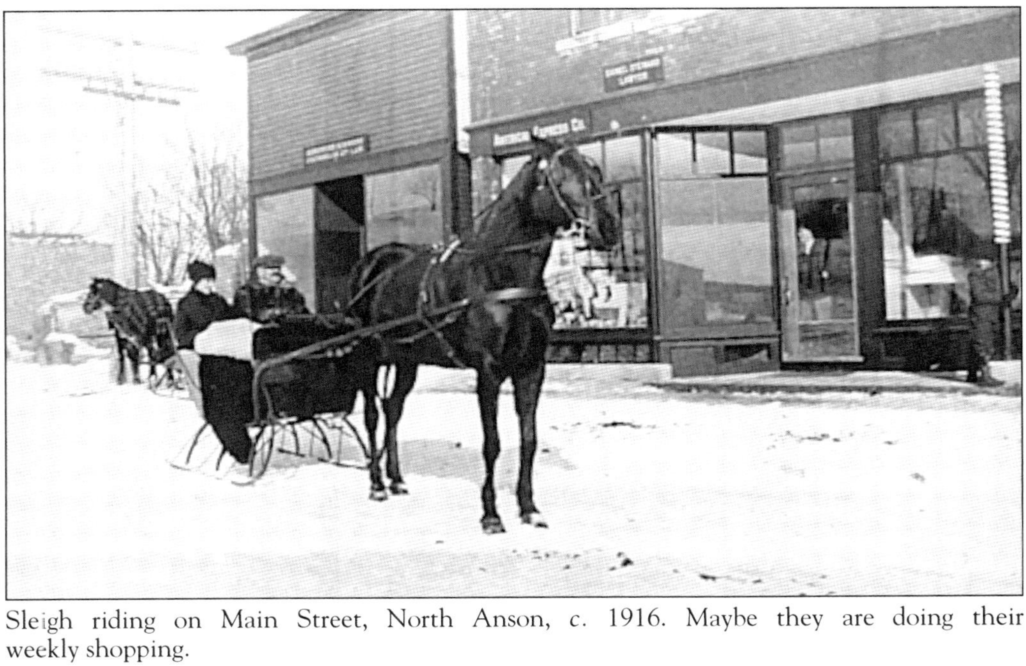

Sleigh riding on Main Street, North Anson, *c.* 1916. Maybe they are doing their weekly shopping.

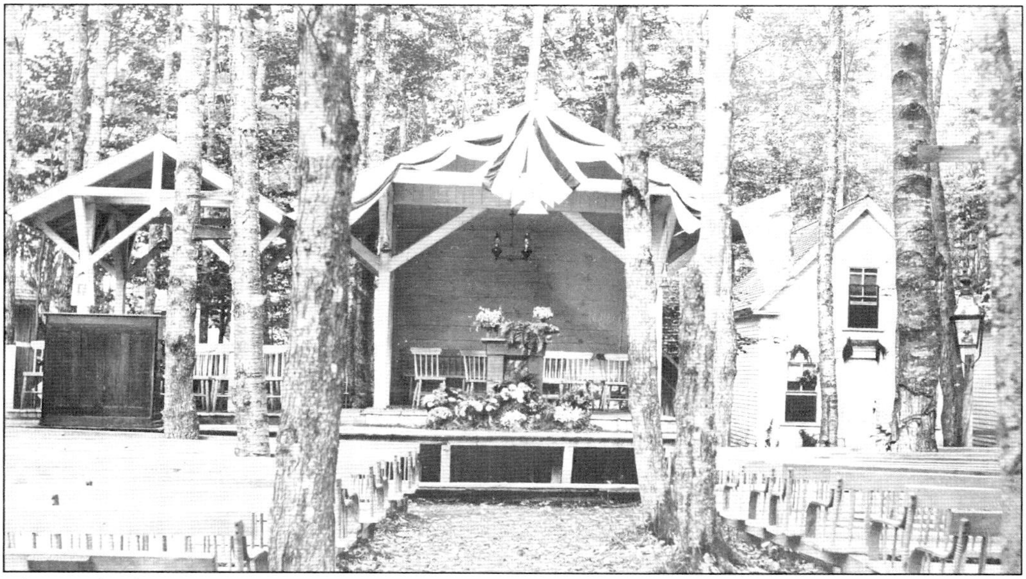

The Methodist Camp Ground, located off the Camp Ground Road, North Anson, c. 1900.

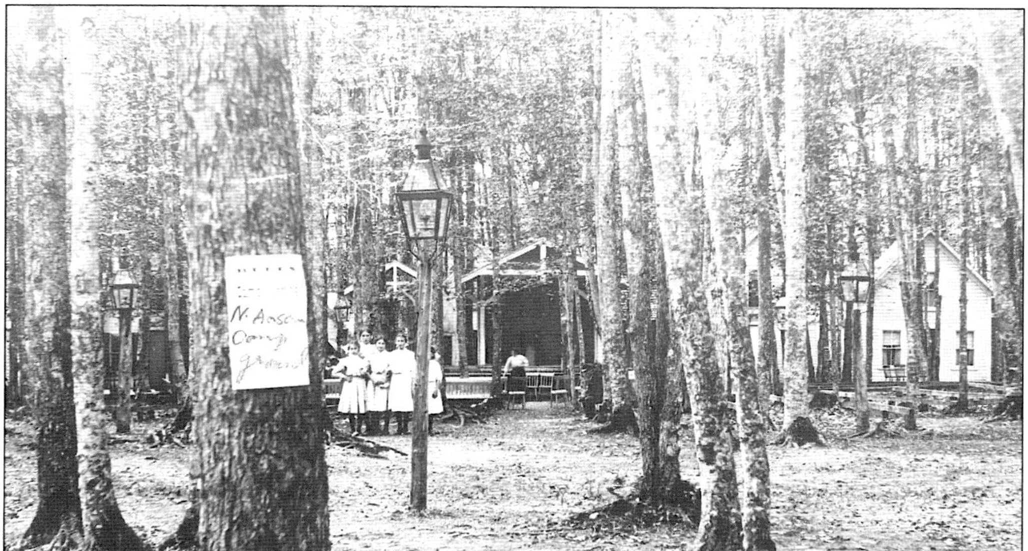

A view from the Methodist Camp Ground, opened in 1872 and closed in 1920.

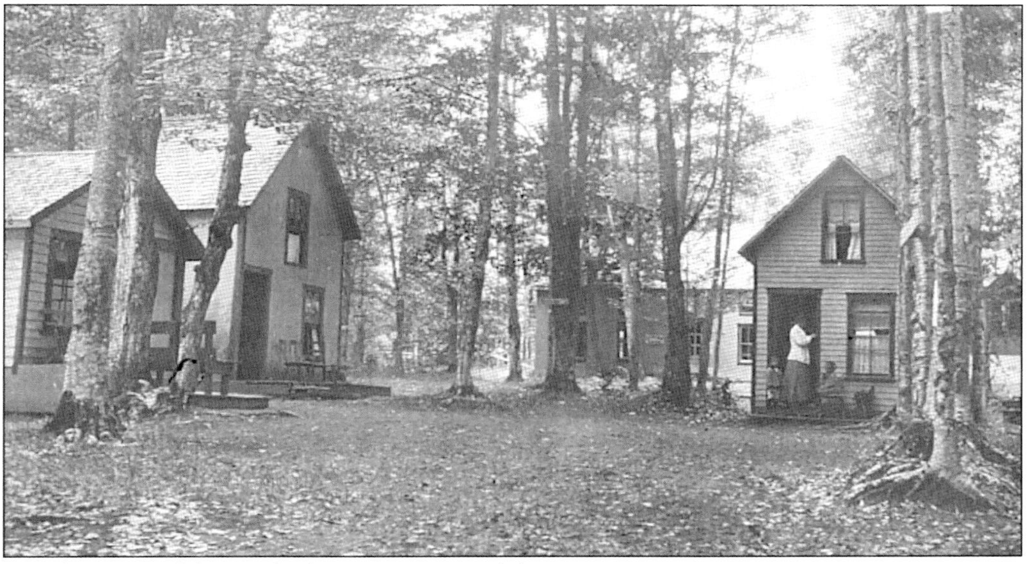

Another view of the Methodist Camp Ground showing cottages.

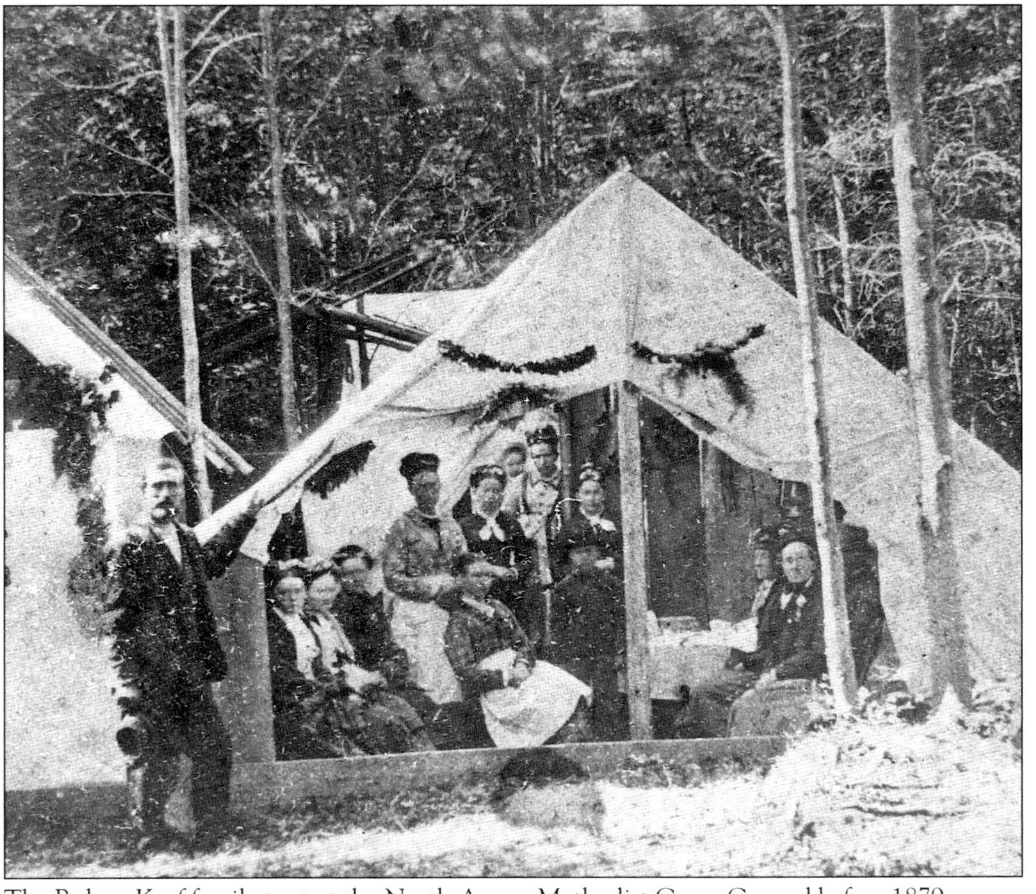

The Robert Keef family tent at the North Anson Methodist Camp Ground before 1879.

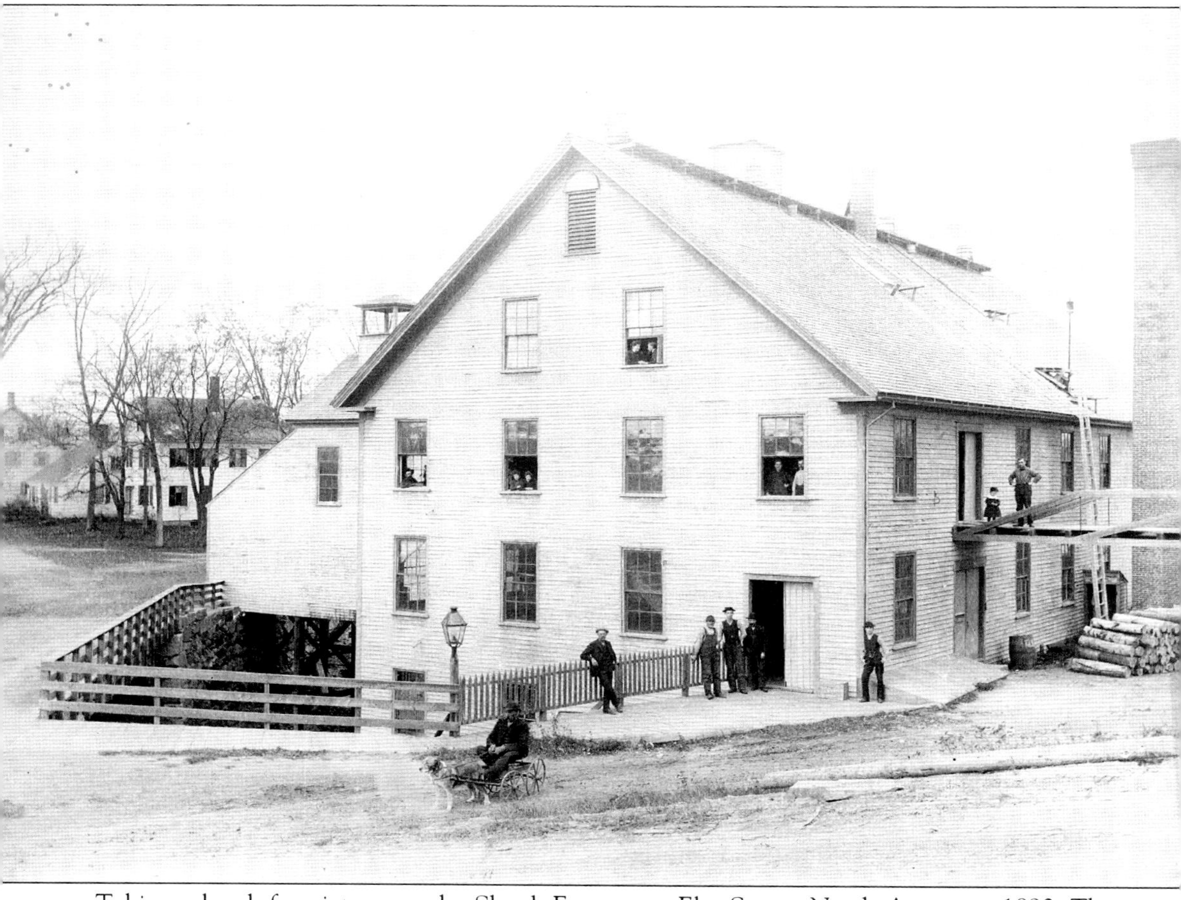

Taking a break for pictures at the Shank Factory on Elm Street, North Anson, c. 1890. The factory was located on Mill Stream, and was where wooden shoe shanks were made. Twenty to 25 men and women were employed here. The equipment was moved to Bingham 1906–1908. The factory was torn down in later years. In the center of the picture is Henry Perry, along with his dog and wagon.

The town's International TD-18 tractor, making the most of the devastating snow of February 1969. This tractor with plow was purchased in 1946 and has been used extensively in severe storms and driving conditions. It is still held in reserve—it is slow but sure and much in demand when the heavy storms come and the wind blows.

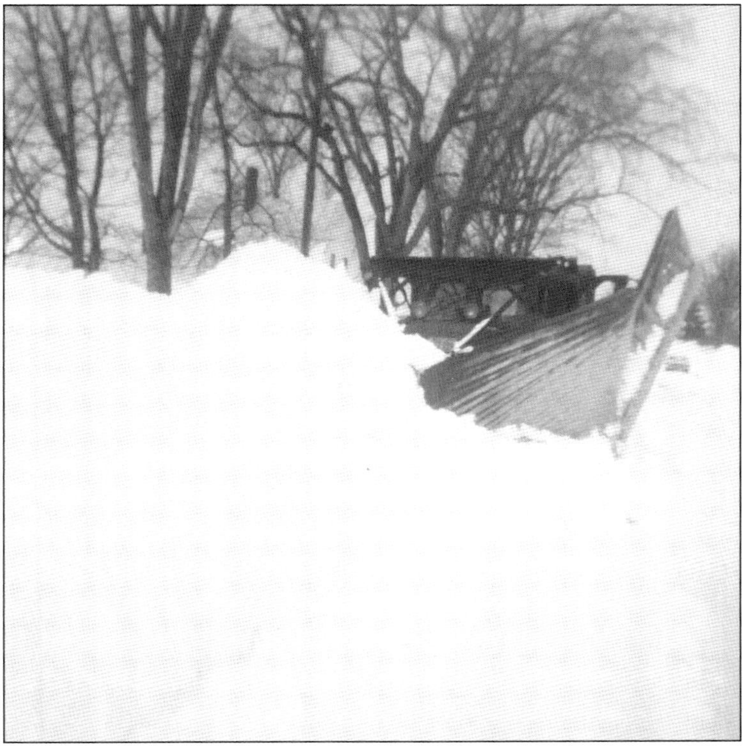

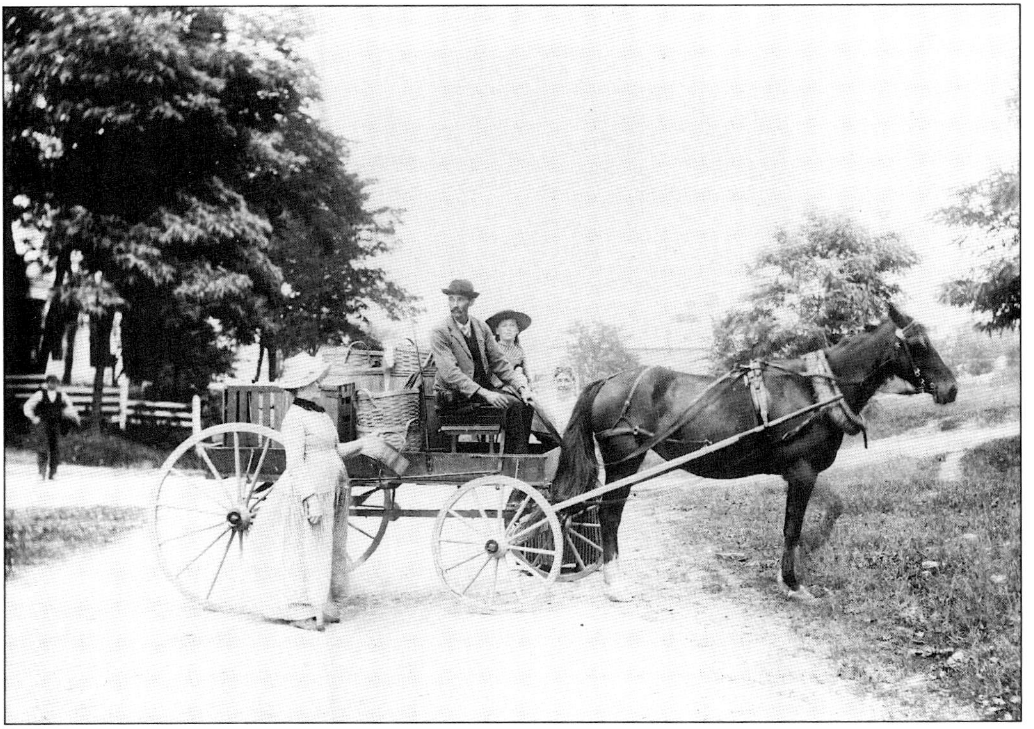

G.W. Spalding, grower of fruits and vegetables, North Anson, *c.* 1890.

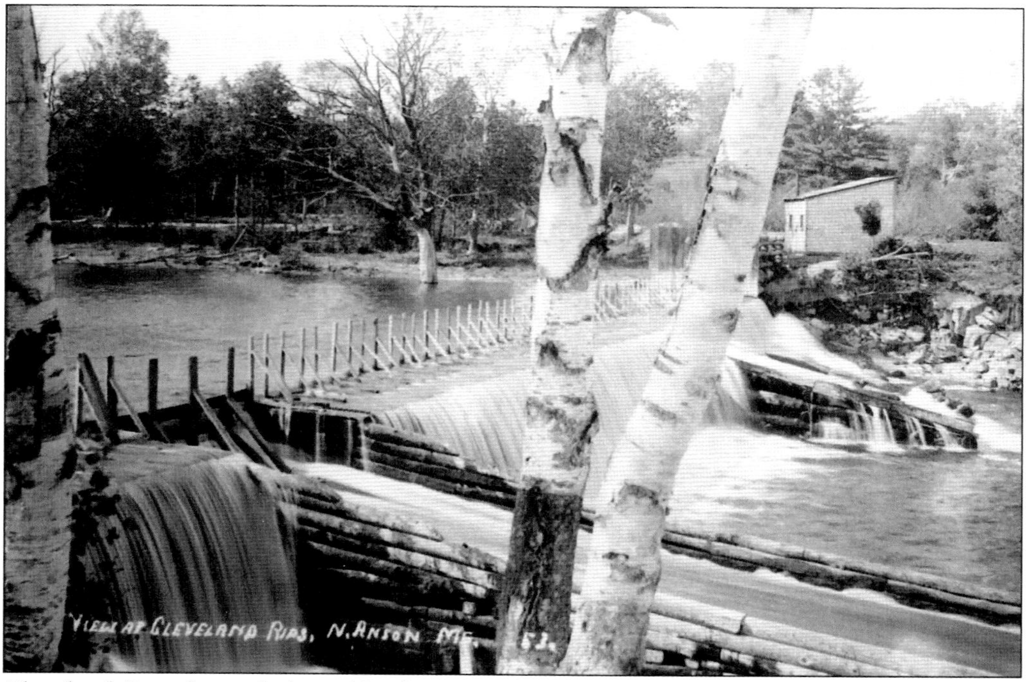

Cleveland Rips, located above North Anson on the Carrabassett River, c. 1920–1930s. An early dam was built here for generating electricity. The lines extended to Farmington. The dam is no longer in use.

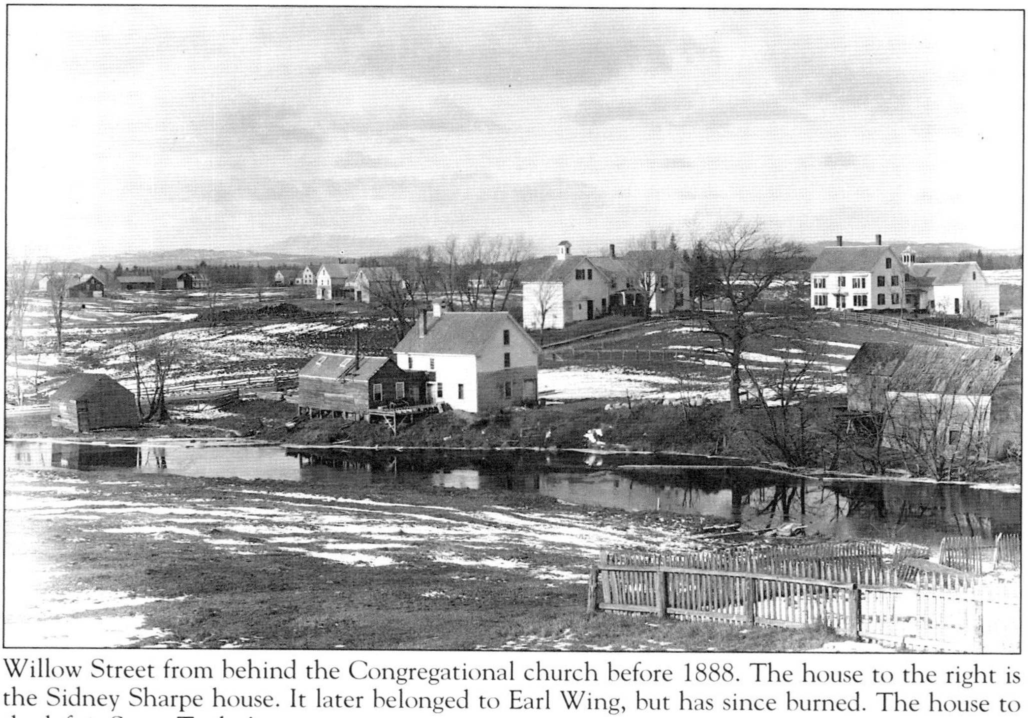

Willow Street from behind the Congregational church before 1888. The house to the right is the Sidney Sharpe house. It later belonged to Earl Wing, but has since burned. The house to the left is Steve Taylor's.

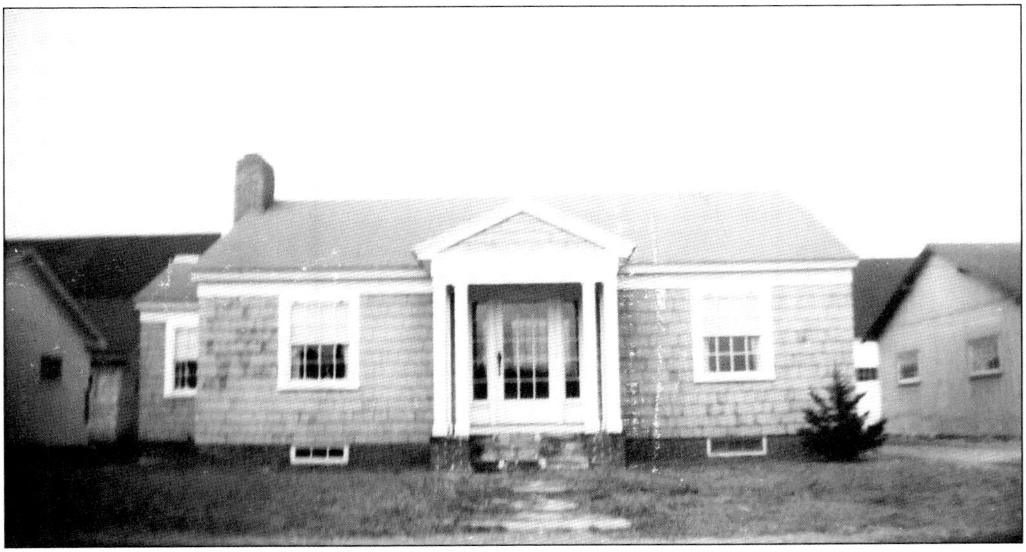

The Beaver Wood Products Office, *c.* 1945.

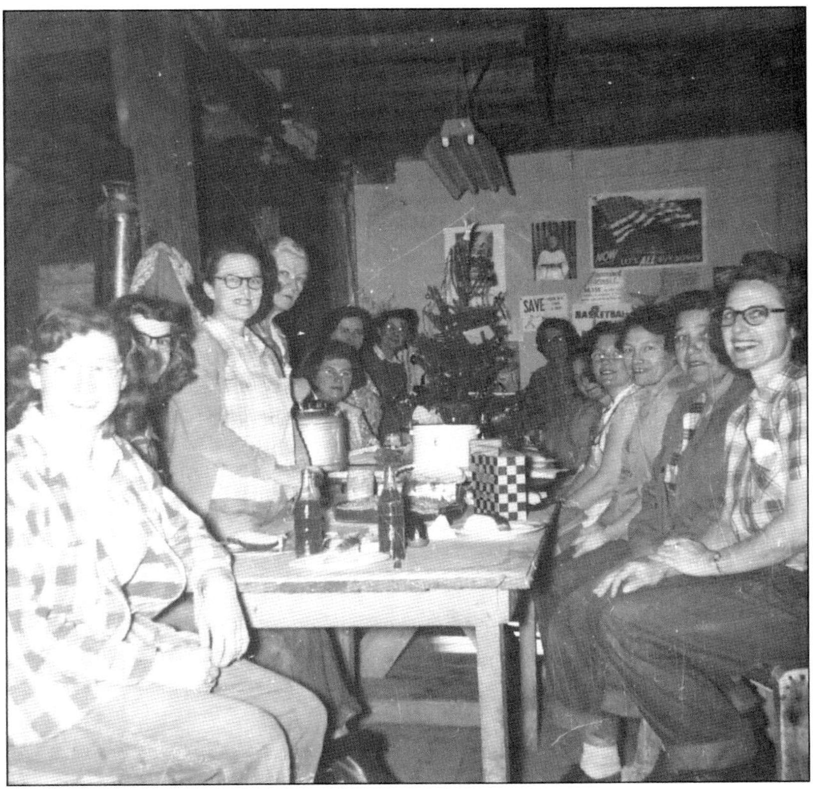

A Christmas party at Beaver Wood Products, *c.* 1940.

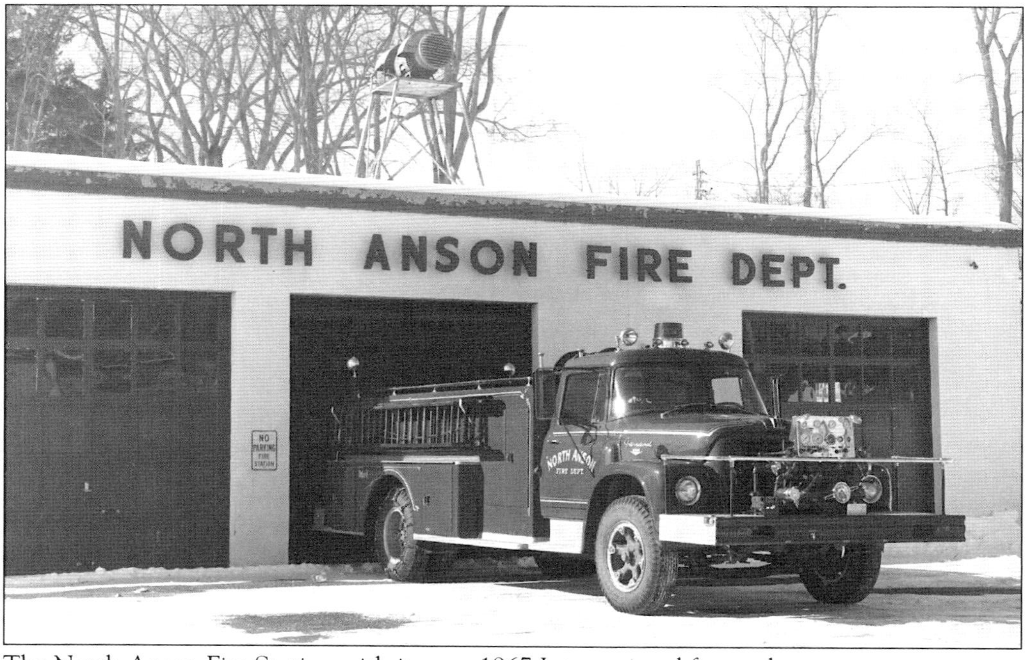

The North Anson Fire Station with its new 1967 International firetruck.

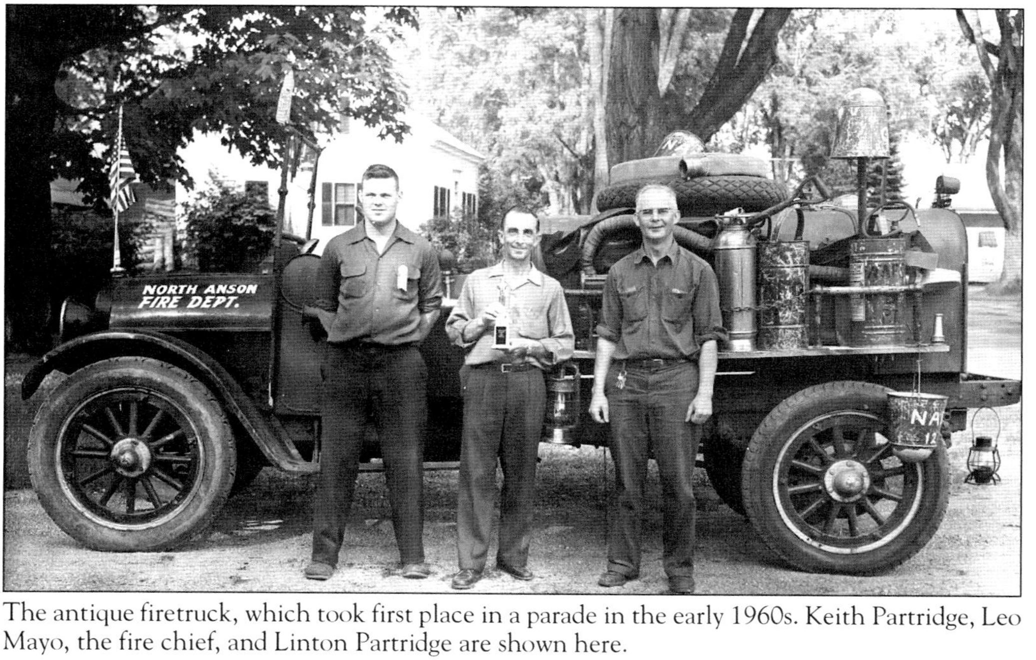

The antique firetruck, which took first place in a parade in the early 1960s. Keith Partridge, Leo Mayo, the fire chief, and Linton Partridge are shown here.

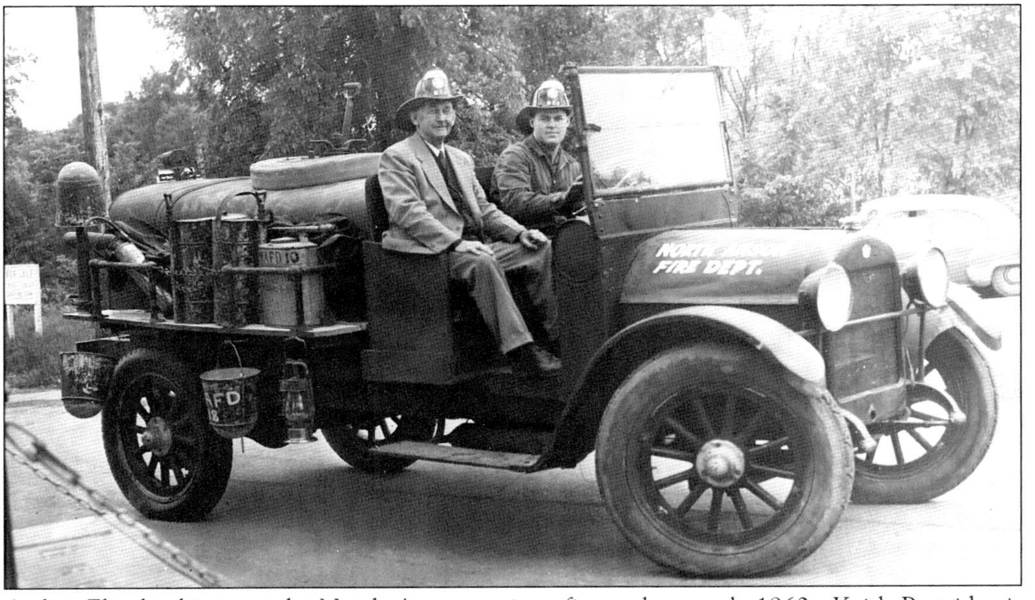

Arthur Ela checking out the North Anson antique firetruck, *c.* early 1960s. Keith Partridge is the driver. The truck is a 1920 REO.

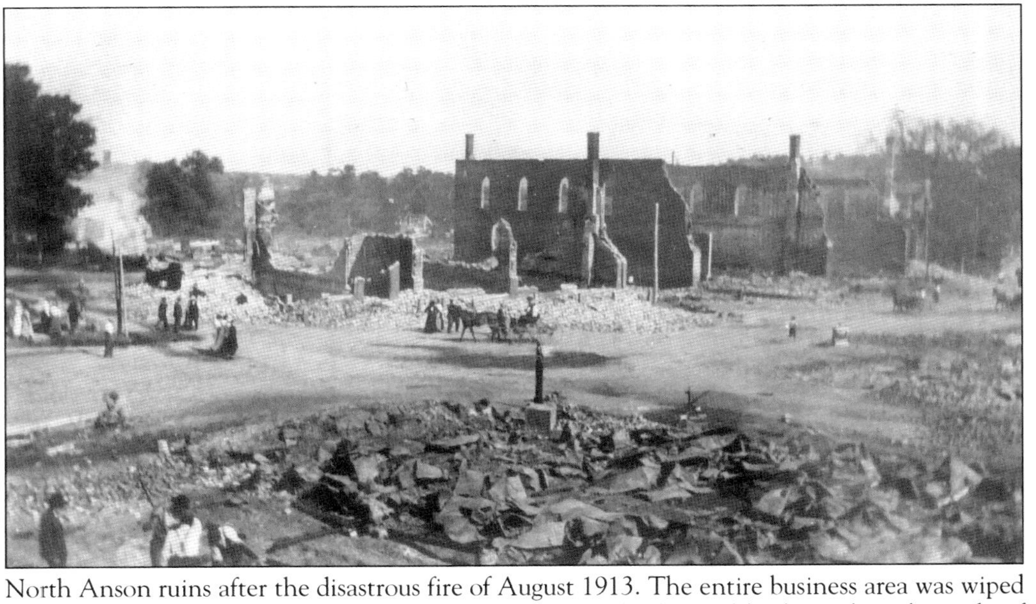

North Anson ruins after the disastrous fire of August 1913. The entire business area was wiped out, on Main Street from the Methodist church to the bridge and back up the other side of Elm Street to the Grange Hall. Twenty-three blocks were destroyed along with about a dozen dwelling houses.

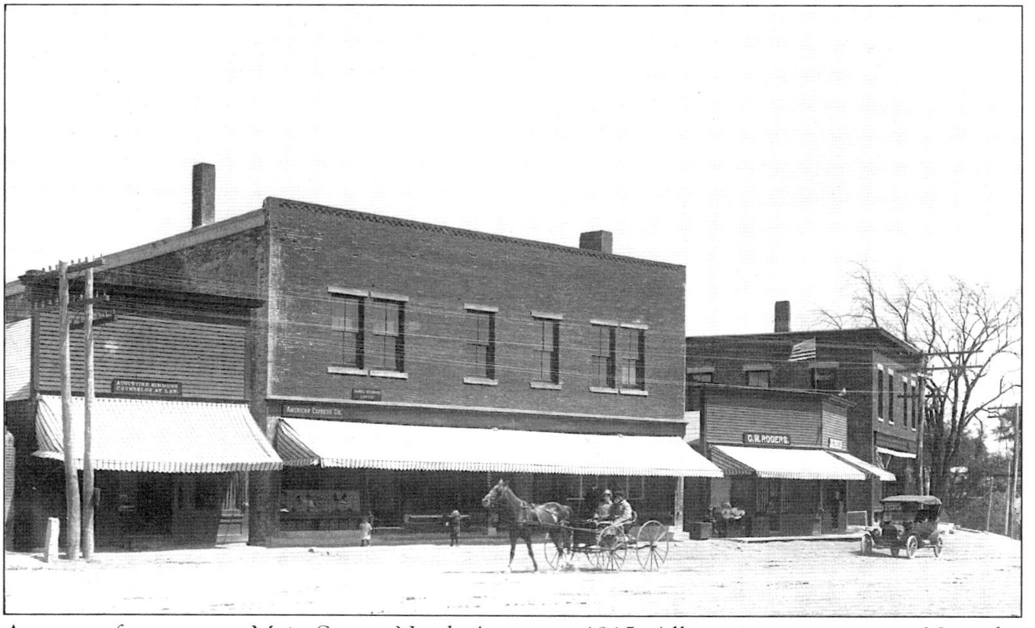

A sunny afternoon on Main Street, North Anson, *c.* 1915. All awnings were in use. Note the old and new transportation vehicles.

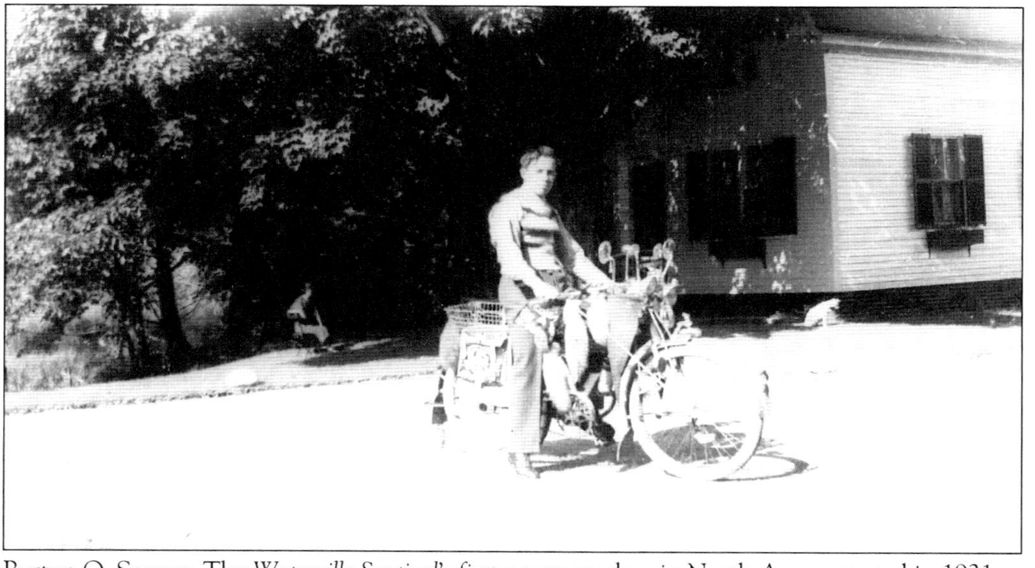

Burton O. Savage. The *Waterville Sentinel*'s first newspaperboy in North Anson started in 1931.

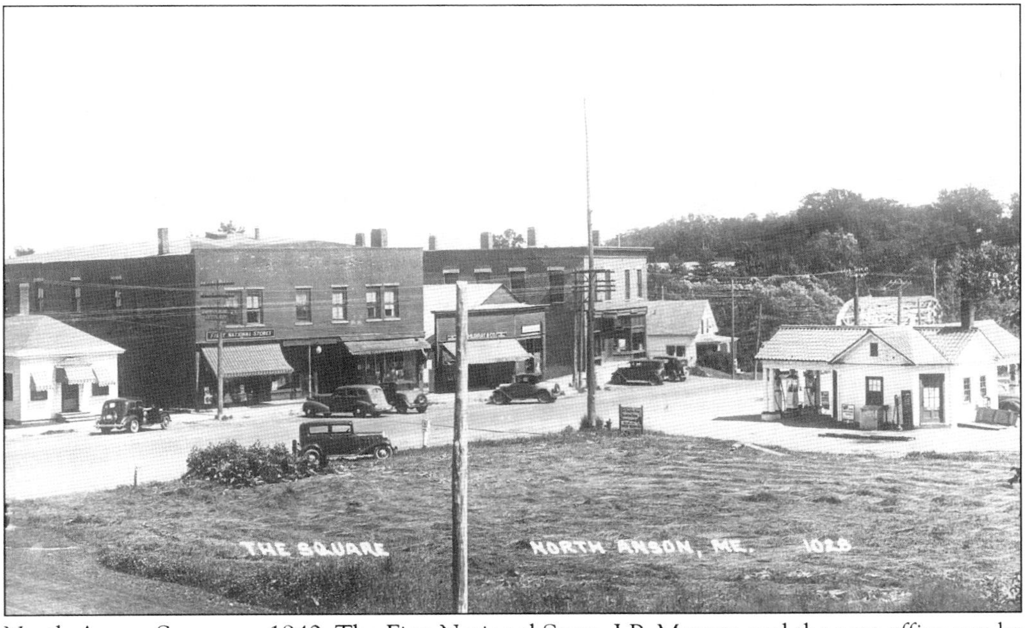

North Anson Square, *c.* 1940. The First National Store, J.P. Murray, and the post office can be seen in the center of the picture. To the right is Dean's filling station.

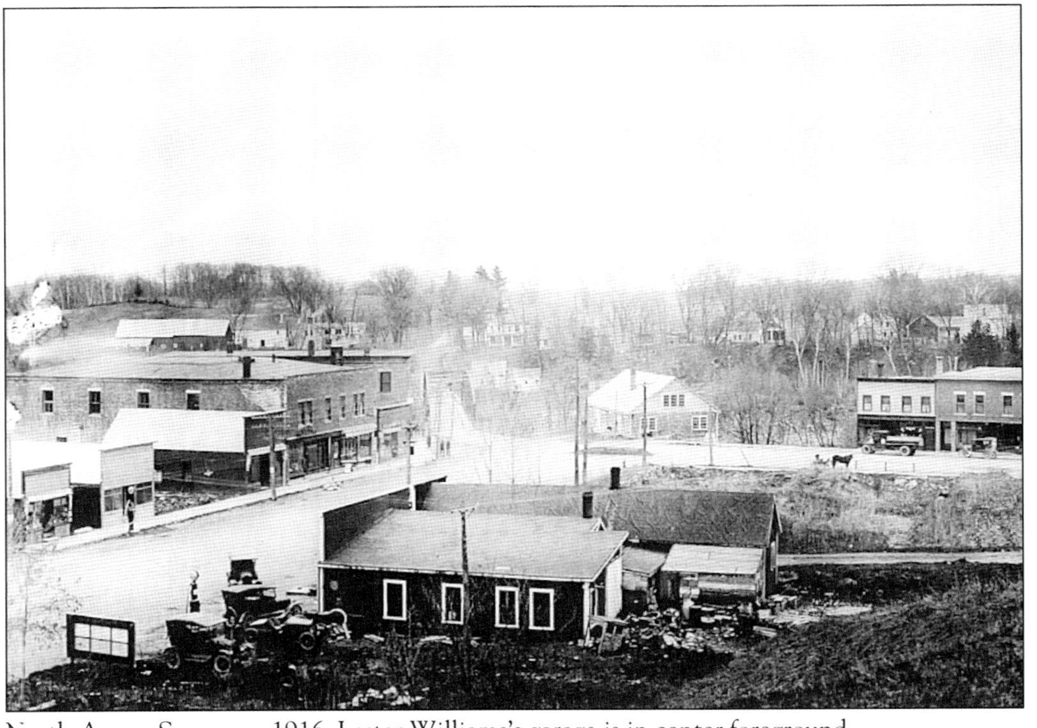

North Anson Square, *c.* 1916. Lester Williams's garage is in center foreground.

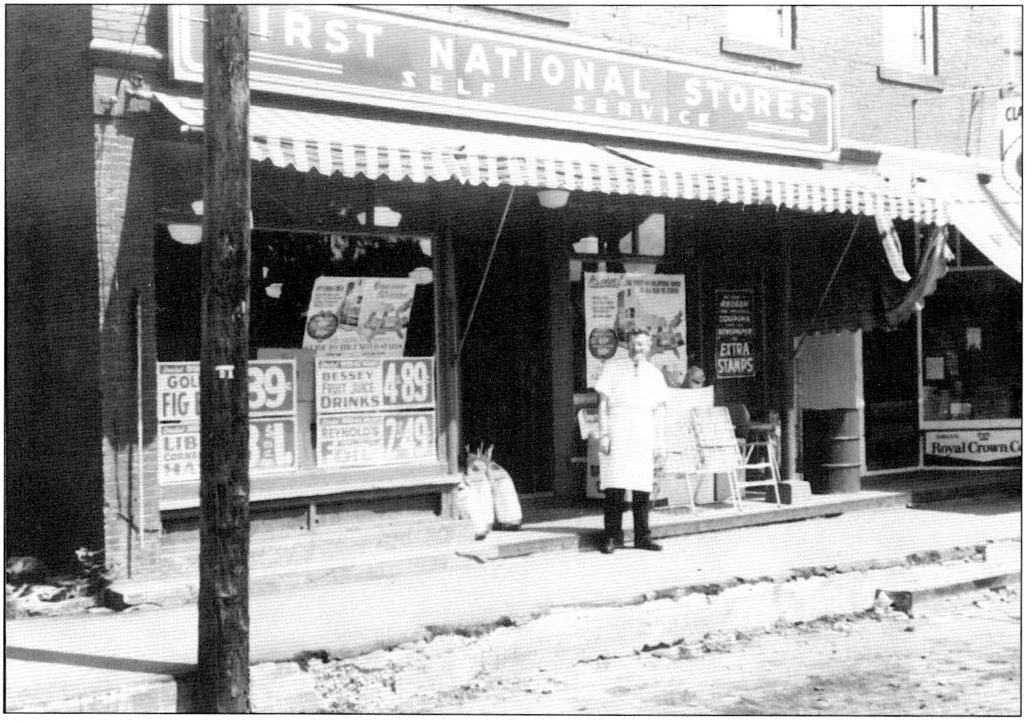

The First National Store on Main Street, North Anson, late 1950s. Store clerk Clifford Daggett is on the sidewalk.

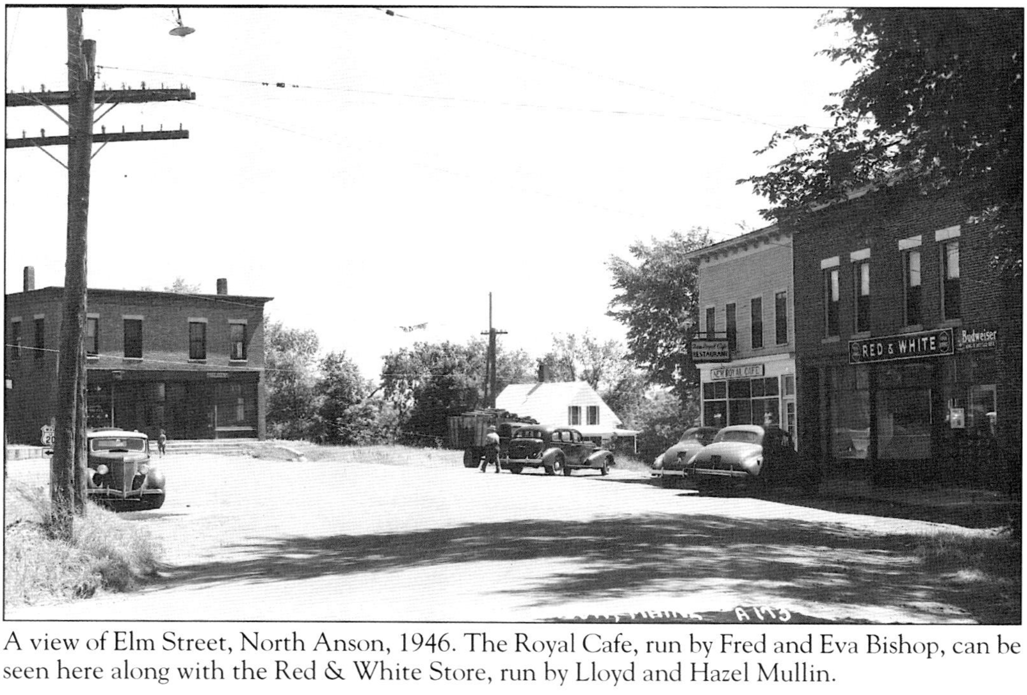

A view of Elm Street, North Anson, 1946. The Royal Cafe, run by Fred and Eva Bishop, can be seen here along with the Red & White Store, run by Lloyd and Hazel Mullin.

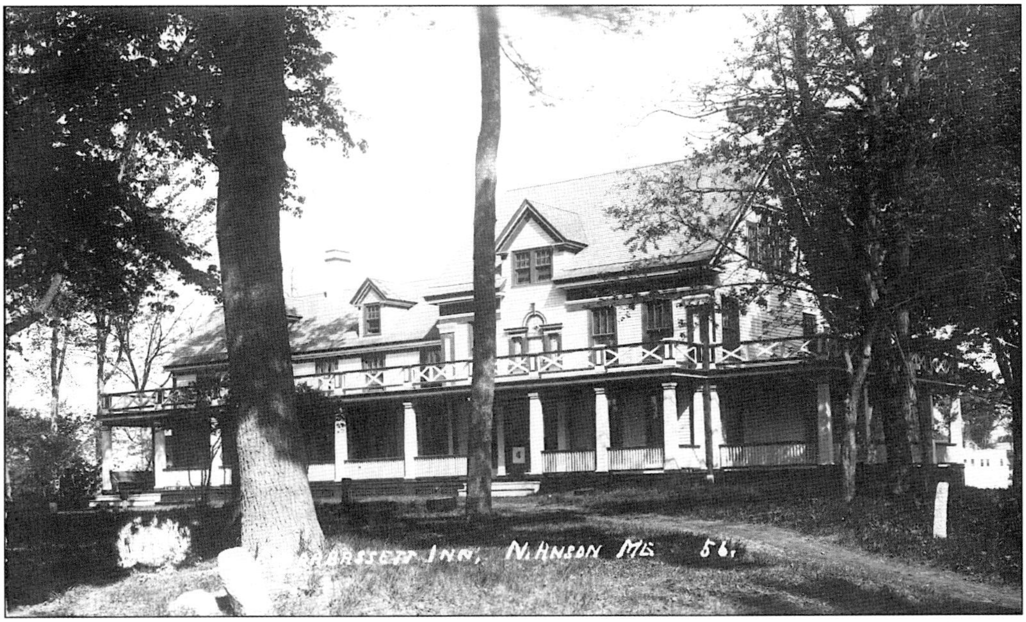

The old Carrabassett Inn in North Anson on the corner of Union and Main Streets. This was originally a private home that was extensively altered and expanded into a grand inn in 1900. It was operated as an inn until 1946, when a section of the inn was moved on logs up Union Street to become a separate residence. The inn is now a private residence with features that still retain its former grandeur.

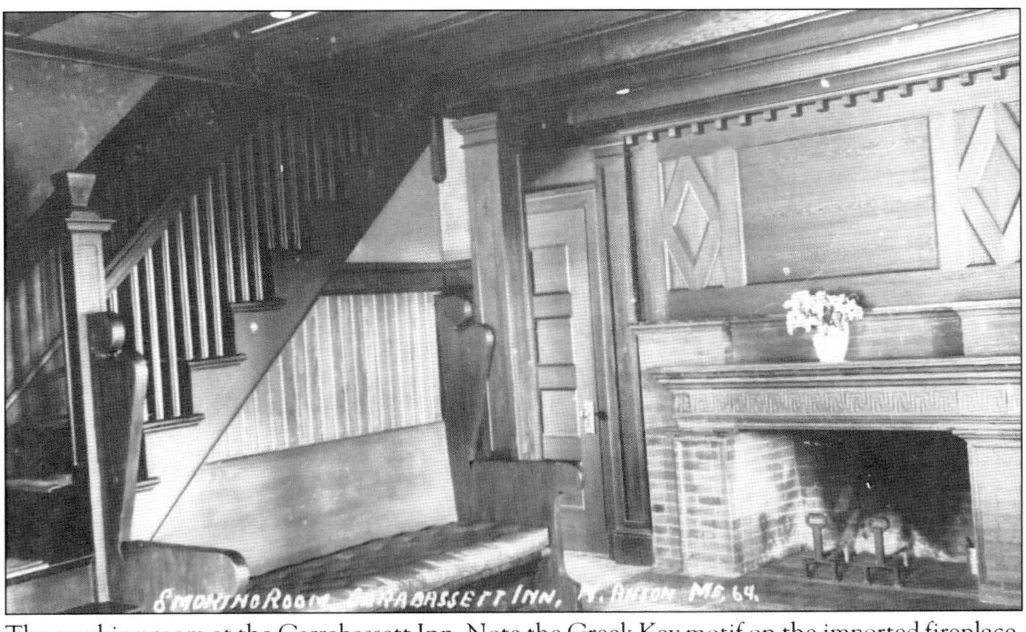

The smoking room at the Carrabassett Inn. Note the Greek Key motif on the imported fireplace. The area is resplendent with dark Southern pine wood.

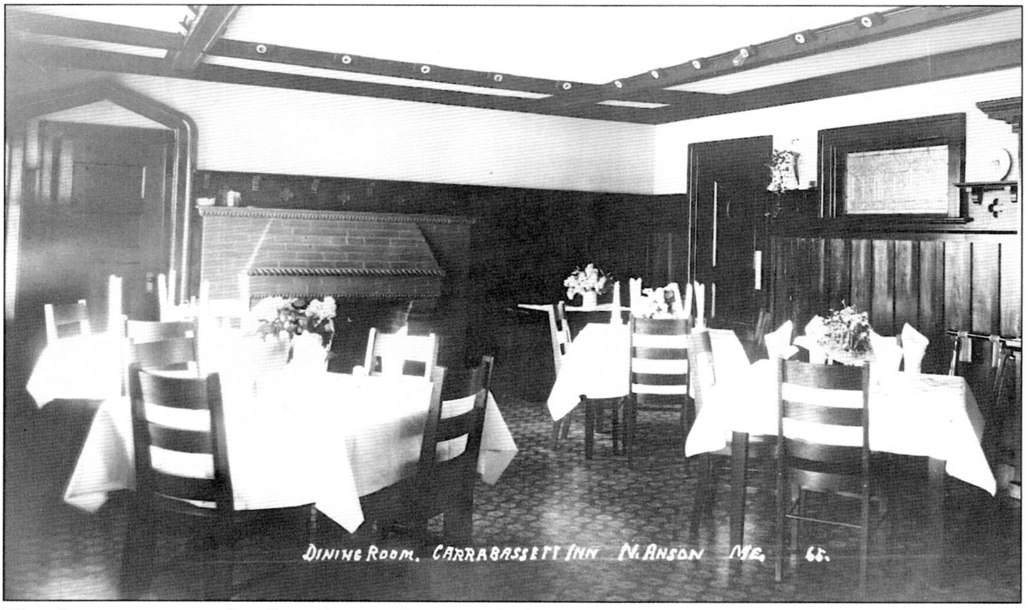

The dining room at the Carrabassett Inn, *c.* 1920–1930.

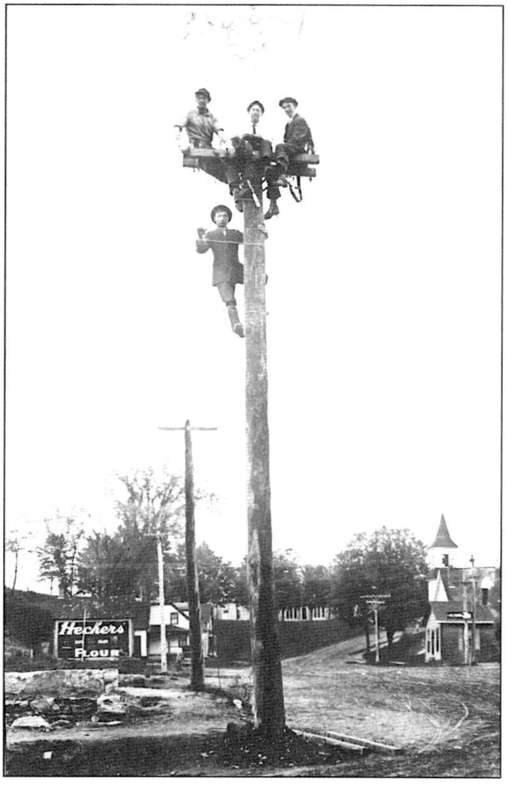

Bringing lights back to North Anson after the fire of 1913. The line crew poses for a picture. They had no hard hats in those days. Edwin Quint is in the upper left.

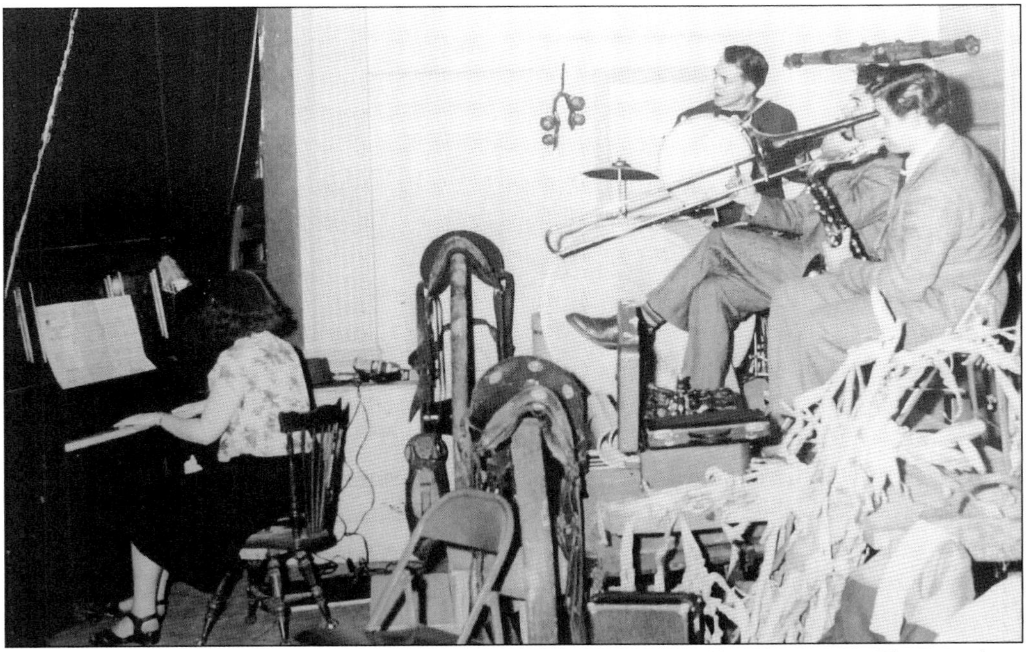

A dance band which played at dances in North Anson and neighboring towns. The members of the band are Avis Luce (on the piano), Ted King (on the drums), Harold Alpert (a music teacher at Anson Academy, on the trombone), and Buddy Sterling (on the saxophone), c. 1947–1948.

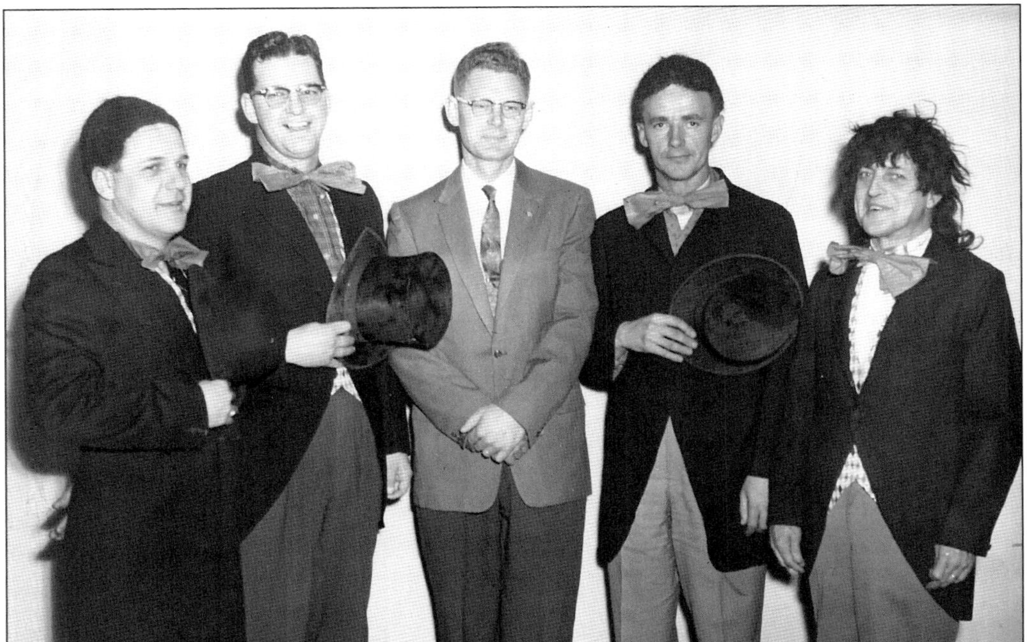

Donald Pickett, Harold Bubar, Raynard Morrell, Larry Maheu, and Ted King, members of a minstrel show that was performed in May 1960.

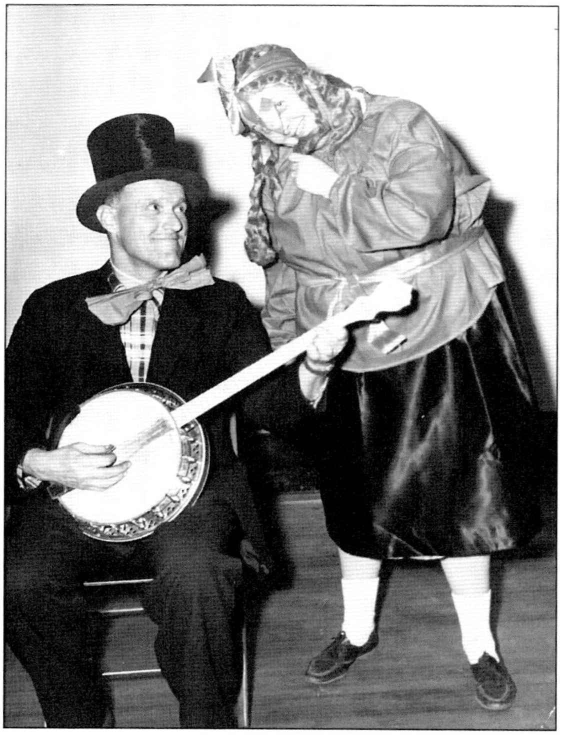

William Allen and Avis Luce, members of a minstrel show that was performed in May 1960.

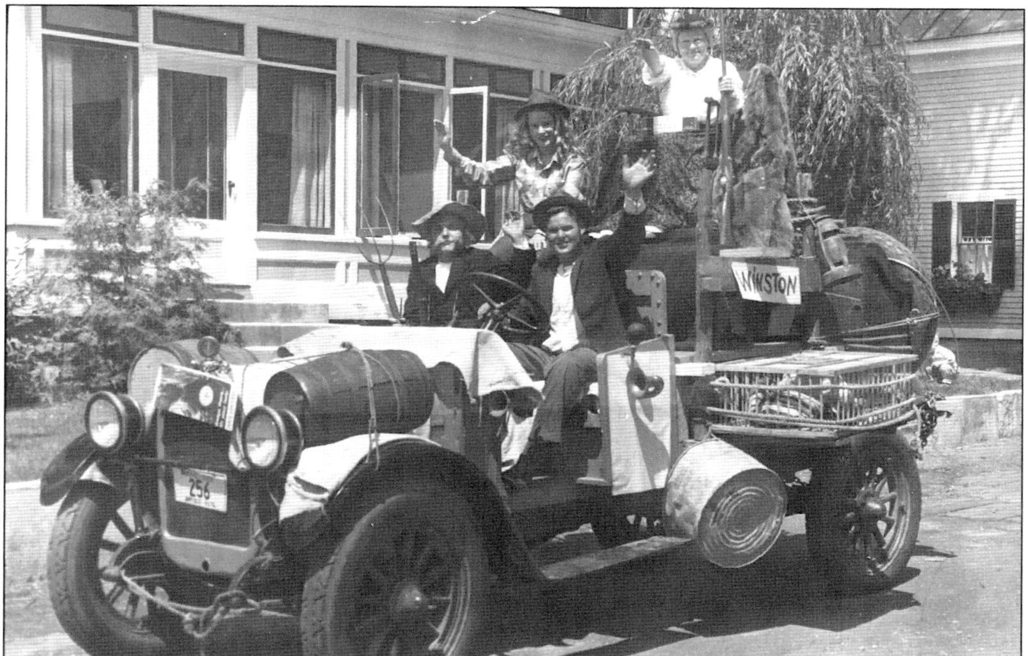

The Clampet family loaded up in their truck, heading for the parade (not California!), early 1960s. Jed Spear is Uncle Jed, Keith Partridge is Jethro, Terry Dyer is Ellie May, and Genevieve Partridge is Grannie.

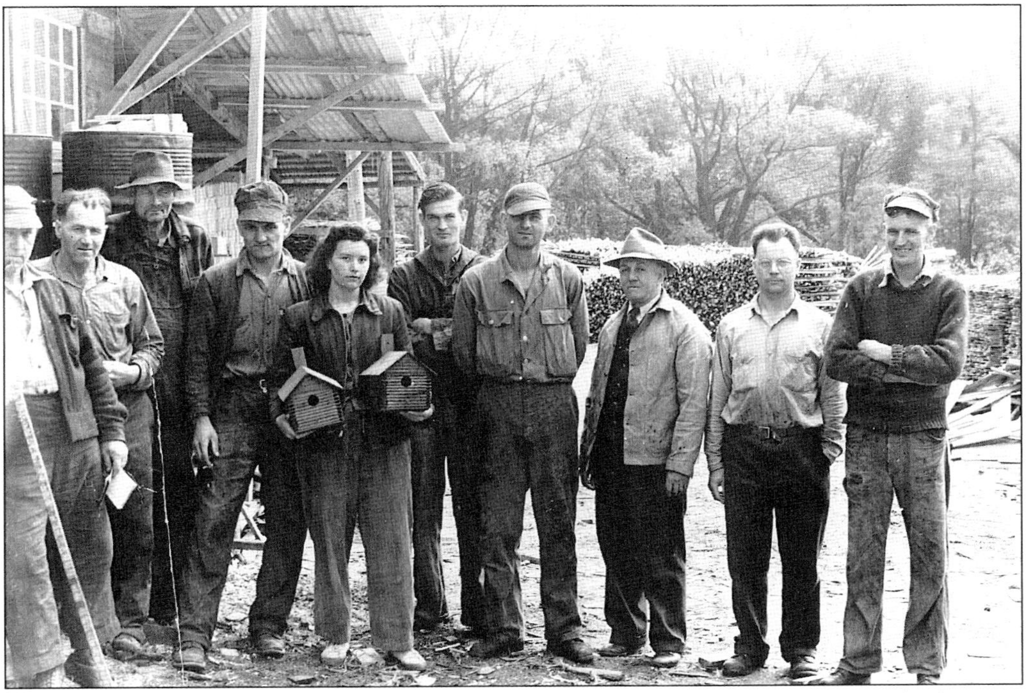

Earl Wing's mill crew, 1947. Leeman Mullin, James Flaherty, Horace Skillings, Willard Freeze, Shirley Engelborge Atwood, Walter Lightbody, Lyman Smith, Earl Wing, Cecil Engelborg, and Ainslie Lightbody are shown here.

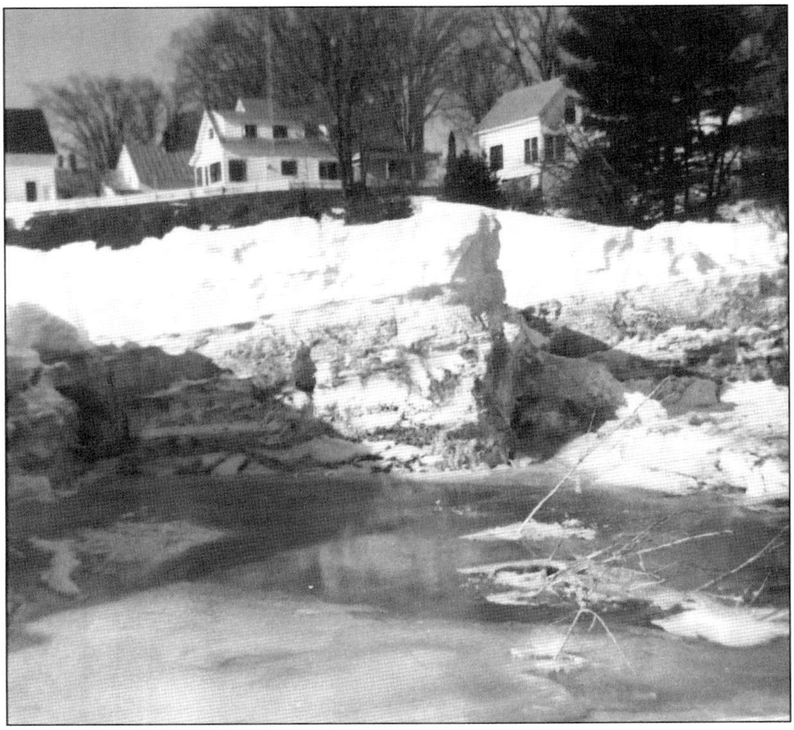

Ice along the Carrabassett River, below the bridge, North Anson, 1970.

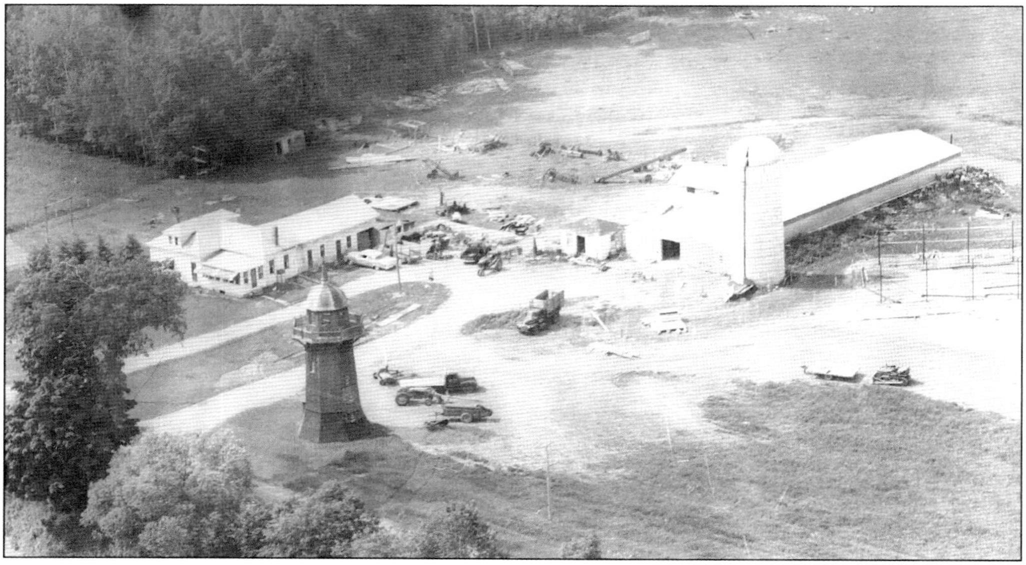

The McLean Farm, after the fire of November 1962, showing new barn. The windmill is the only original structure left. Built in 1904 by the Bailey Brothers, it has been in the McLean family since 1924, and is on the National Register of Historic Places. It was used as a lookout for enemy planes during WW II and was manned 24 hours a day. It was originally built to pump water from the well on the lawn. The farm is now owned by the Seavey family.

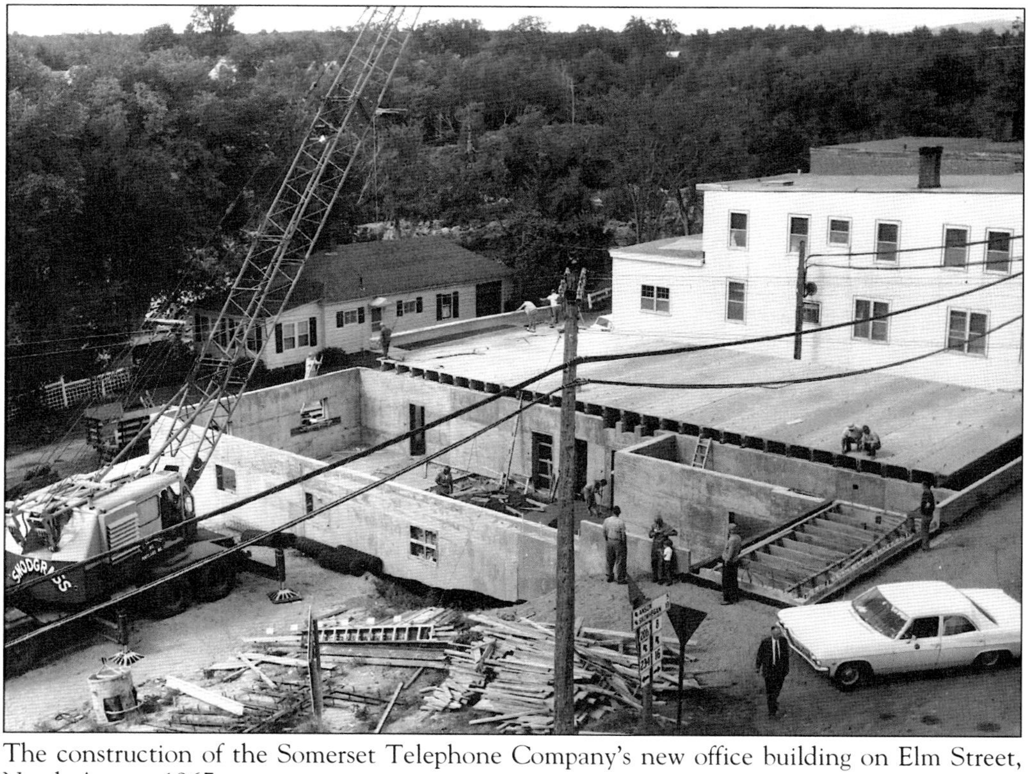

The construction of the Somerset Telephone Company's new office building on Elm Street, North Anson, 1967.

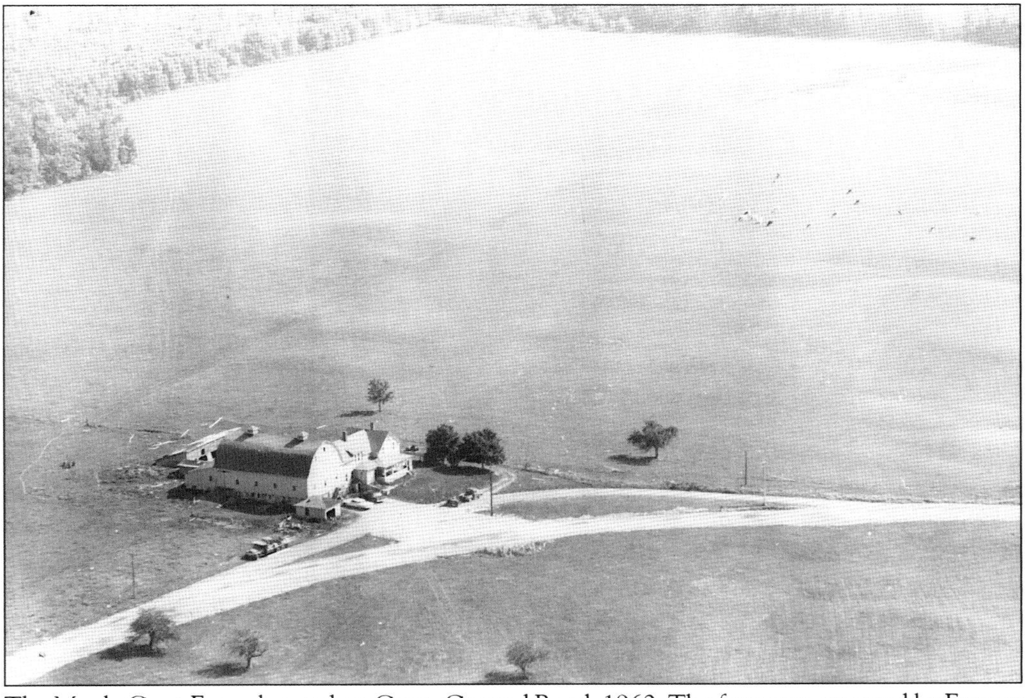

The Maple Crest Farm, located on Camp Ground Road, 1960. The farm was operated by Everett and Hazel Billing.

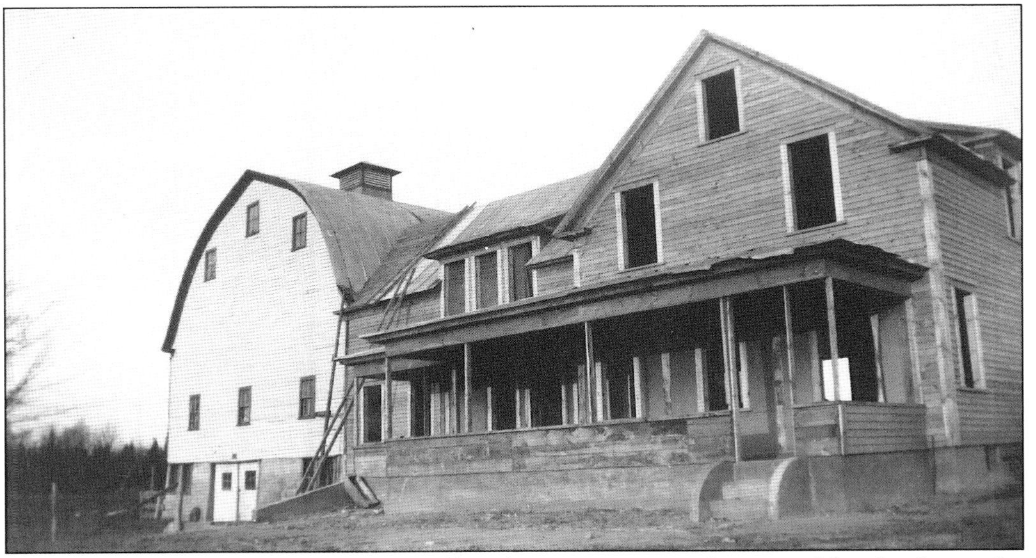

The completed barn, with the house still under construction, after a total loss by fire at the Billing Farm, 1926.

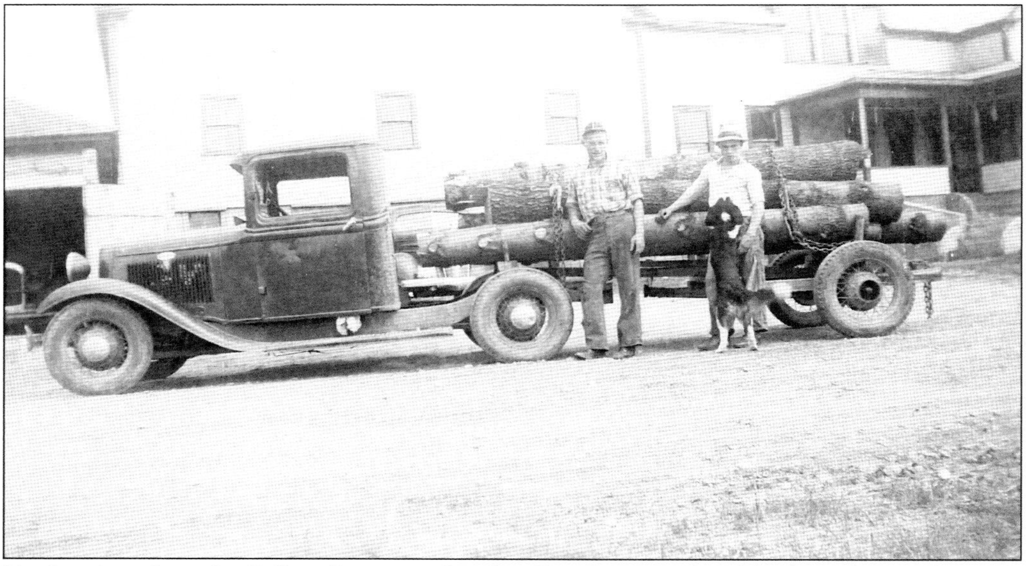

Hauling logs from the Billing Farm to a local mill with a mini hand-built trailer truck. Clyde and Harold Billing are shown here *c.* mid-1930s.

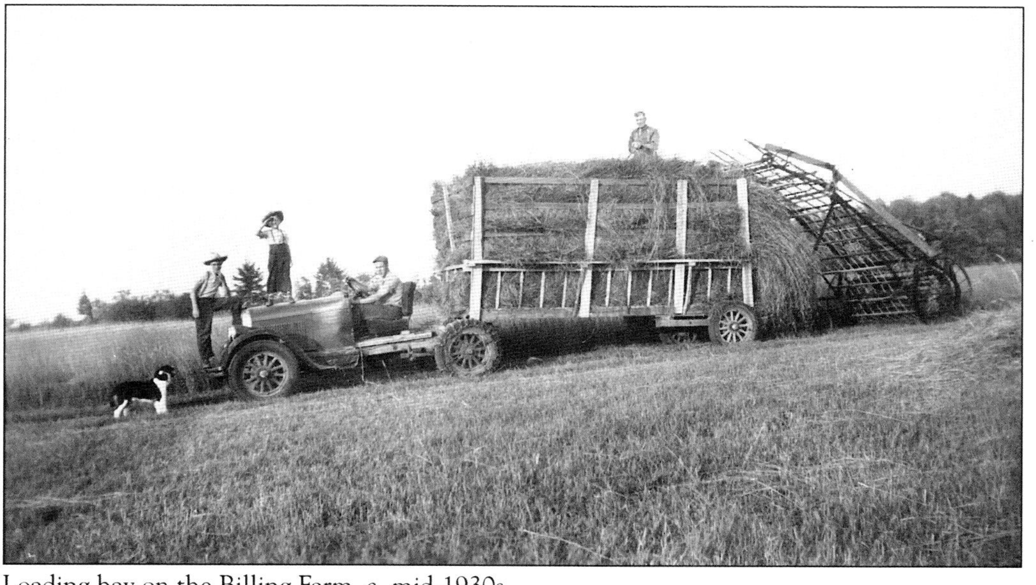

Loading hay on the Billing Farm, *c.* mid-1930s.

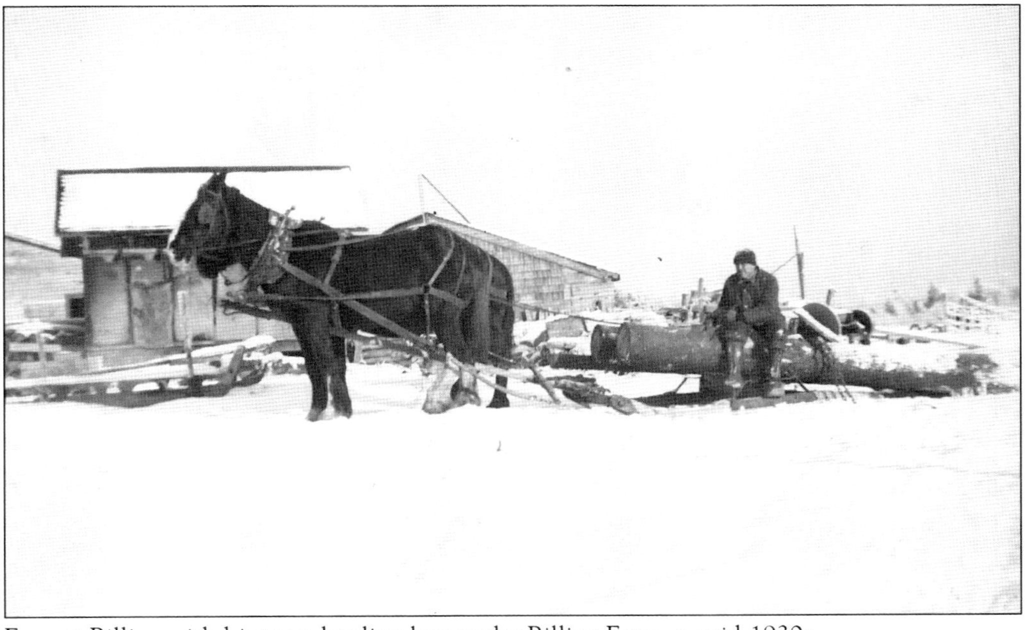

Everett Billing with his team hauling logs at the Billing Farm, *c.* mid-1930s.

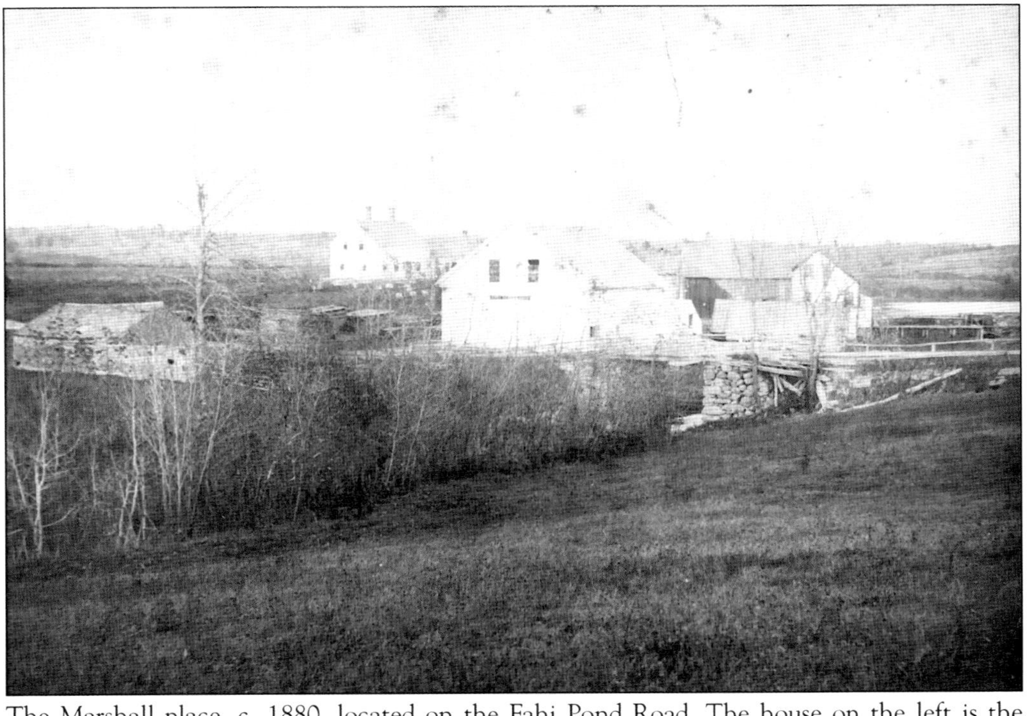

The Marshall place, *c.* 1880, located on the Fahi Pond Road. The house on the left is the Moody house. The barn is located where Elizabeth Oliver's house now stands. The building to the right is part of the saw- and gristmill. In 1883 it was listed as the Marshall and Wasson shovel-handle factory (note the mill pond on the right).

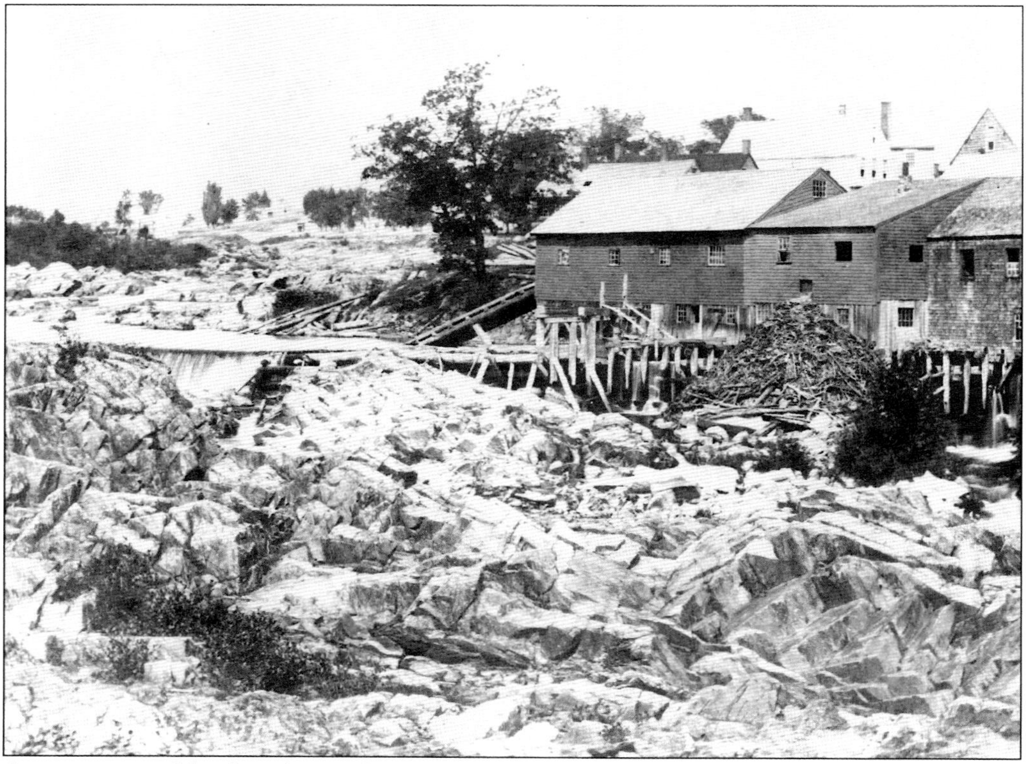

A stereo view of the Carrabassett River in North Anson, looking upriver from the bridge before 1863. Early mills, a sawmill, and the N.B. Buxton Grist and Card Mill can all be seen here.

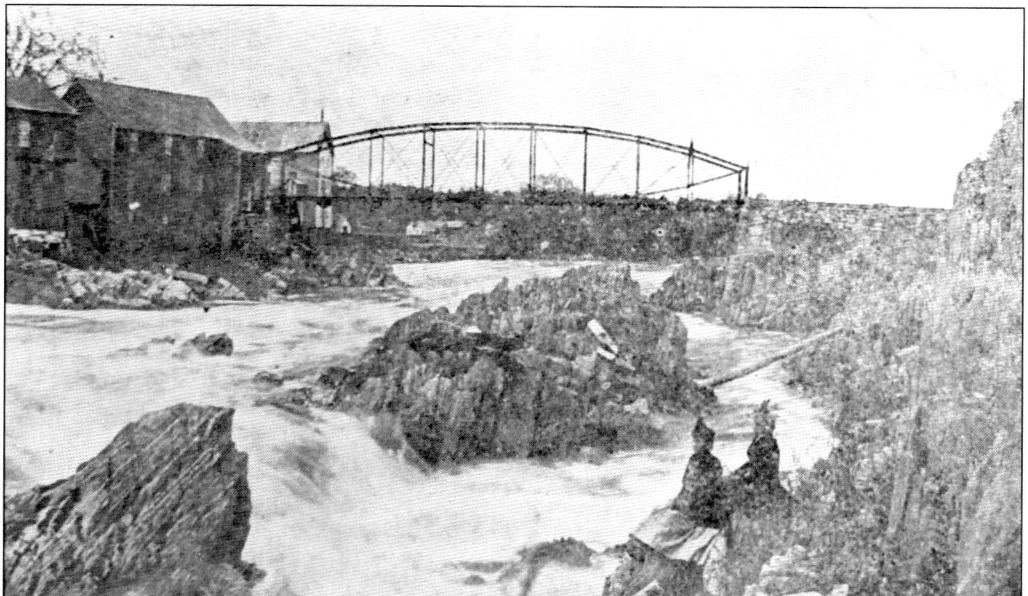

An early view of first iron bridge crossing the Carrabassett River, erected in 1886. To the left can be seen some of the early mills.

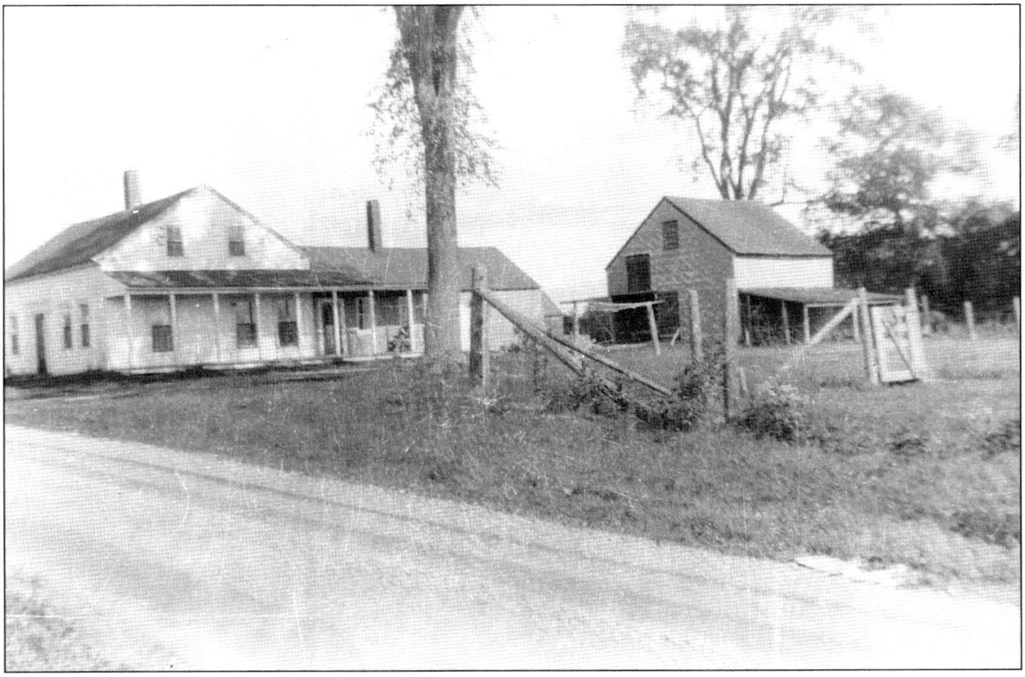

An early home, believed to be built in 1791, located near Patterson Bridge. Previous owners were C. Patterson, the Fletchers, and the Great Northern Paper Co. It was also the home of Herbert and Polly Rogers for many years. It is now owned and much remodeled by Michael Adams.

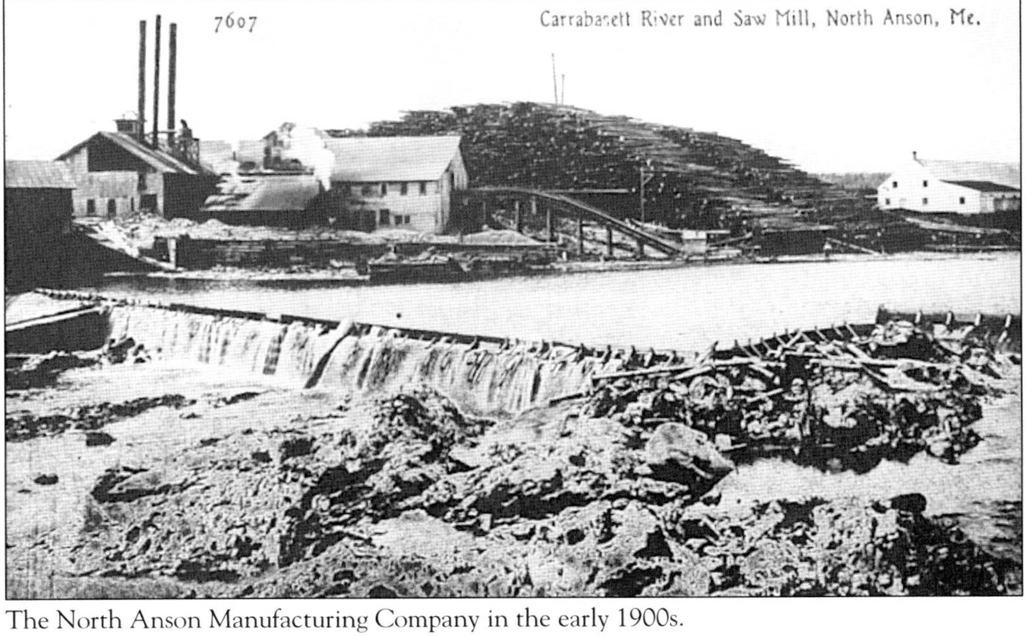

The North Anson Manufacturing Company in the early 1900s.

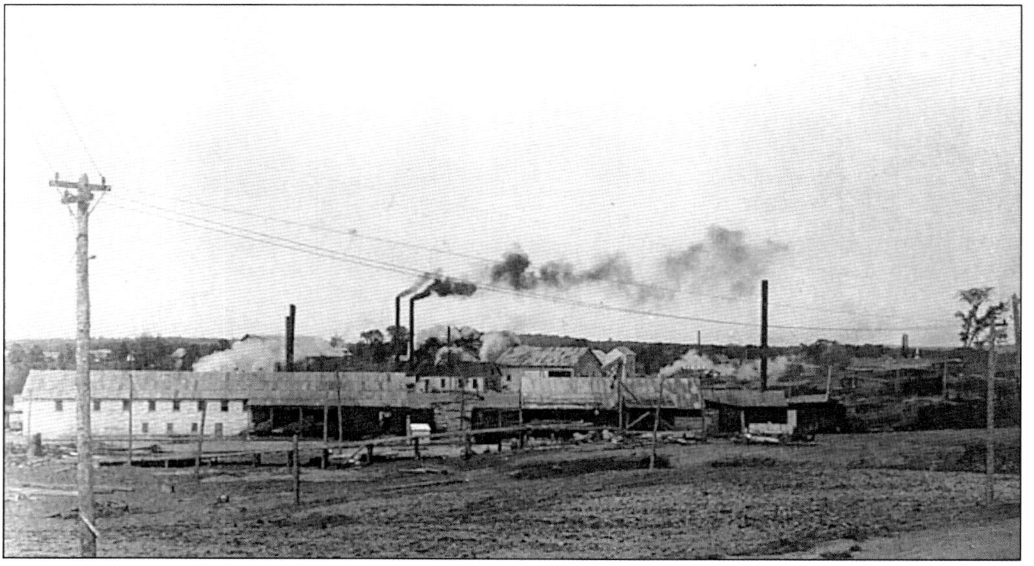

The Newcastle Lumber Co., North Anson, *c.* 1920s, manufacturer of lumber, boxes, and cable reels.

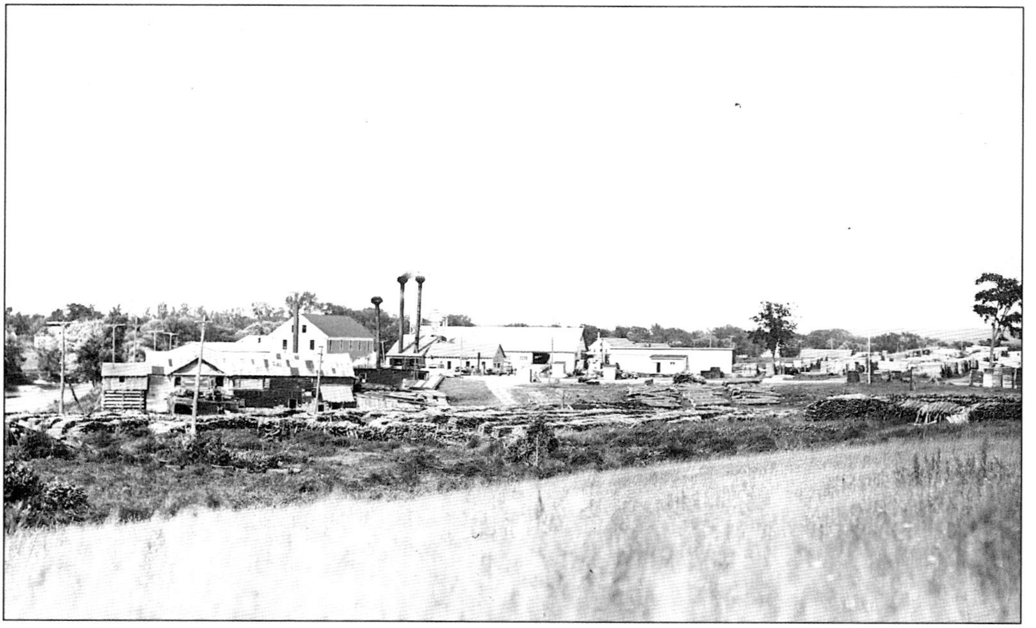

The North Anson Reel Co., North Anson, *c.* 1940s, manufacturer of lumber, cable reels, and croquet sets.

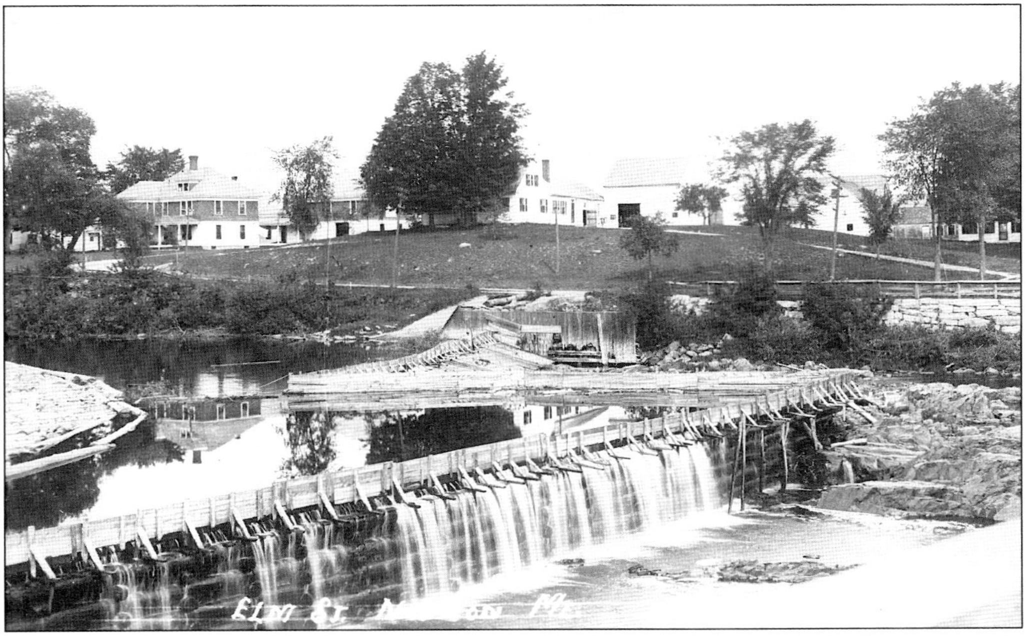

The mill pond and dam on the Carrabassett River, North Anson, *c.* 1910. Elm Street is in the background.

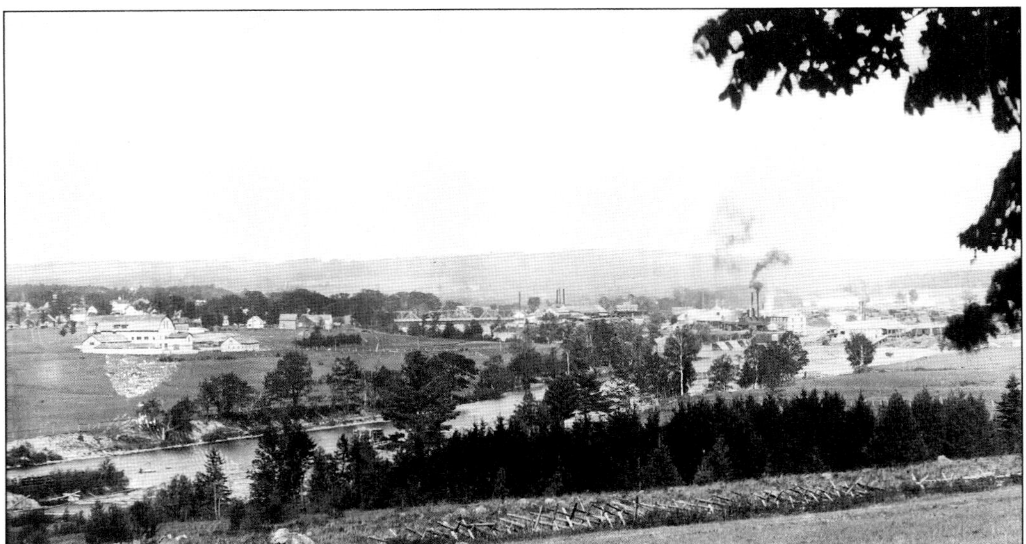

A view of North Anson Village from Union Street. The Bailey Brothers Farm is to the left, the railroad bridge is in the center, and woodworking mills are to the right.

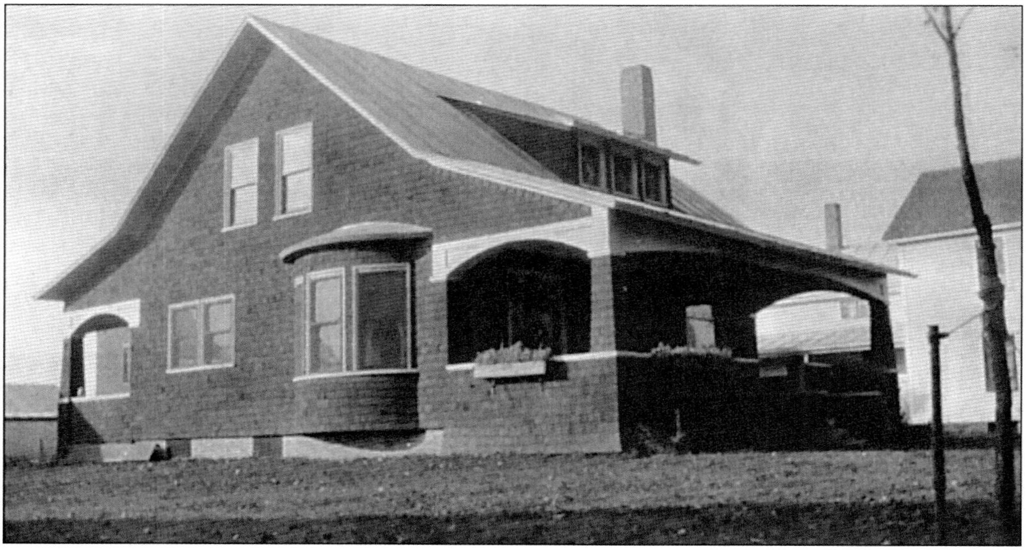

The home of Earl and Carrie Wing on Center Street. Built in 1921–22, it was designed in the Craftsman style (Sears and Roebuck) by Earl Wing. The house, now owned by his daughter, Virginia Wing Moore, stands on the land where two houses were destroyed by the fire of 1913. One was owned by Carrie Wing's grandfather, Stickney Gray; the other was owned by Bert Witham.

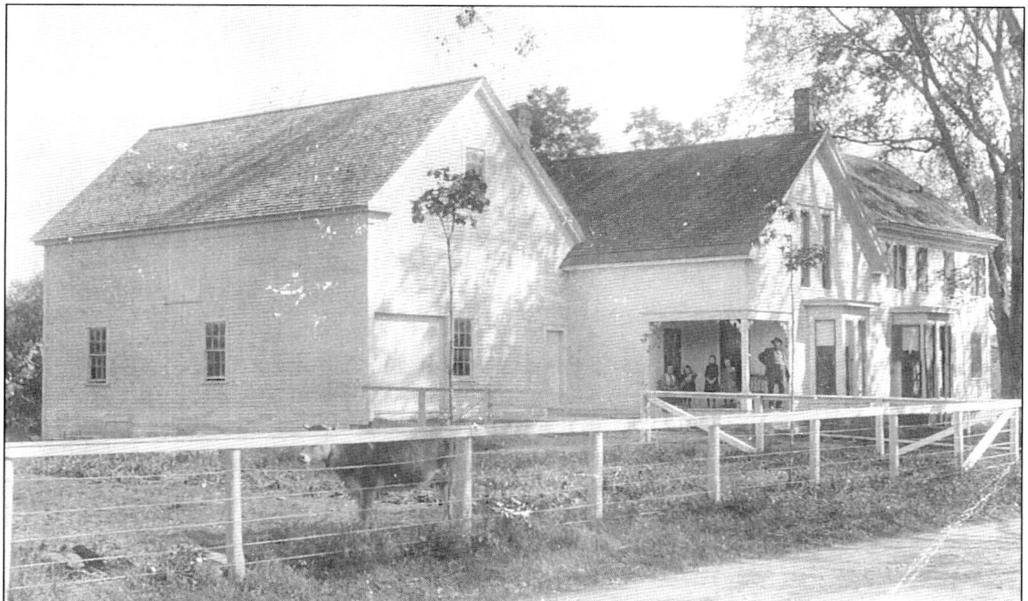

The home of William and Evie Robinson on Summer Street from the 1890s to the 1930s. Known as a great storyteller and active in railroad building, William Robinson was superintendent of transportation when the White Pass & Yukon Railway was built in Alaska in 1899. Upon retirement, he became an avid orchardist. Evie H.G. Robinson was recognized for her extensive knowledge of North Anson history and genealogy. The house's previous owner was A. Coleman. More recent owners were Howard Abbott and Dr. Jolda.

Three

CHURCHES AND SCHOOLS

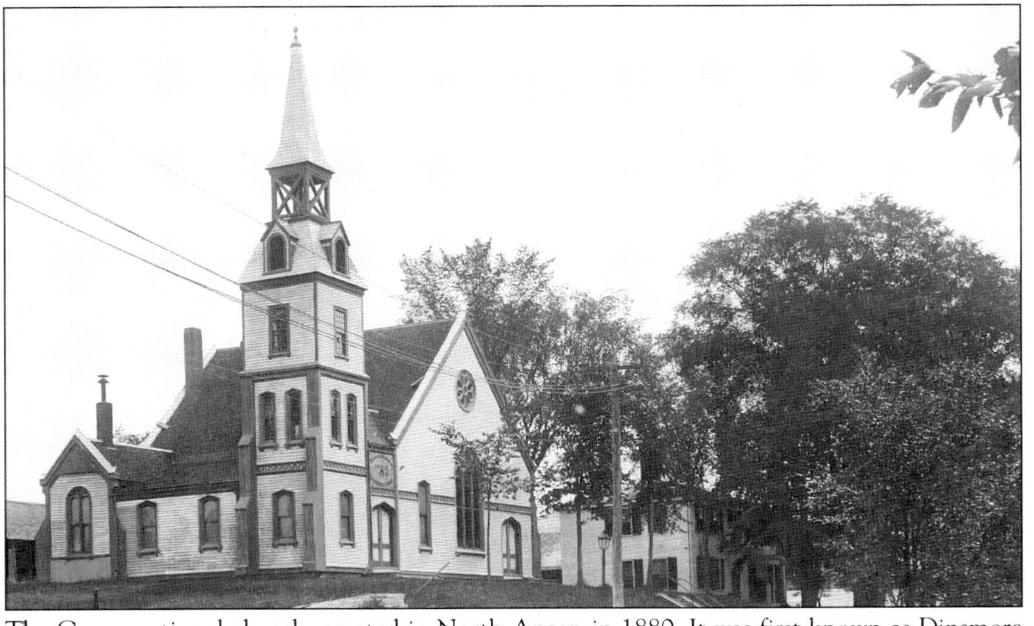

The Congregational church, erected in North Anson in 1880. It was first known as Dinsmore Memorial Church.

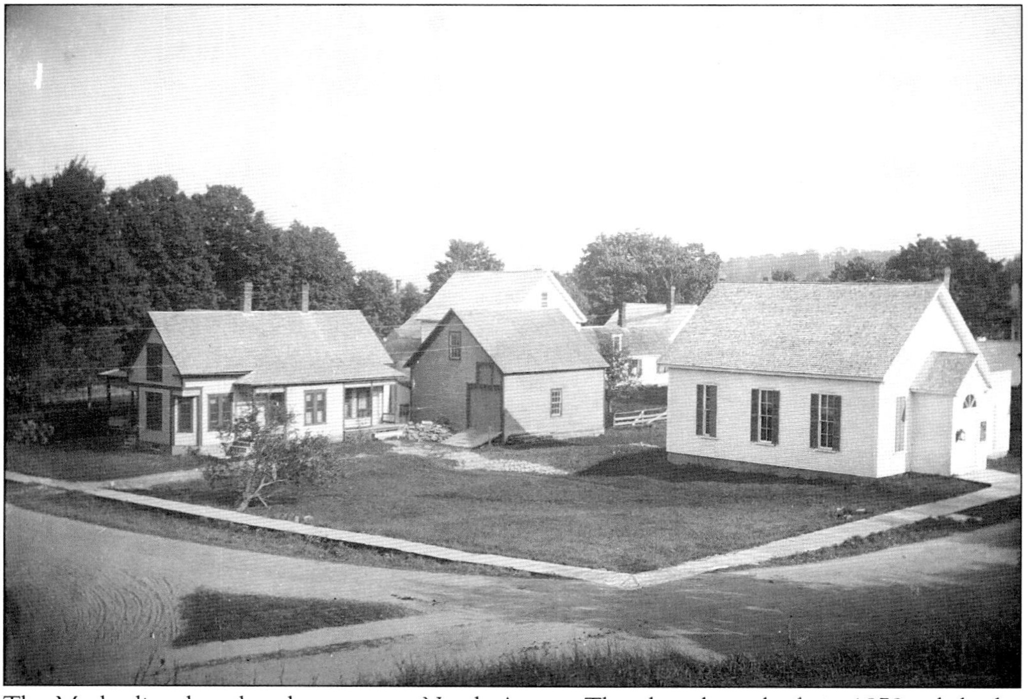

The Methodist chapel and parsonage, North Anson. The chapel was built in 1879, while the parsonage was erected in 1892–93.

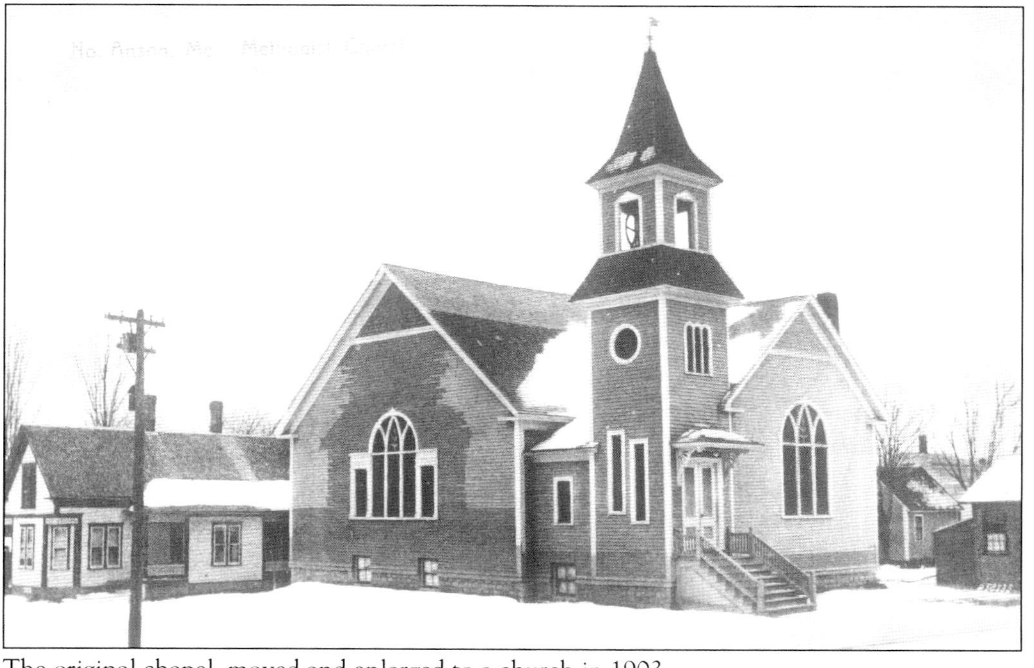

The original chapel, moved and enlarged to a church in 1903.

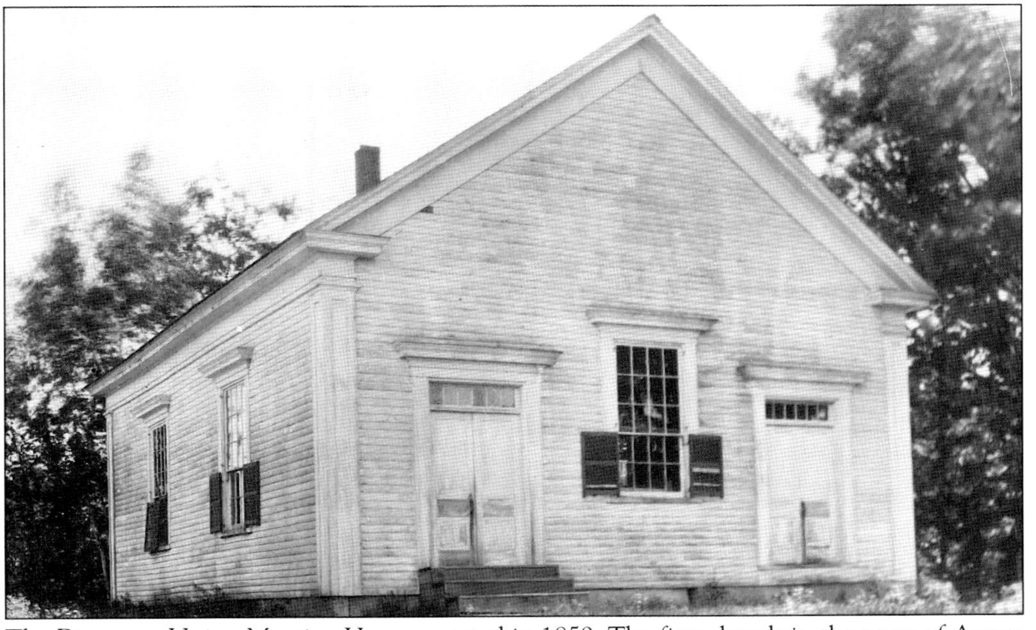

The Dinsmore Union Meeting House, erected in 1859. The first church in the town of Anson (south) was organized on April 19, 1804, at the home of Mr. Arthur Dinsmore. Original membership was six. Mr. Dinsmore was the first settler in that part of the town, coming with his wife and nine children from Chester, New Hampshire, in 1794.

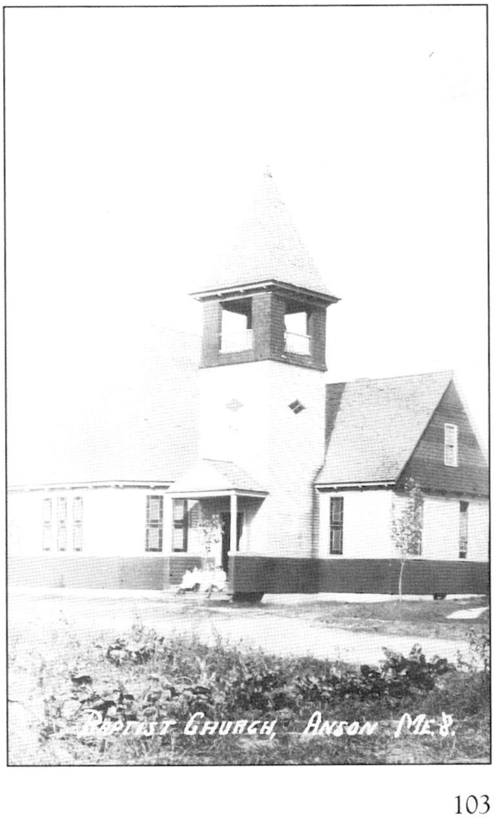

The Baptist church, Anson, erected 1898 at a cost of $2,800. Active in the erection of the church were Asa Gilman, Hiram Gilman, Lysander Berry, and the Macklin family. The first pastor was Rev. John Longley. After many years of being vacant, it was purchased by the Nazarene Church in 1941. It was again vacated in the 1970s, and has been occupied by the Maranatha Church since 1981.

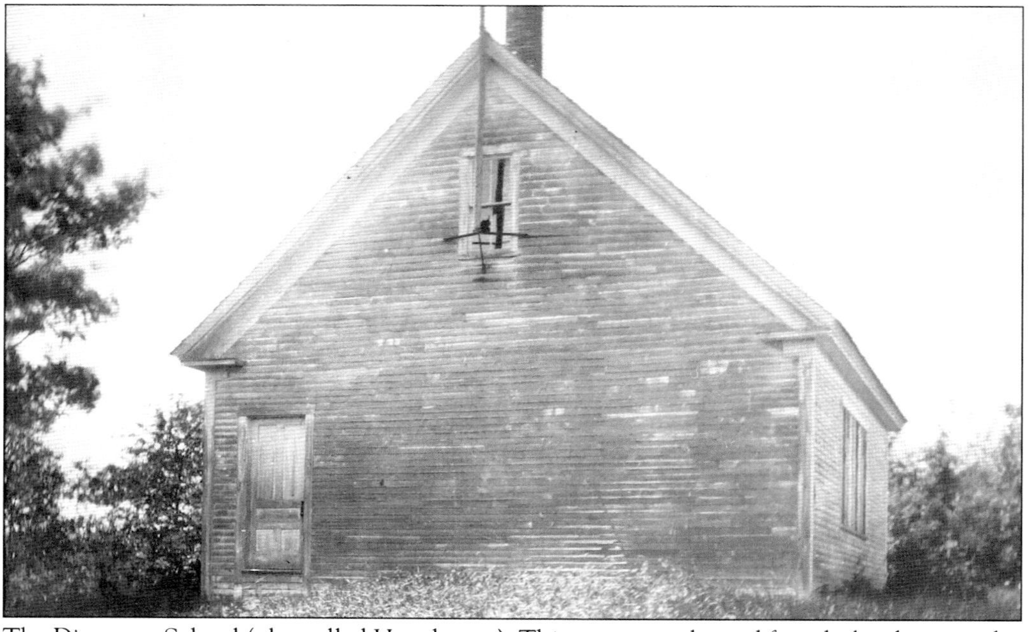

The Dinsmore School (also called Hawthorne). This was not only used for scholars but was also a meeting house for Sabbath congregations. It was used for church purposes until 1859, when a union church was built on another lot not far from it. The schoolhouse was then moved to a spot near the church. The record gives no date of the erection of the schoolhouse but the Dinsmore genealogy records that it was in use prior to 1819.

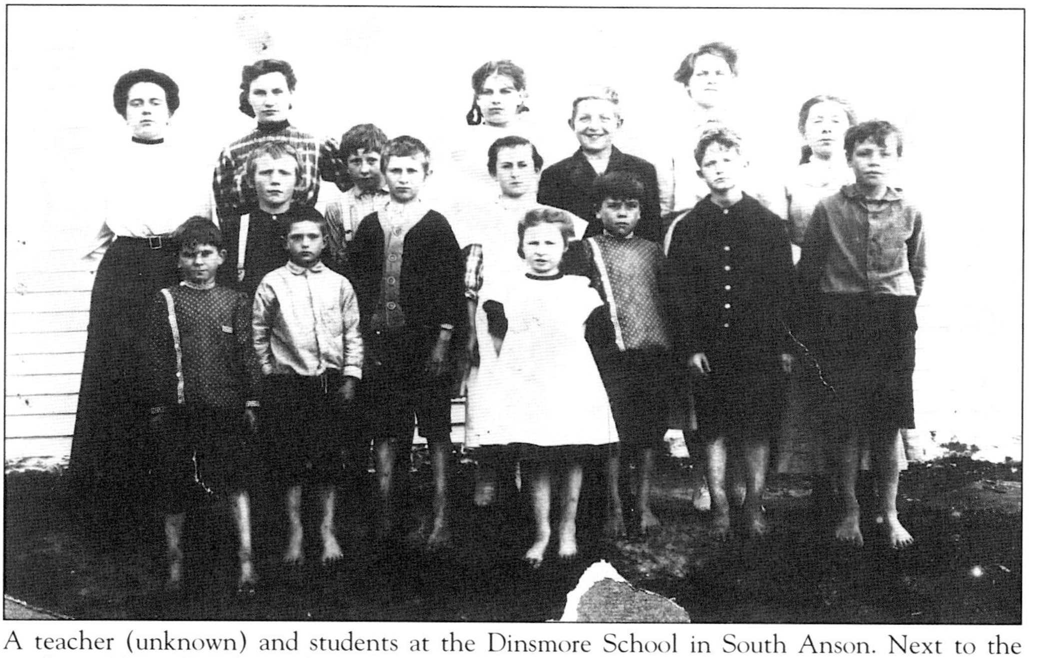

A teacher (unknown) and students at the Dinsmore School in South Anson. Next to the teacher is Hattie Beryl Moody Barron. Some of the other students are Gerald Goodwin, Beatrice Goodwin, Florence Hilton, John Longley, Omar Dawes, Eula Nevens, and Chris, Guy, Charles, and Lester Hilton.

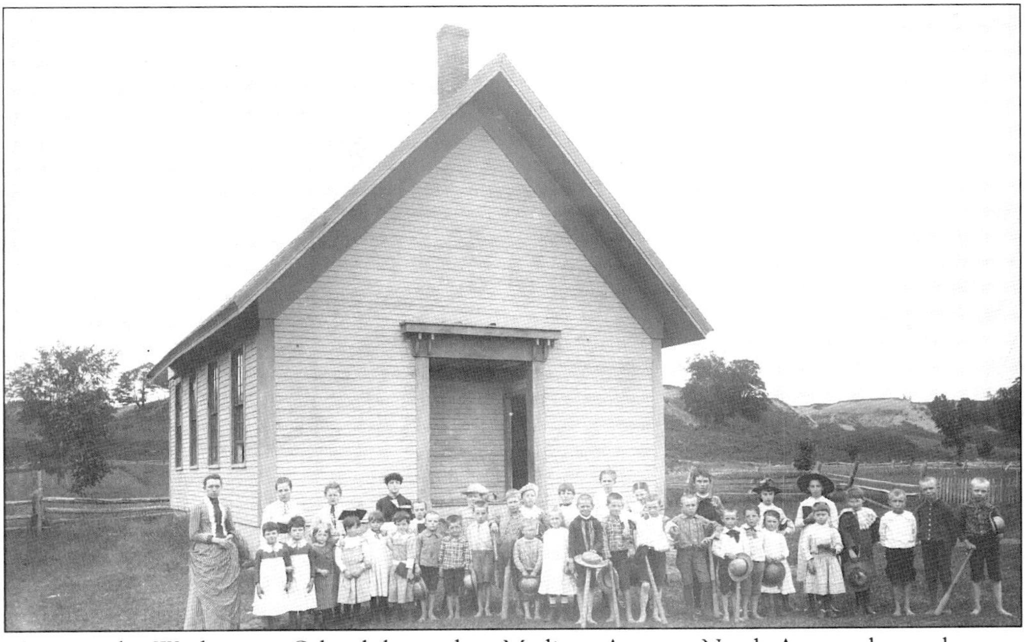

The Lincoln, Washington School, located on Madison Avenue, North Anson, date unknown. The building was later made into a home and was occupied by the Ted King family for many years.

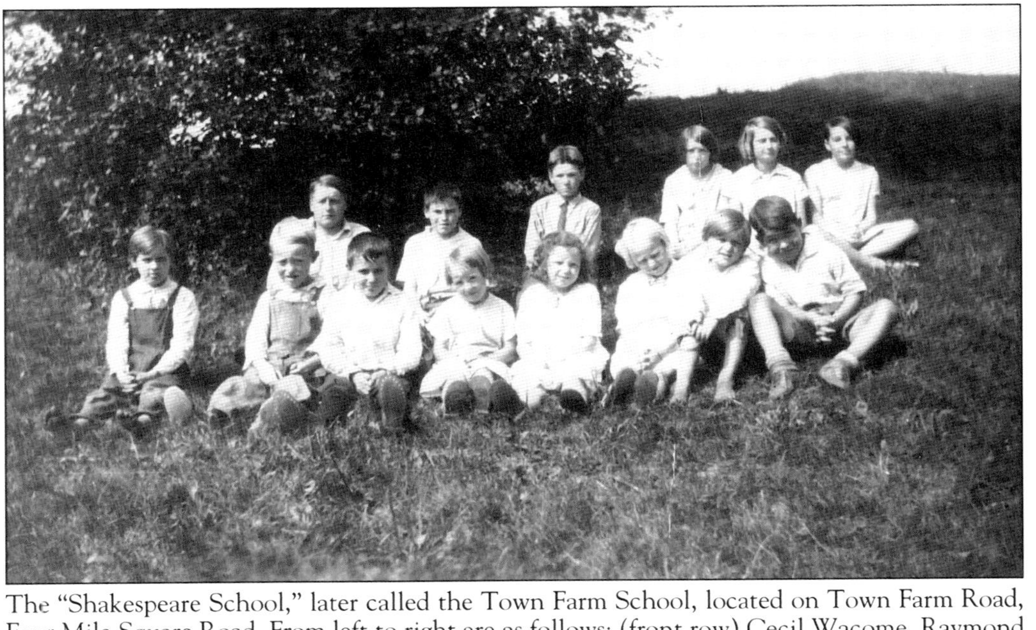

The "Shakespeare School," later called the Town Farm School, located on Town Farm Road, Four Mile Square Road. From left to right are as follows: (front row) Cecil Wacome, Raymond Greenleaf, Ivan Hoyt, Frances Greenleaf, Mae Hoyt, Ruth Greenleaf, Ralph Wacome, and Frank Paine; (back row) Stanley Wacome, George Hoyt, Phillip O'Reiley, Rosella Wacome, Virginia Shepardson, and Marjorie Paine.

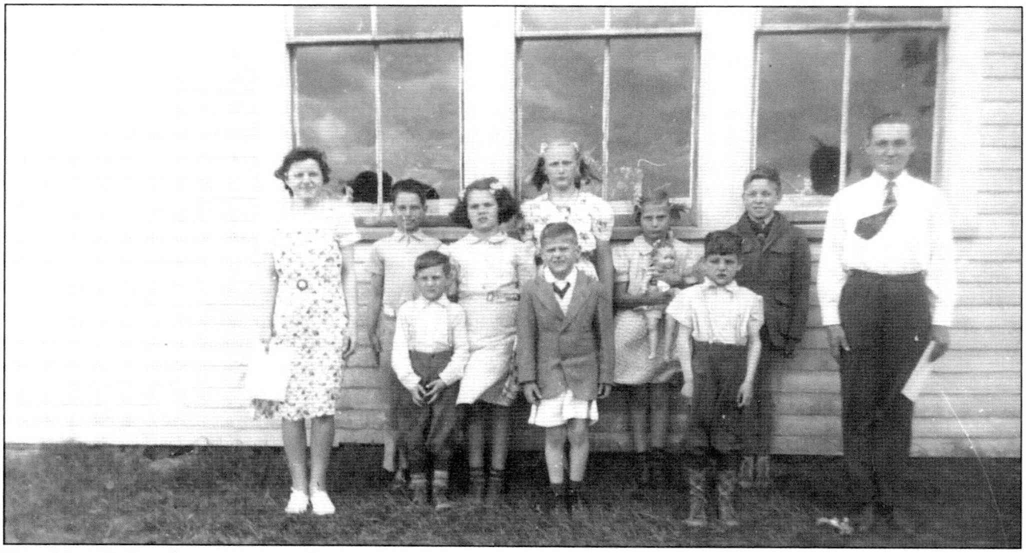

Franklin School, 1938. Franklin School was located on the Fletcher Road, West Anson. From left to right are as follows: (front row) Richard Frazer, Benjamin Pinkham, and Ronald Frazer; (back row) Ava Pinkham, Robert Hewey, Ruth Frazer, Pearly Hewey, Rosalie Hewey, Norman Brackett, and Hurley Fletcher.

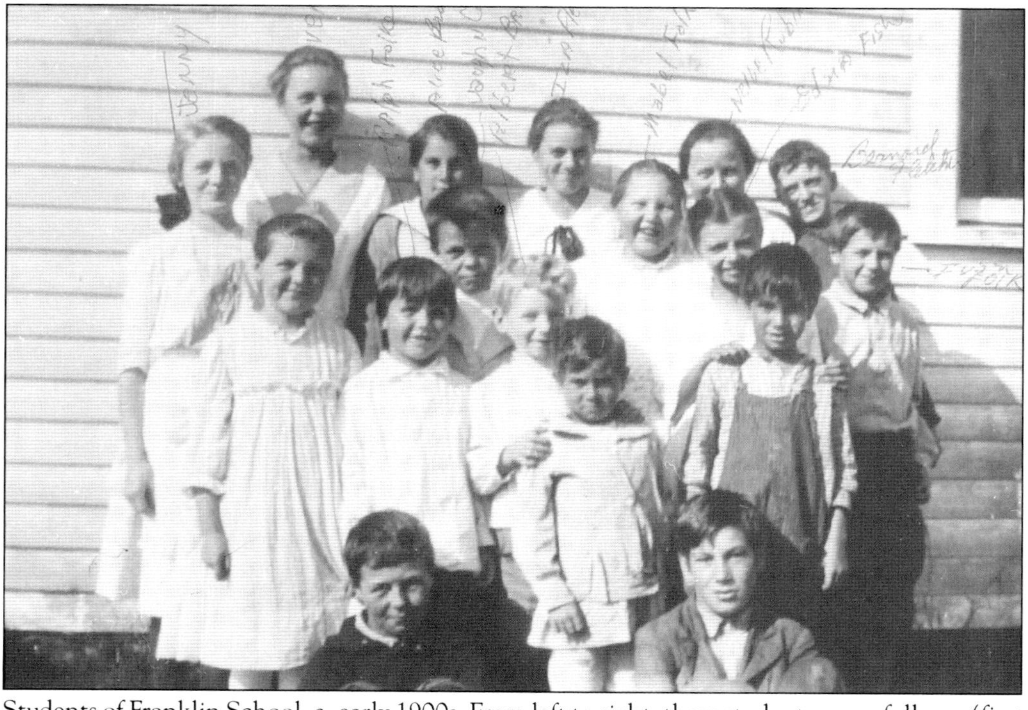

Students of Franklin School, *c.* early 1900s. From left to right, these students are as follows: (first row) Henry Harrington and Lorenzo Brown; (second row) Sylvia Fowke, Ralph Fowke, Albert Brackett, Pearly Brown, and Blendon Brown: (third row) Jenny Fish Morse, Vaughn Cooper, Mabel Fowke, Edna Fish, and Ivan Fowke; (fourth row) Vera Cooper Page, Alice Brown, Izzie Fletcher, Nellie Robinson, and Bernard Fletcher.

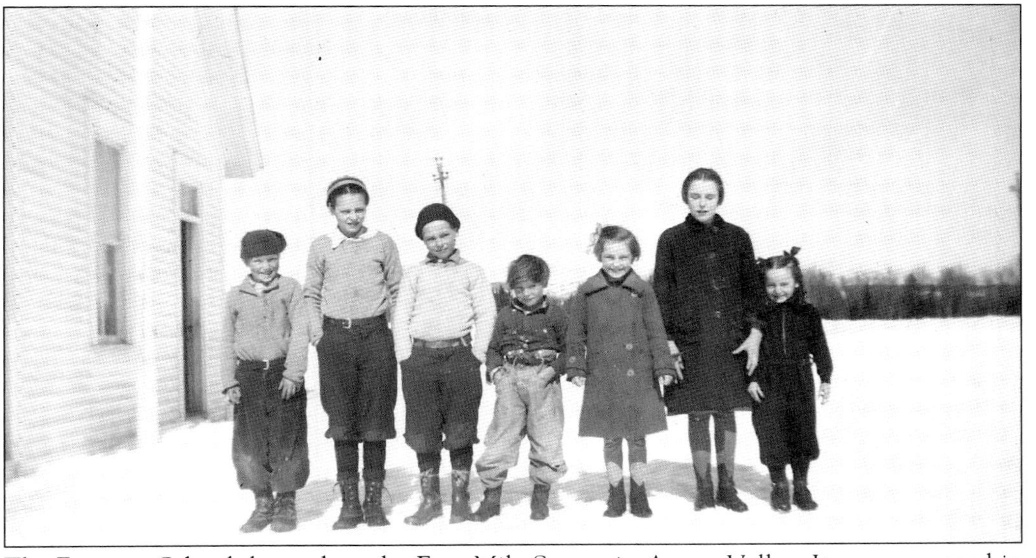

The Emerson School, located on the Four Mile Square in Anson Valley. It was re-opened in 1937 with only seven students attending. Although the enrollment would grow during the next few years, the school was closed for good in 1944 and the students were bussed to North Anson. The students, from left to right, are: Erland Clark Jr., Charles Schwarz, Howard Schwarz, Manix Clark, Louise Schwarz, Erma Hoyt, and Shirley Viles.

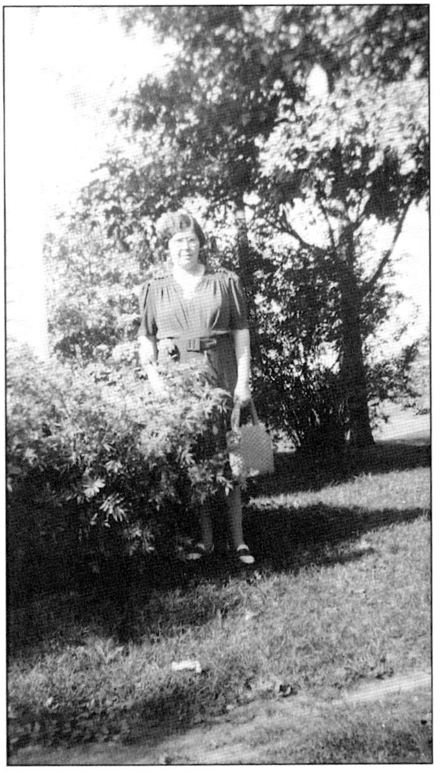

Flossie Jones, who lived in Anson Village and taught several years at the Emerson School, c. 1937–44. She would board with a family in the valley and walk over a mile to school, sometimes wading through deep snow or mud.

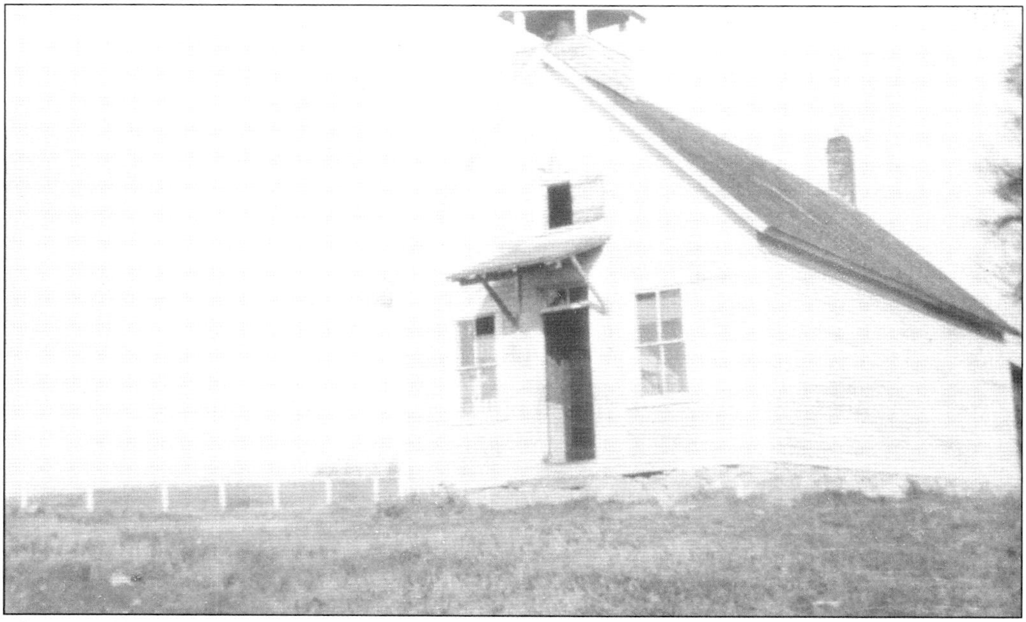

The Lowell School at Bixby Corner, 1930.

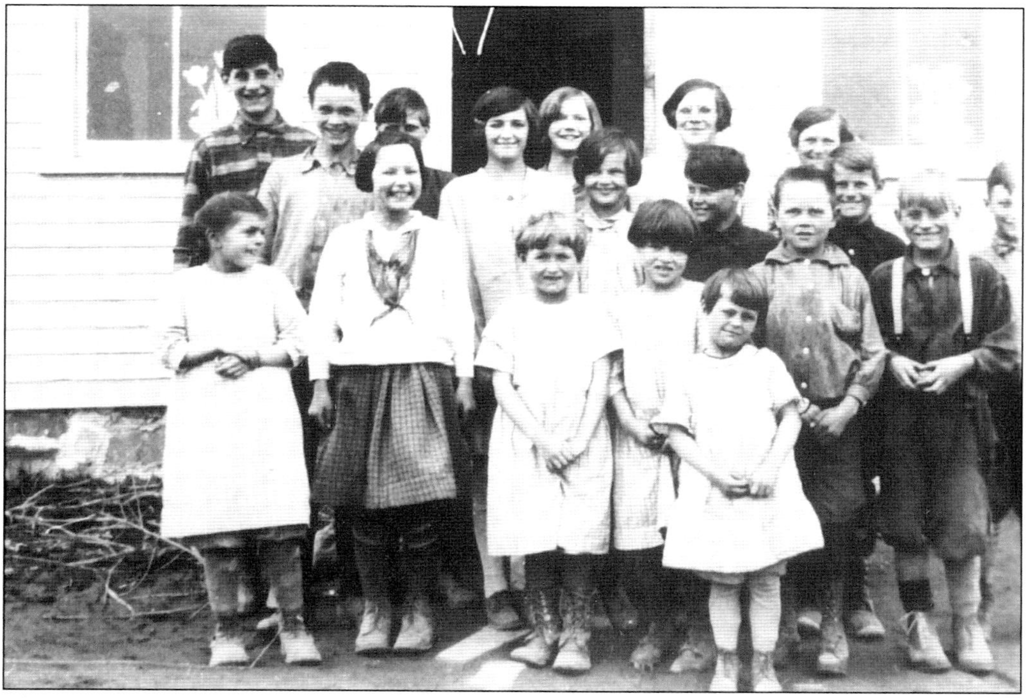

The Lowell/Bixby School on the West Mills Road in Anson, 1928. From left to right, are as follows: (front row) Kathleen Bradley, Irma Caldwell, Nellie Bradley, Evelyn Heald, Muriel Burns, ? Heald, and Carroll Bradley; (middle row) Roy Heald, Justina Kimball, Arlene Heald, Leslie Burns, Fred Bradley, and Everett Caldwell; (back row) Walter Trask, William Burns, Gertrude Miller, unidentified, and Isabelle Bradley.

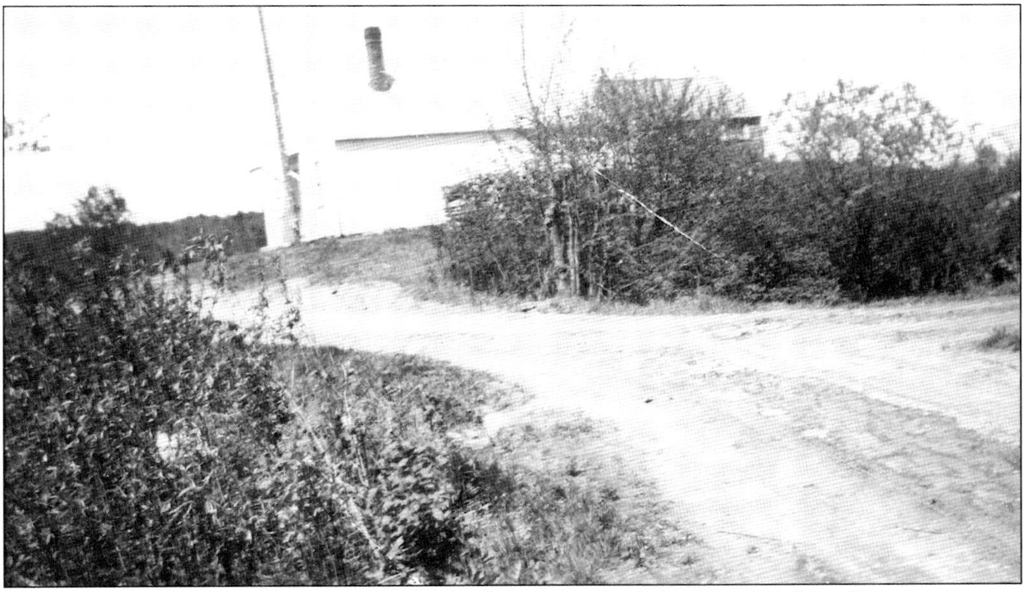

The Longfellow School, 1939–40, located off the Horseback Road in Bookerville.

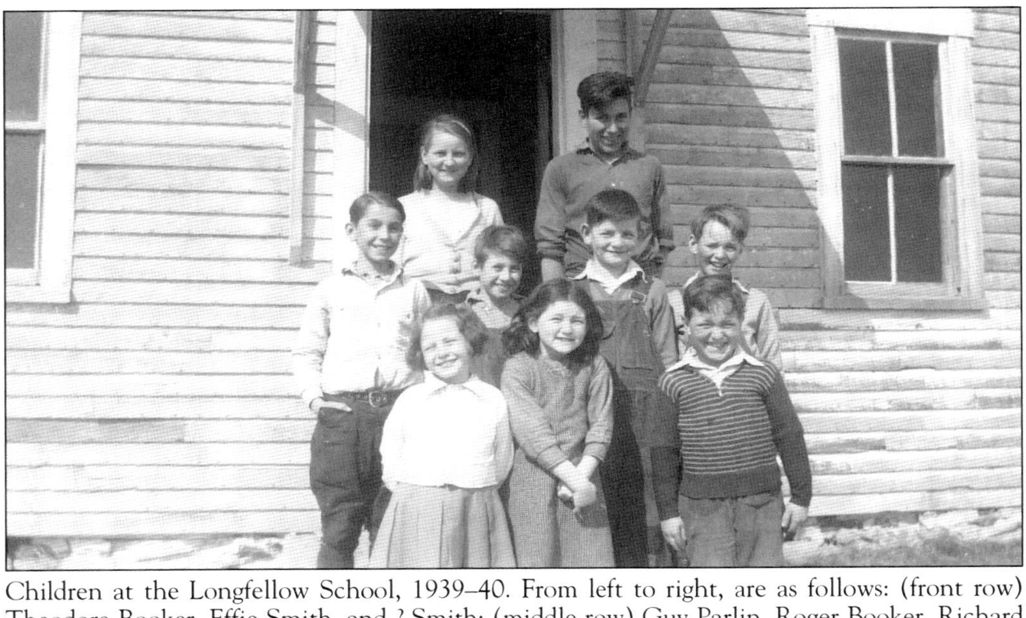

Children at the Longfellow School, 1939–40. From left to right, are as follows: (front row) Theodore Booker, Effie Smith, and ? Smith; (middle row) Guy Parlin, Roger Booker, Richard Smith, and Jack Smith; (back row) May Smith and Neil Foster.

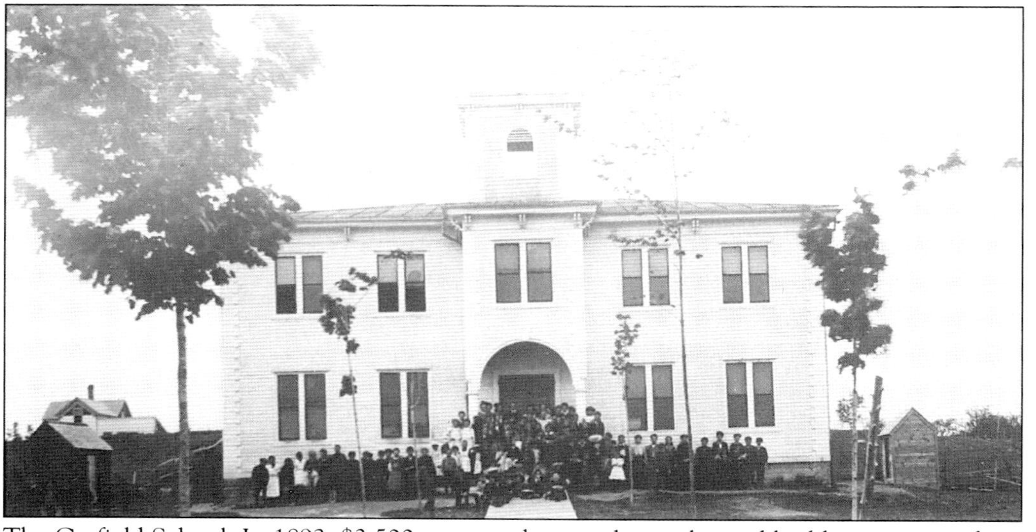

The Garfield School. In 1892, $3,500 was voted to purchase a lot and build a two-story, four-room school for elementary students. It was named Garfield and was also used for a few years as a high school. It was located where the town garage now stands.

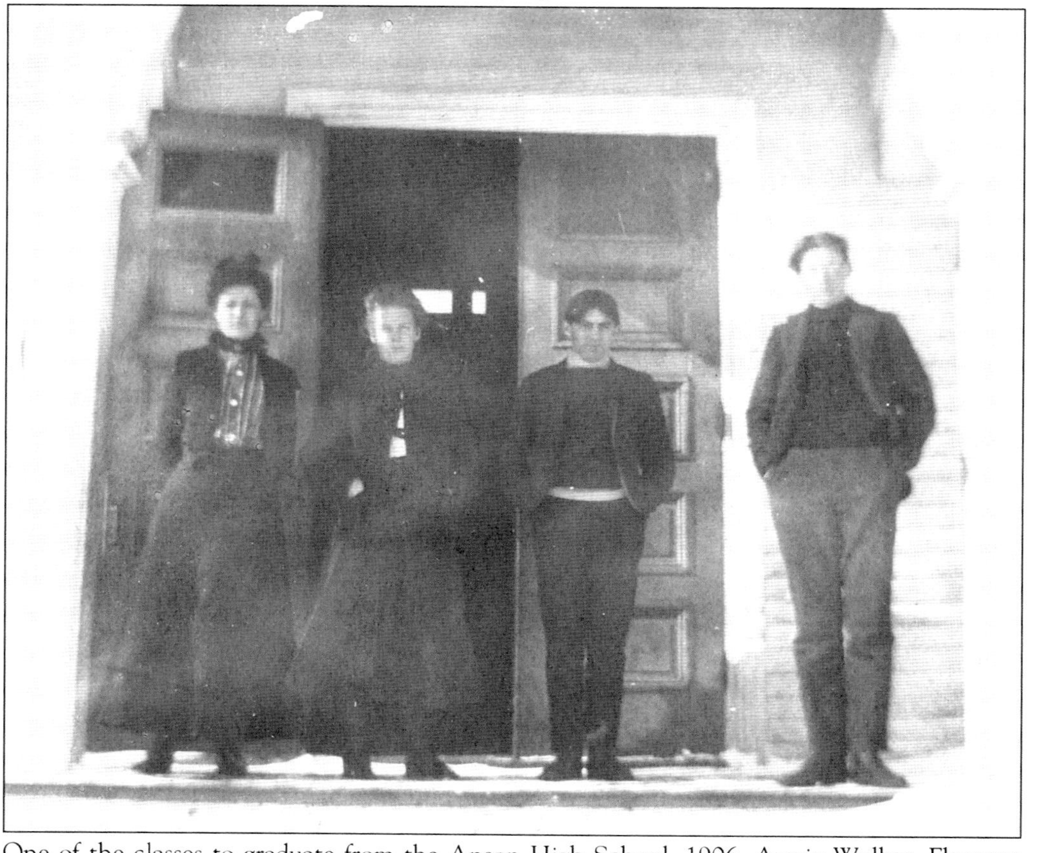

One of the classes to graduate from the Anson High School, 1906. Annie Walker, Florence Roberts, Ralph Gilman, and Willis Viles are shown here.

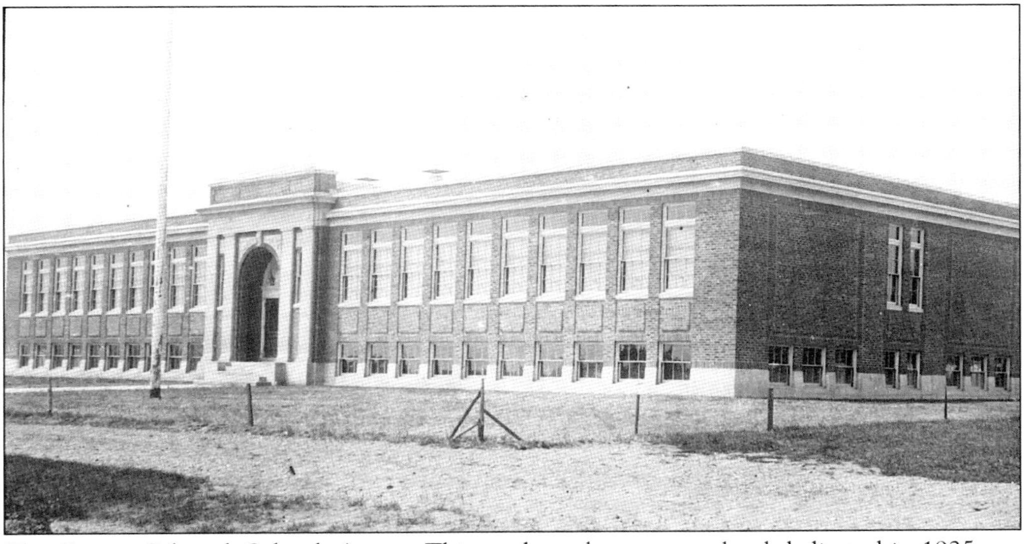

The Garrett Schenck School, Anson. This modern elementary school dedicated in 1925 was ahead of its time for a rural area. It has been of great benefit to the students over the years and is in use today with an addition.

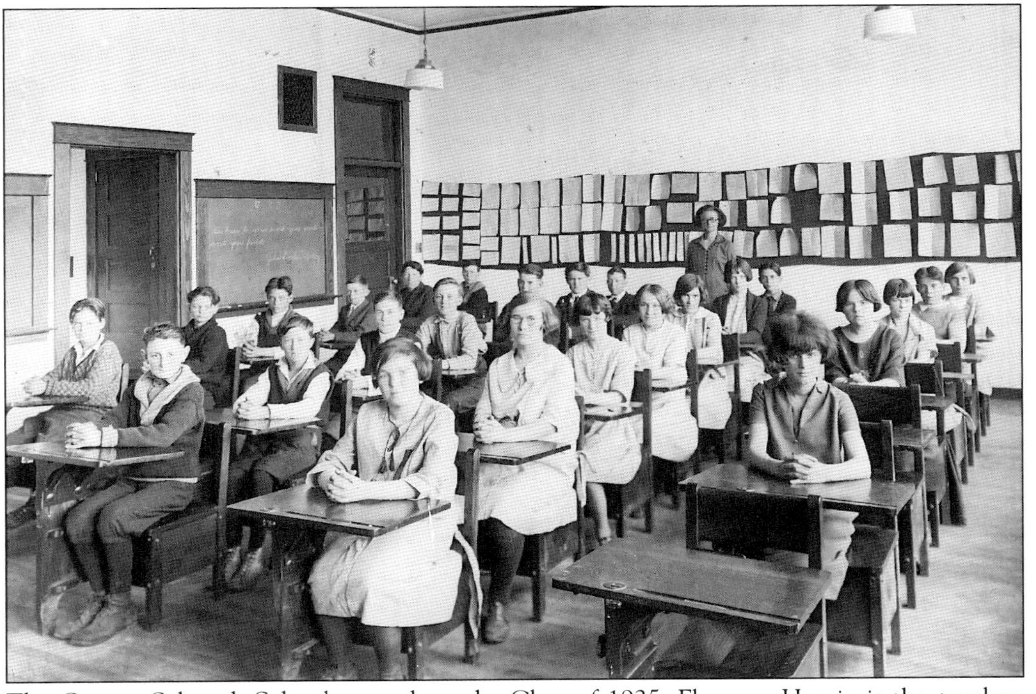

The Garrett Schenck School seventh grade, Class of 1925. Florence Harvie is the teacher. From the left row (front to back) to the right row, are as follows: (first row) Joseph Murray, Craig Welch, Chester Merrill, Leigh Collins, Patrick Flaherty, and Maurice Welch; (second row) George Viger, Donald Perkins, Homer Nichols, Joseph Ellis, Ronald Redmond, Philip Baker, and William Devalt; (third row) Adeline Viger, Cora Newton, Ruth Tranten, Mary Demchak, Clara Newton, Ethelyn Collins, and John Macklin; (fourth row) Florence Dugas, Ruth Henry, Grace Welch, Freeman Cote, and Emily Gilman.

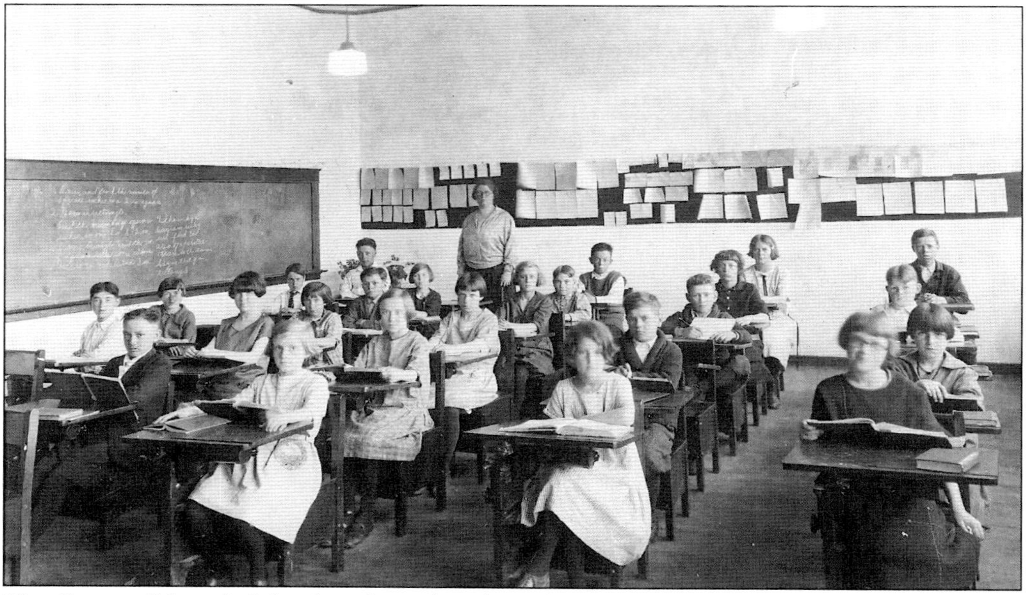

The Garrett Schenck School sixth grade, Class of 1925. Ethel Luce Viles is the teacher. The students, from the left row (front to back) to the right row, are as follows: (first row) Wilfred Cote, Jeanette Savoy, Bernard Davis, and Stephen Moran; (second row) Mike Jacobs, Muriel Connors, Irene Sawyer, George Serencha, and Elva Duplissea; (third row) Bertha Viles, Evelyn Demchak, Beulah Petley, Dorothy Bosworth, Jeffrey Coro, and William Ramsey; (fourth row) Lauretta Connors, Melvin Carter, George Demko, Beatrice Ellis, and Alice Hilton; (fifth row) Emma St. Peter, Annie Welch, Ralph Matthews, and Philip Punty.

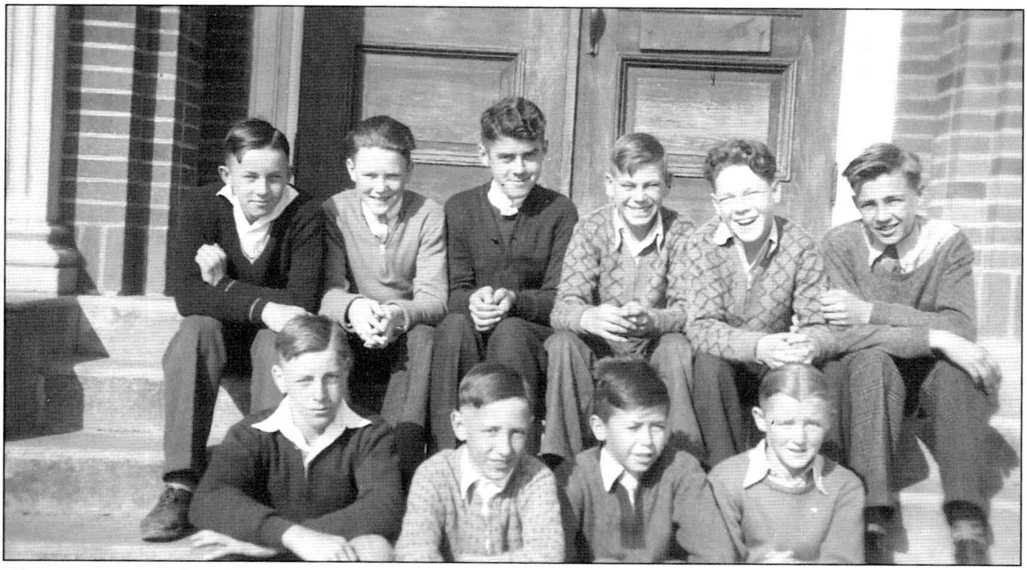

The Garrett Schenck School eighth grade boys, Class of 1937. From left to right, are as follows: (front row) Robert Ray, Richard Walker, Ralph Conners, and Elwin "Sam" McKinney; (back row) Fred Taylor, Gordon Page, Norman Cote, Edward Davis, Erlon Barron, and Rodney Petley.

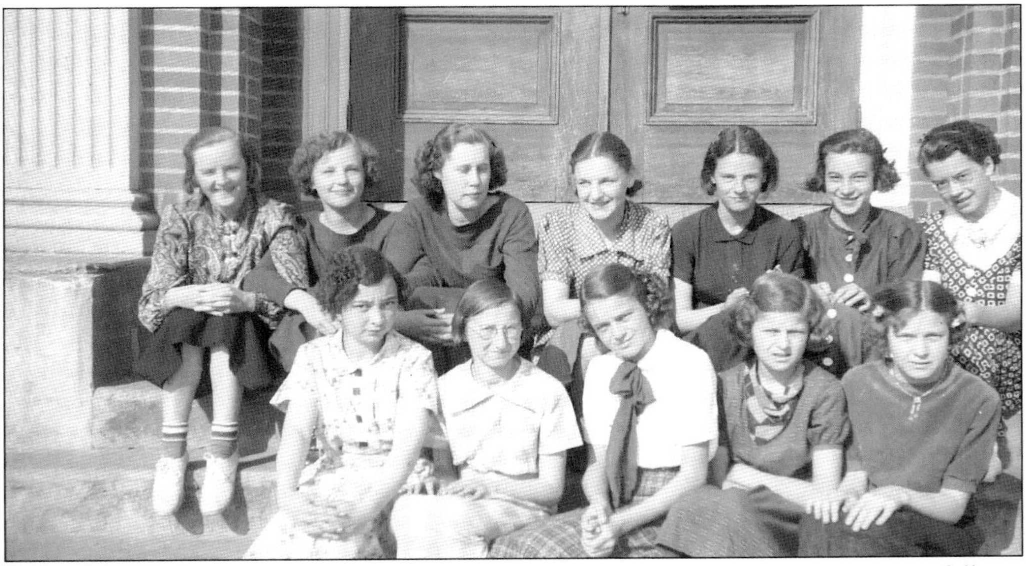

The Garrett Schenck School eighth grade girls, Class of 1937. From left to right, are as follows: (front row) Rosalie Delile, Regina Devalt, Genevieve Albert, Beverly Albert, and Barbara Ingalls; (back row) Lorraine Barron, Priscilla Duley, Pauline Waddell, Alvina Morin, Hazel Walker, Charlene Bearor, and Barbara Dunlap.

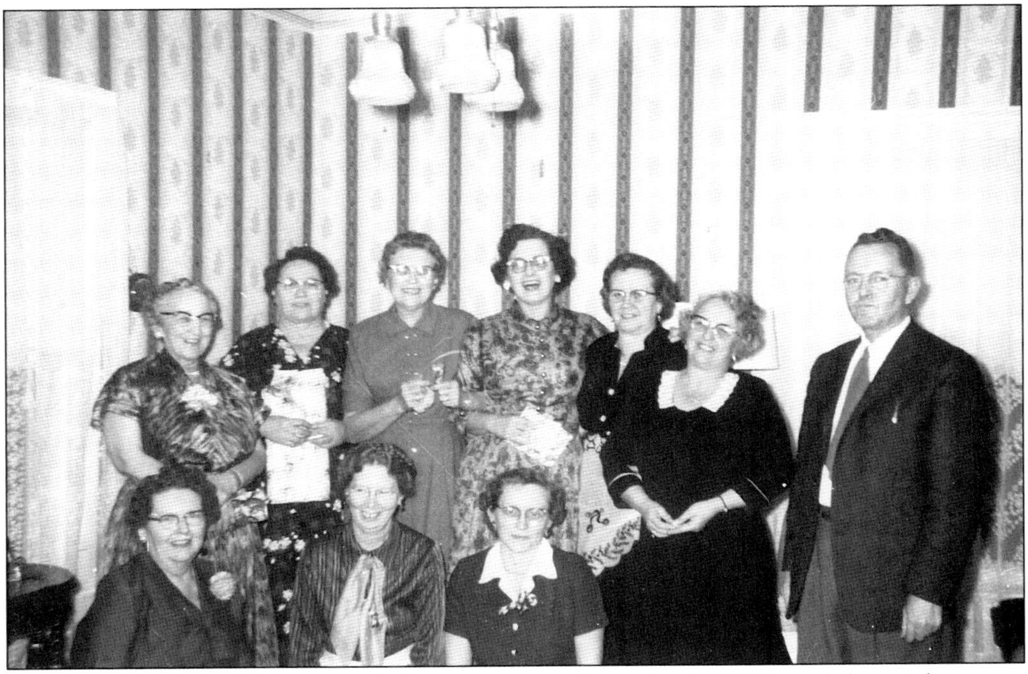

The Garrett Schenck School staff Christmas party, December 1957. From left to right, are as follows: (front row) Ethel Viles (office), Olena Taylor (gr. 3), and Bertha Welch (s.p.); (back row) Mabel Brackett (gr. 5), Annie Sabol (cook), Amy Gavett (gr. 7), Barbara Garland (gr. 2), Alta Danforth (gr. 1), Alta Safford (gr. 6), and Kenneth Taylor (gr. 8 and principal).

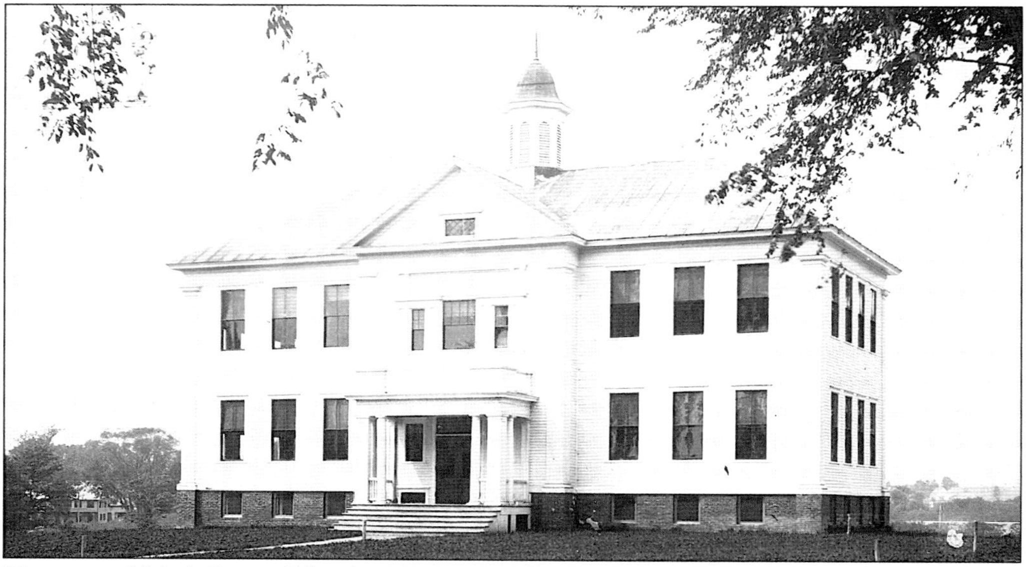

The original Mark Emery School in the upper village, grades K-8. Completed in 1910, it is still in use today with additions.

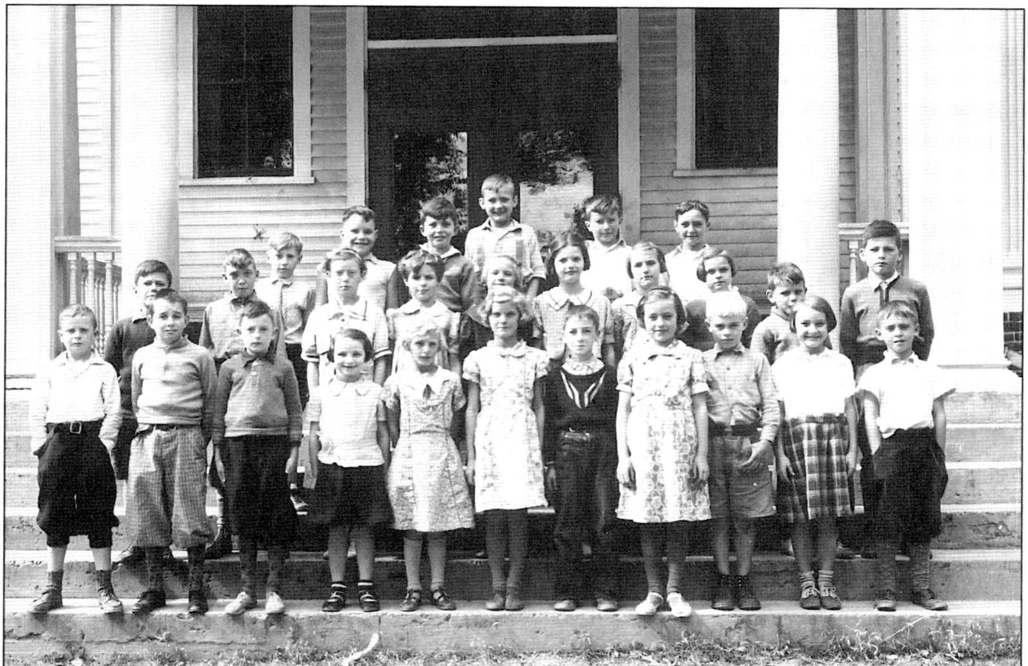

Mark Emery students, *c*. 1937. From left to right, are as follows: (front row) Claude Dunton, John Fletcher, Merle Skillings, Maxine Paine, Phyllis Coro, Florence Coro, Verne Berry, Helen LeClair, Harold Billing, Katherine Ela, and Calvin Otis; (middle row) Daniel Oliver, Wendal Oliver, Doris Skillings, Eunice Hibbert, Isabelle Green, Joan Wing, Ruth Green, Betty Petty, Richard Green, and Bennie LeClair; (back row) Warren Adams, Wendal Paine, Alan Wing, Walter Ela, Bruce Paine, and William Carl.

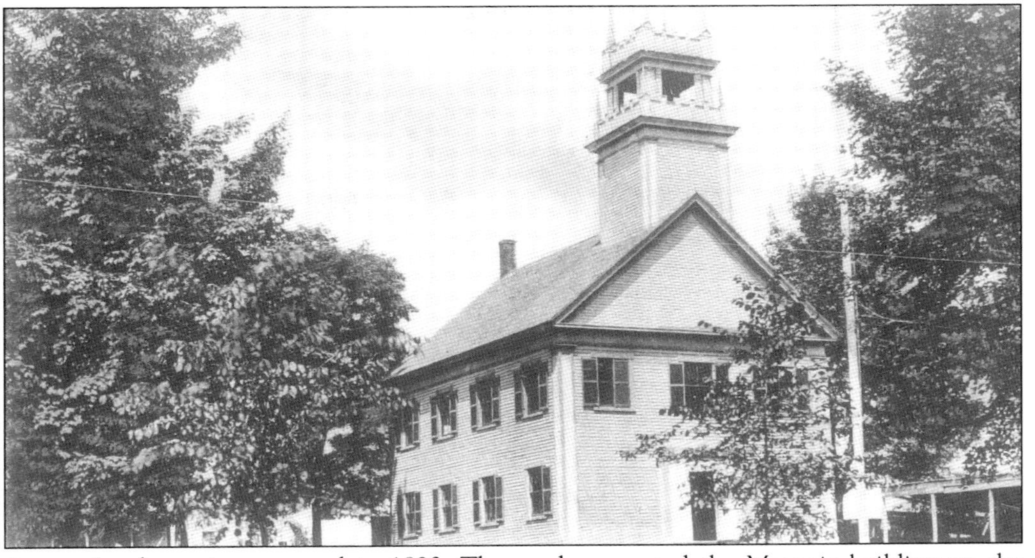

Anson Academy, incorporated in 1823. The academy rented the Masonic building on the corner of Main and Center Streets for 25 years. The building pictured here was erected in 1848 and was later enlarged and a basement added. It was destroyed by fire in 1946.

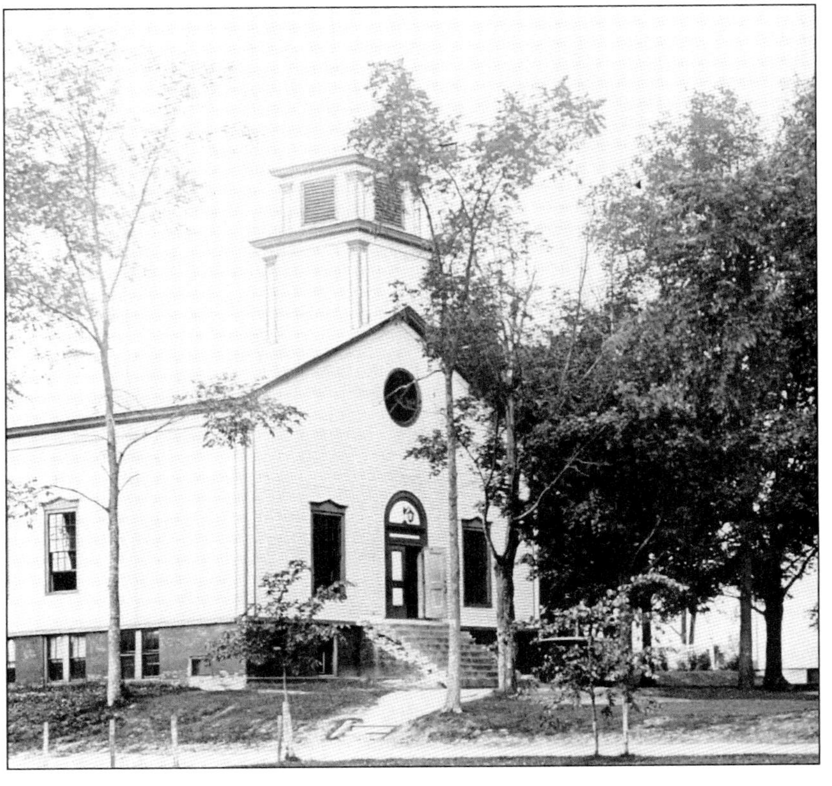

The adjoining property, known as Academy Hall. Academy Hall, erected in 1829, was acquired from the Universalist Church in 1917 and remodeled for school use. It burned in 1976.

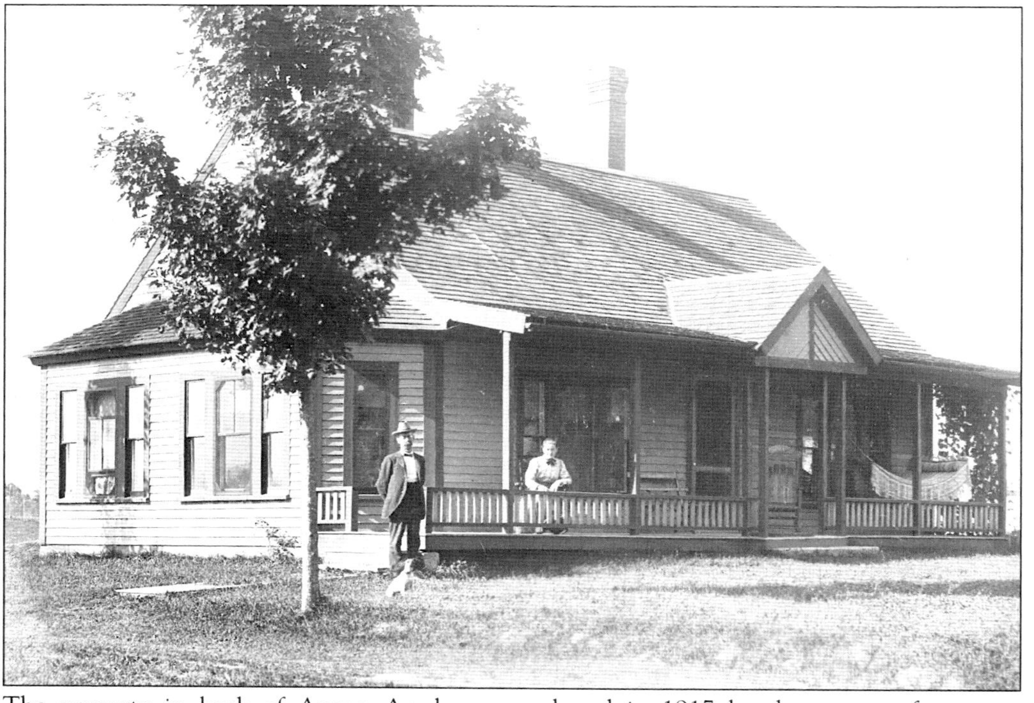

The property in back of Anson Academy, purchased in 1917 by the trustees for use as a teacherage.

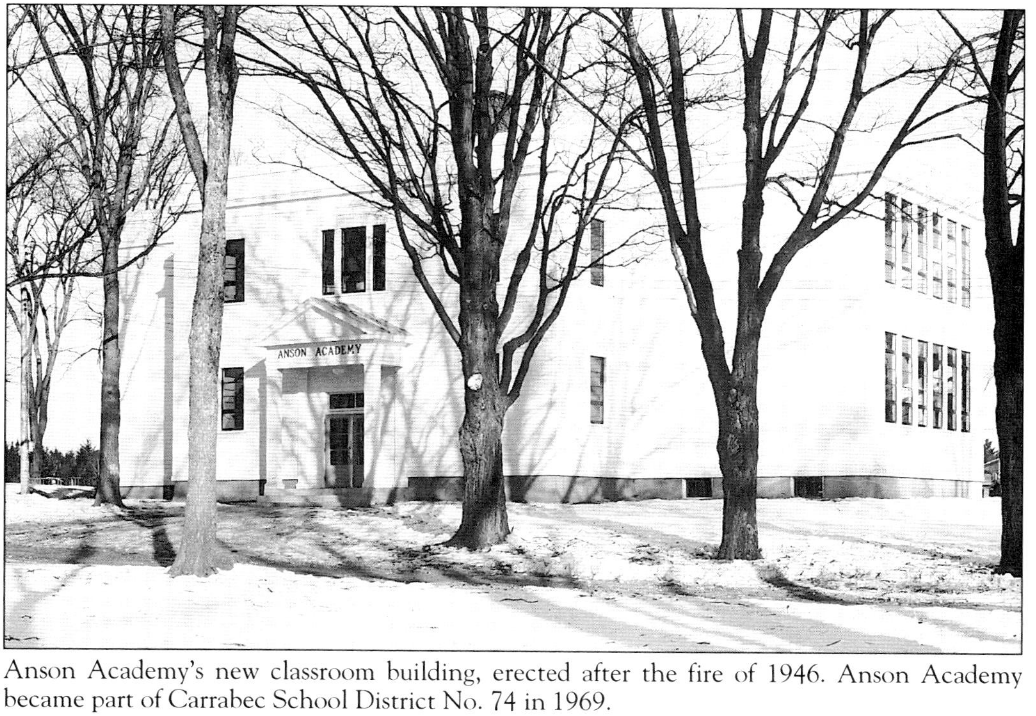

Anson Academy's new classroom building, erected after the fire of 1946. Anson Academy became part of Carrabec School District No. 74 in 1969.

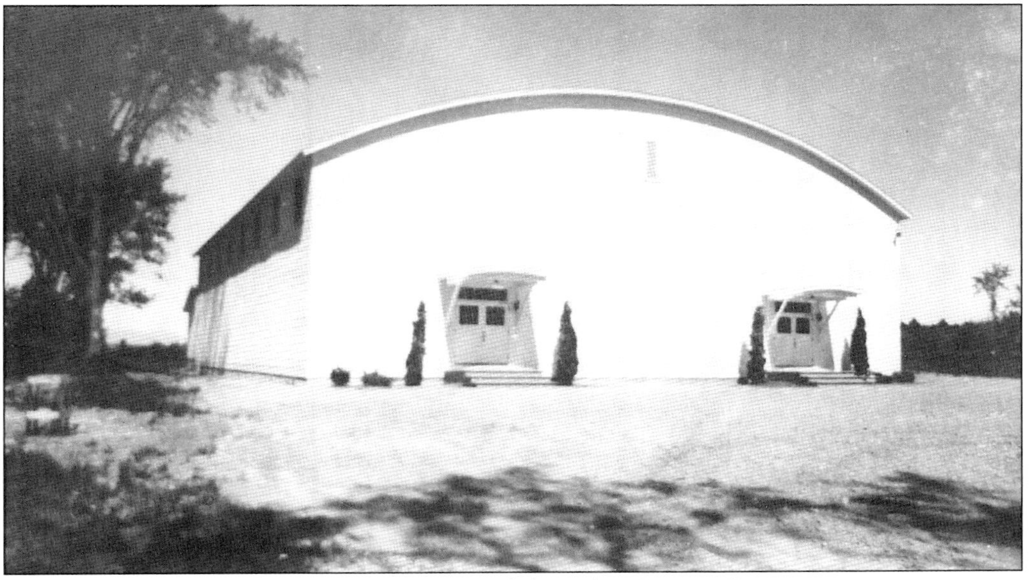

The Anson Academy gymnasium in 1952, a gift from the Hinman Corporation.

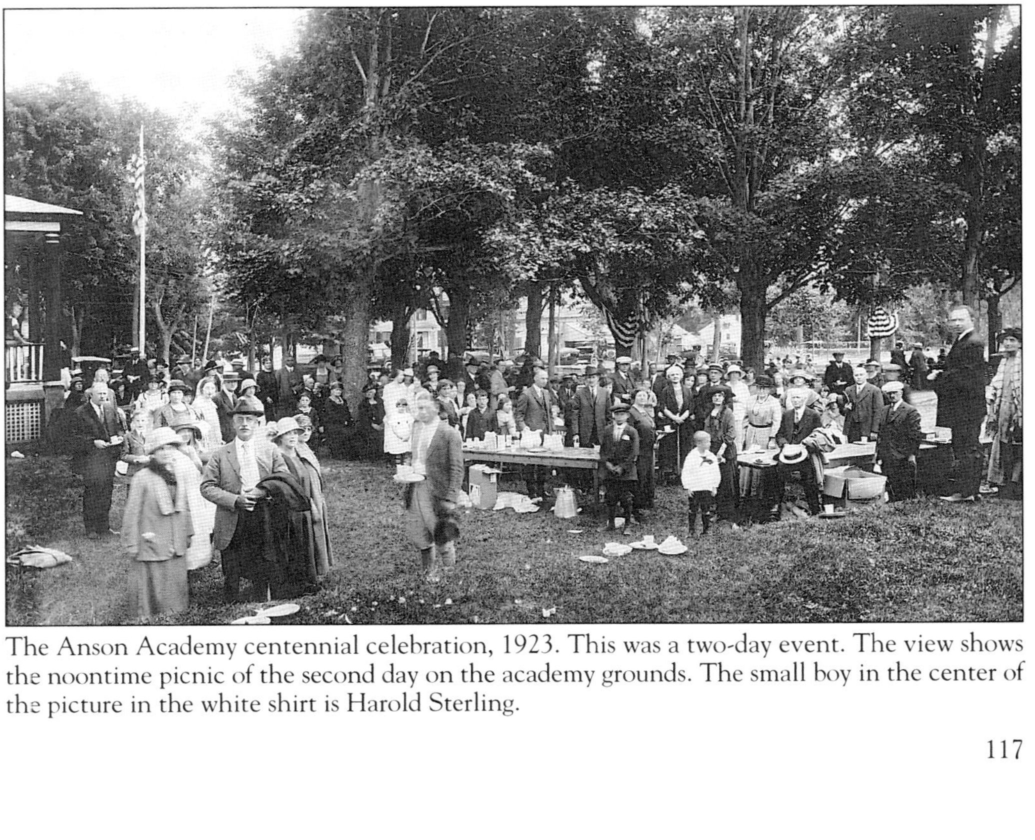

The Anson Academy centennial celebration, 1923. This was a two-day event. The view shows the noontime picnic of the second day on the academy grounds. The small boy in the center of the picture in the white shirt is Harold Sterling.

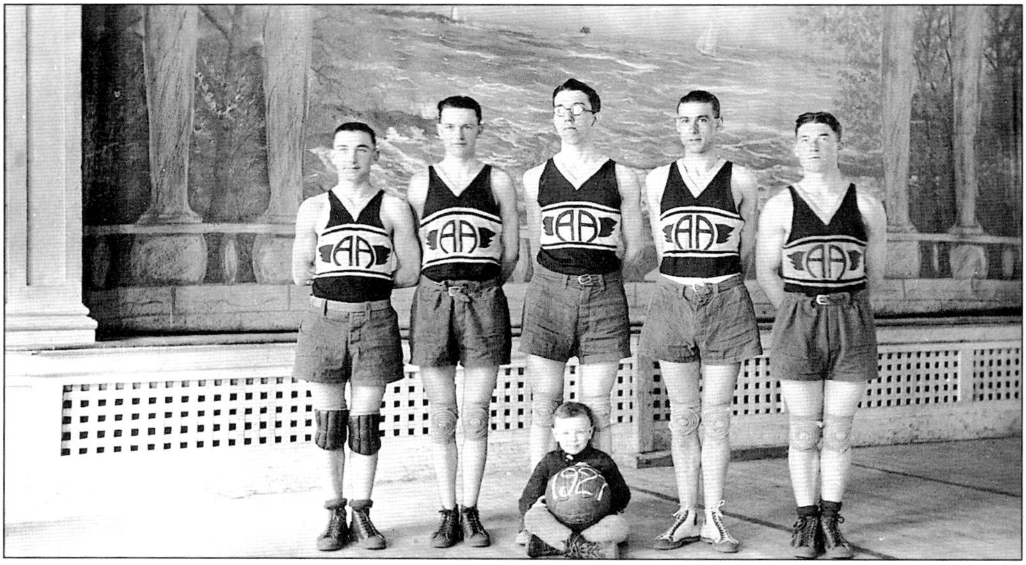

The Anson Academy basketball team of 1921. From left to right are Frank Dickey, Lawrence Shaw, Warren Smith, Whitman Allen, and Roscoe Bigelow. Bobby Haskell is in front.

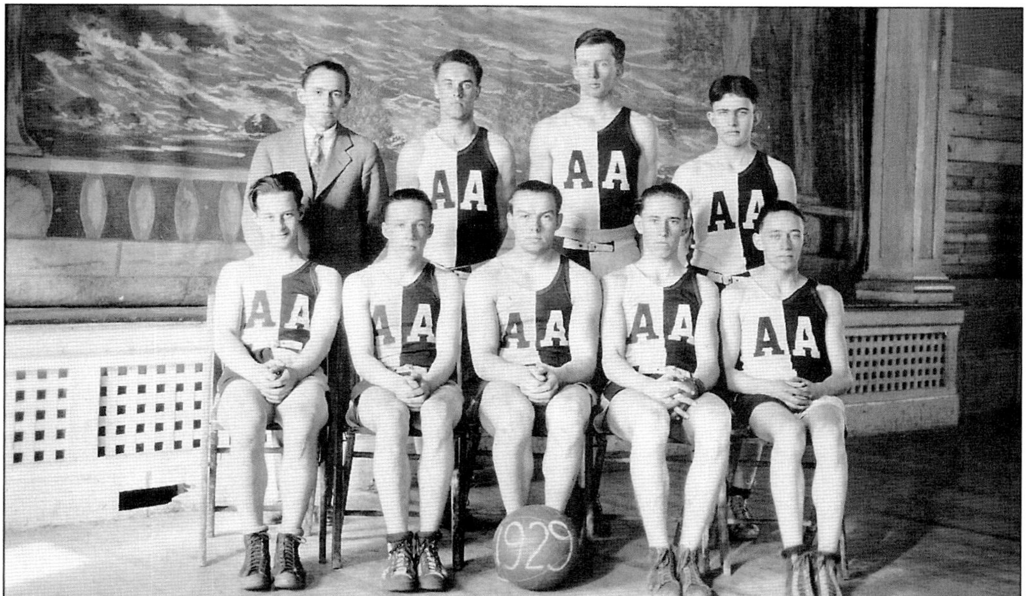

The Anson Academy basketball team of 1929. From left to right are as follows: (front row) Captain John Ellis, Manager Ivan Spencer, Leslie Young, Errold Quint, and Waldo Hartwell; (back row) Coach Wilkins, David Norton, Frank Norton, and Willard Rand.

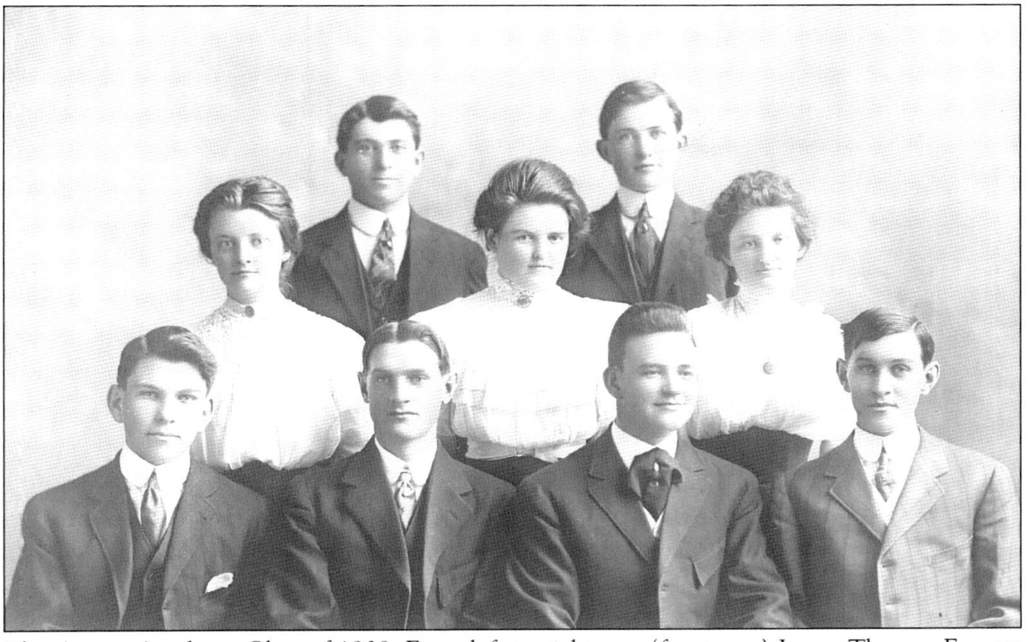

The Anson Academy Class of 1909. From left to right are: (front row) James Thorne, Everett Sawyer, Edmund Danforth, and Archie Danforth; (second row) Josephine Dunton, Bertha Oliver, and Frances Gilbert; (third row) Lester Holway and Elmer Sawyer.

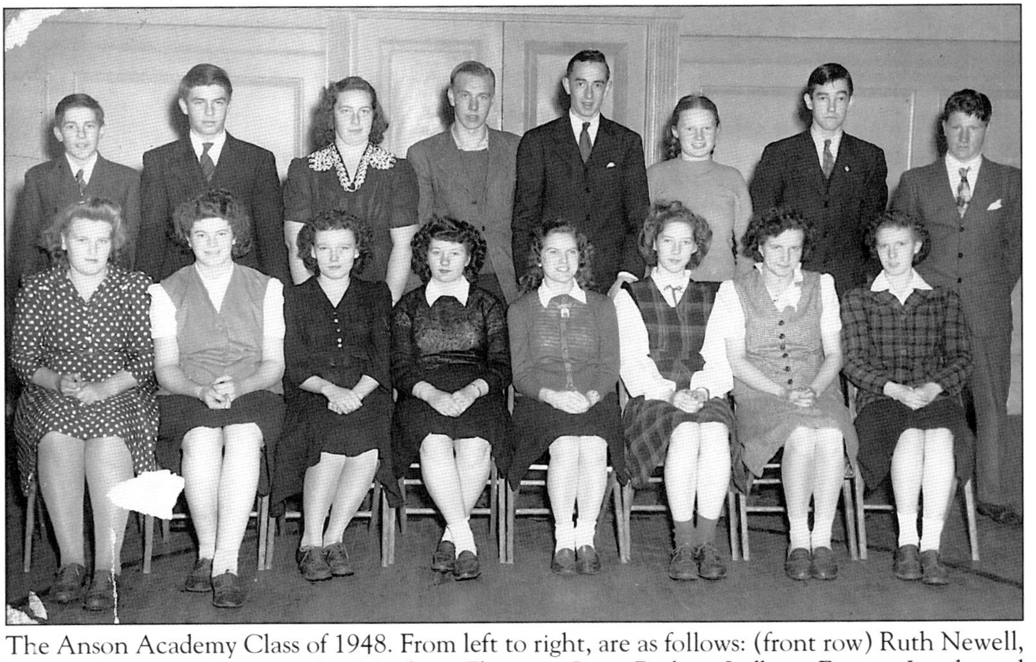

The Anson Academy Class of 1948. From left to right, are as follows: (front row) Ruth Newell, Lucille Berry, Mary Jacques, Iva Moulton, Florence Coro, Barbara Judkins, Frances Lynds, and Sadie Lightbody; (back row) Eldon McLean, Ralph Manzer, Eleanor Ketchum, Leroy Rolfe, Merle Skillings, Hilda Walker, Richard Whitaker, and James Farley.

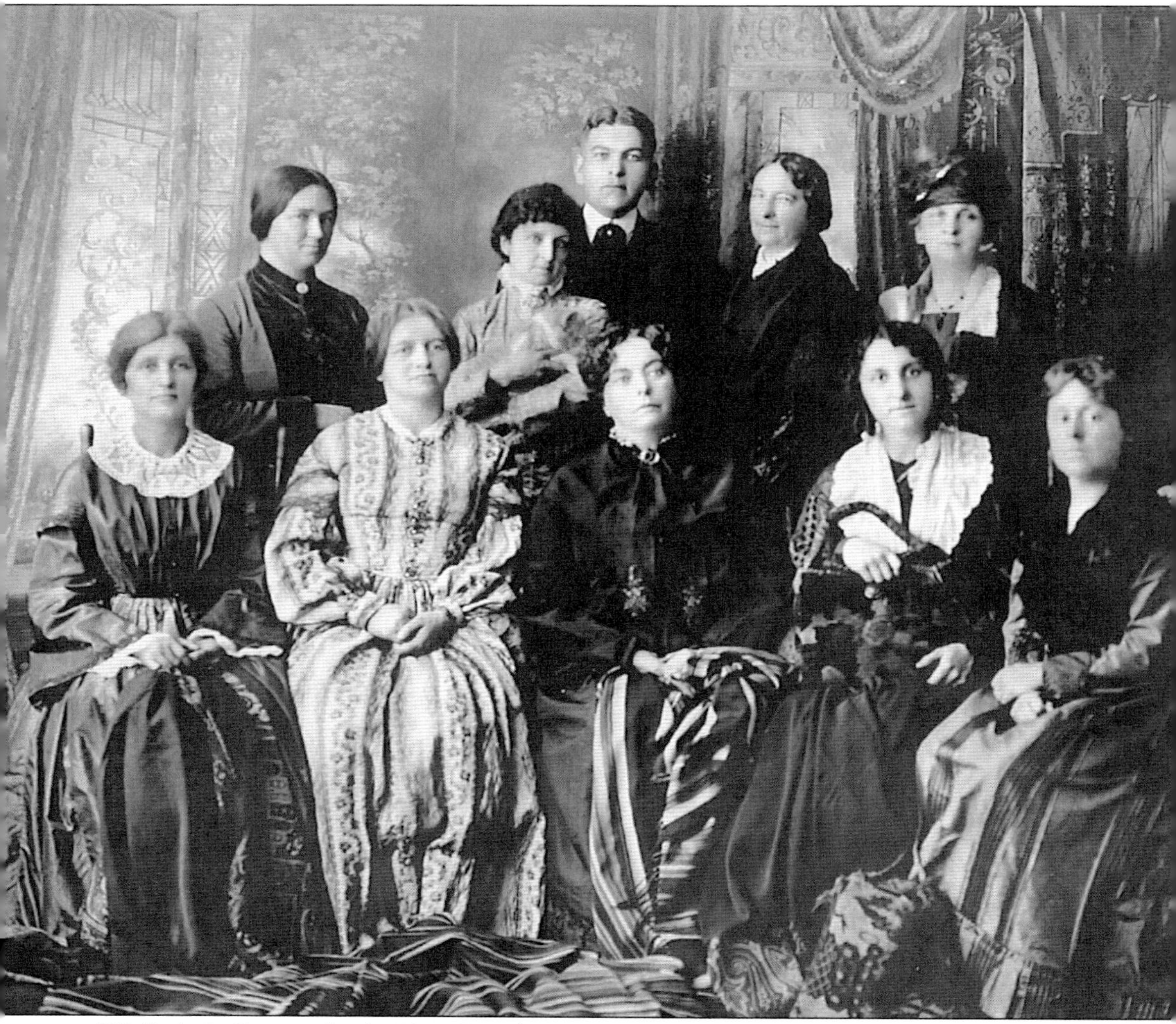

Old Peabody Pew, a play by Kate Douglas Wiggin. This play was performed in North Anson in the summer of 1924. From left to right, are as follows: (front row) Flora Waite, Eva Tarr, Mrs. Spear, Carrie Wing, and Edna Thorne; (back row) Addie Hodgdon, Jane Sawyer, Elmer Sawyer, Julia Clark, and Minnie Mantor.

Four

Organizations and People

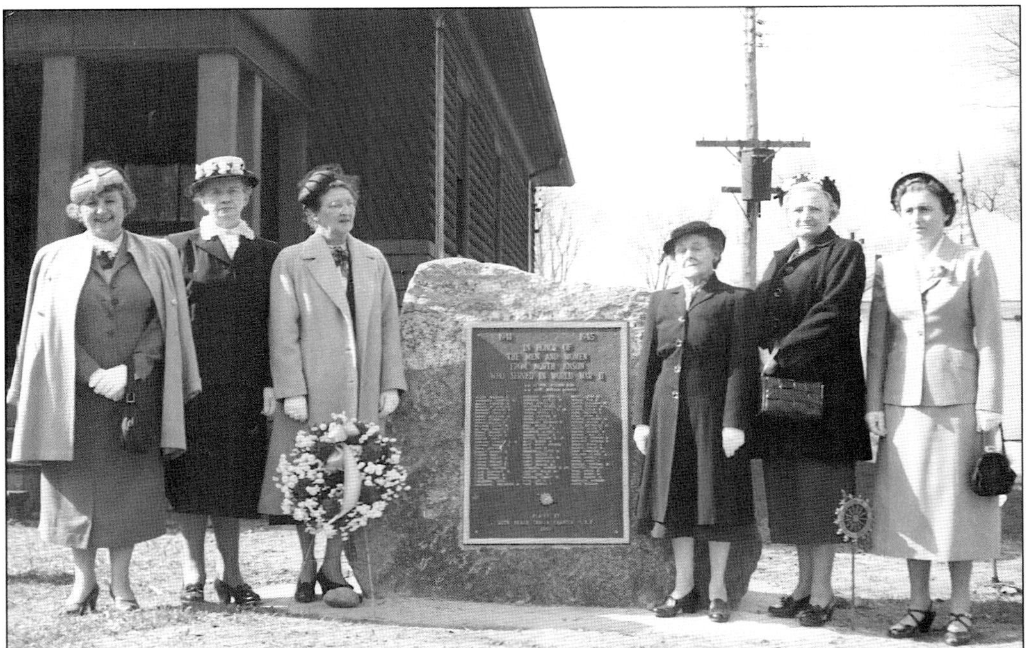

Members of the DAR of North Anson at the dedication of a tablet in honor of the men and women from North Anson who served in WW II. This tablet is located at the Stewart Public Library. From left to right are: Carrie Wing, Bertha Paine, Josie Sawyer, Edna Thorne, Merle Wendell, and Evelyn Edwards.

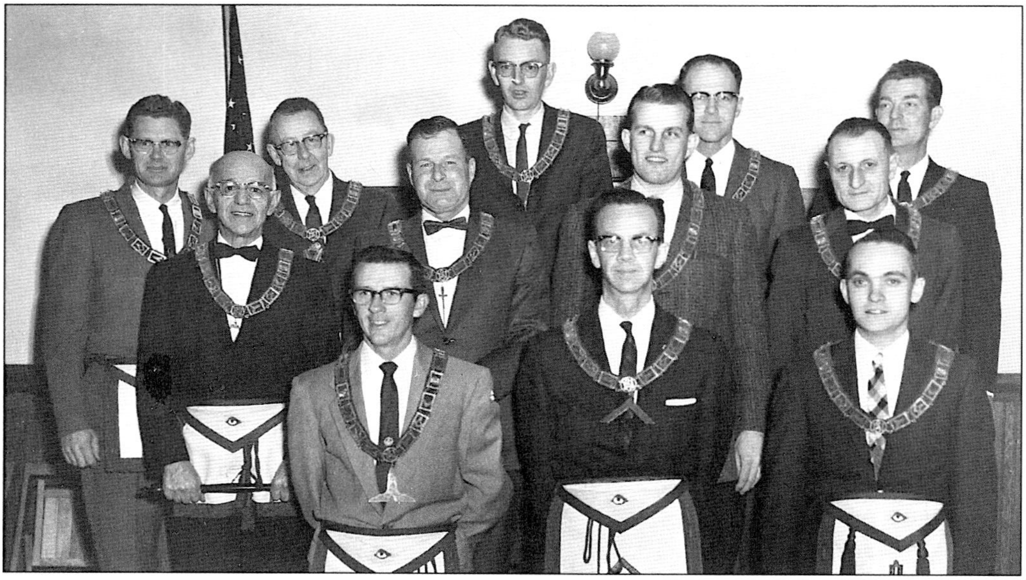

1965 Officers of Northern Star Lodge #28 (Masons). From left to right, are as follows: (front row) Lawrence Harvie, Carroll Goodwin Jr., and David Ela; (middle row) Jack Ducharme, Philip Webber, Charles Qualey, and Ernest Thibeault; (back row) Raynard Morrell, Alfred Holbrook, Clifton Walter, Albert Morrell, and Glendon Durrell.

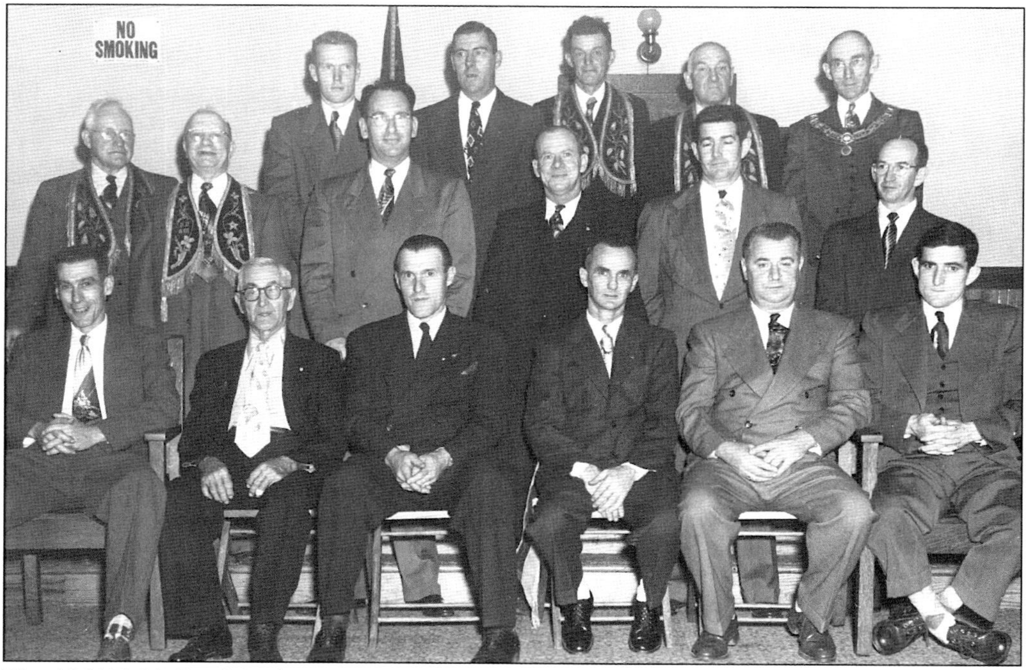

The 1951 Table Rock Lodge No. 100 of the Independent order of Odd Fellows in North Anson. From left to right, are as follows: (front row) Whitman Allen, C. Barnard, William Allen, Cyrus Greenleaf, Leon Young, and Stanley Bragg; (middle row) Elwin Starbird, Lou Koritzy, unidentified, Harold Golding, Elmer Bragg, and Armand Sawyer; (back row) Gordon Page, Ellery Williams, Edwin Carlson, Cyrus Oliver, and Ellery Fletcher.

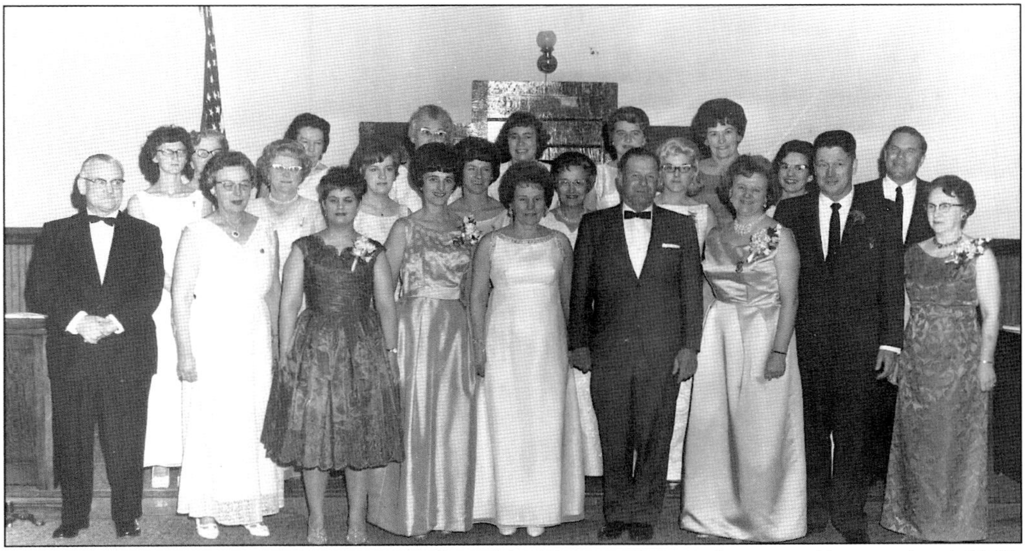

Officers of Mt. Bigelow Chapter #48 Order of the Eastern Star at their installation, April 1968. From left to right, are as follows: (front row) John Agurkis, Elizabeth Agurkis, Marion Blizard (soloist), Betty Withee (installing marshal), Phyllis Webber, Philip Webber, Irja Lehto (installing officer), Arthur Lehto (installing patron), and Mildred Ela (installing chaplain); (middle row) Marjorie Morrell, Genevieve Partridge, Bonnie Pickett, Patricia Andrews, Ruth Houghton, Jean Ela, Mary Kilburn, and James Kilburn; (back row) Dorothy Counce, Florence Durrell, Cora Belle Paine, Helen Viles, Barbara Qualey, and Alyce Corson (installing organist).

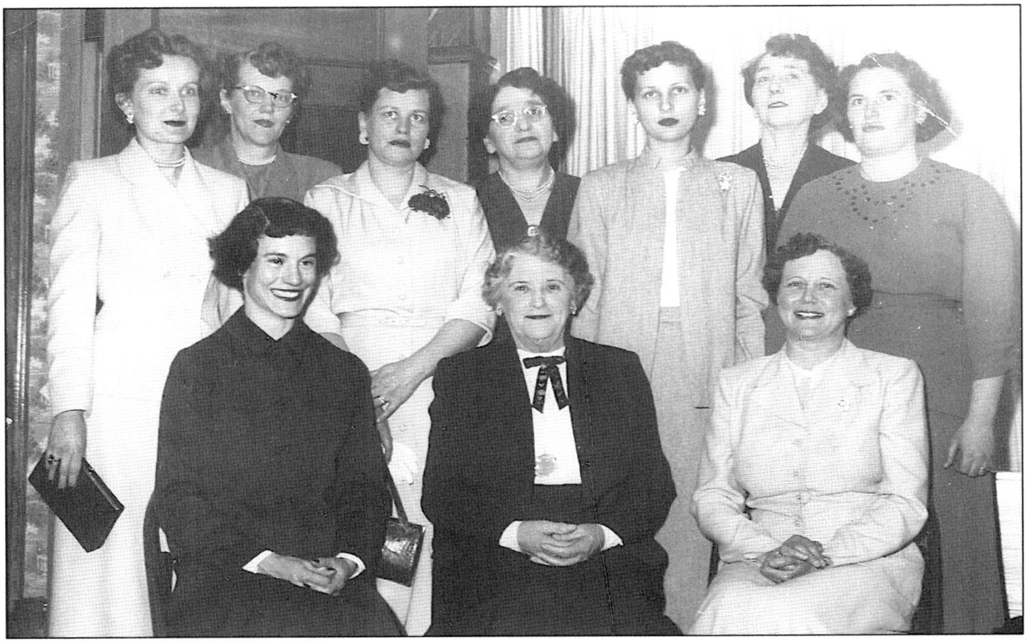

The North Anson Woman's Club, 1953. From left to right, are as follows: (front row) Mary Hill, Ellen Thomas, and Genevieve Partridge; (back row) Marilyn Pelly, Edith Spear, Elinor Hinman, Marion Holbrook, Mary McHenry, Hester Pullen, and Frances Gould. The club was organized on November 15, 1914, and was federated on October 23, 1915.

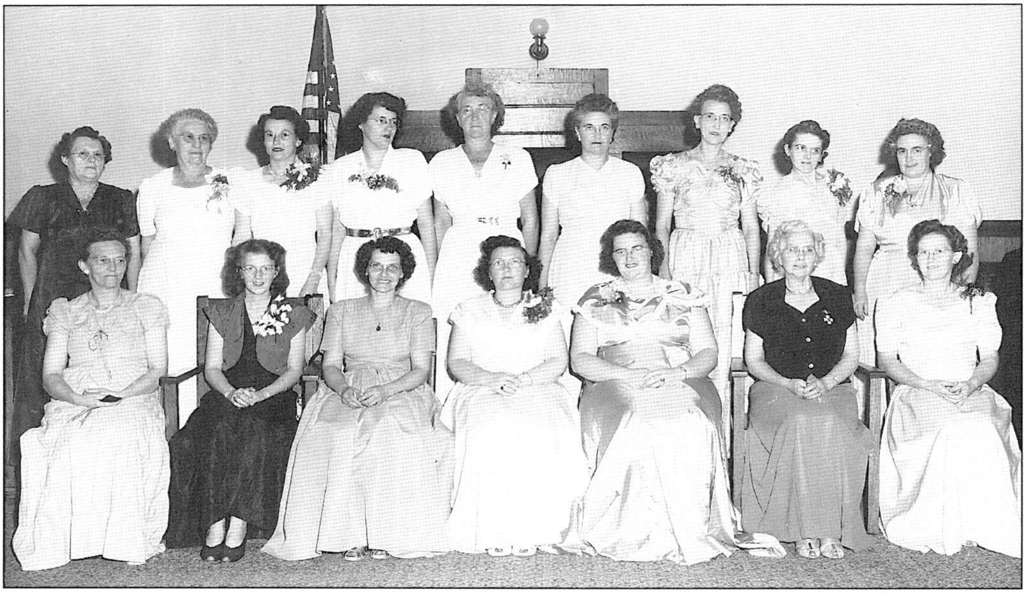

Emerald Rebekah Lodge #65, 1950. From left to right, are as follows: (front row) Erma Rolfe, Anna Pickett, Esther Fletcher, Dorothy Flanders, Mavis Savage, Belle Nye, and Isabelle Carlson; (back row) Esther Spencer, Emma Philpot, Marguerite Otis, Elizabeth Oliver, Hazel Ketchum, Hazel Allen, Humane Parlin, Evelyn Taylor, and Edith Dunbar.

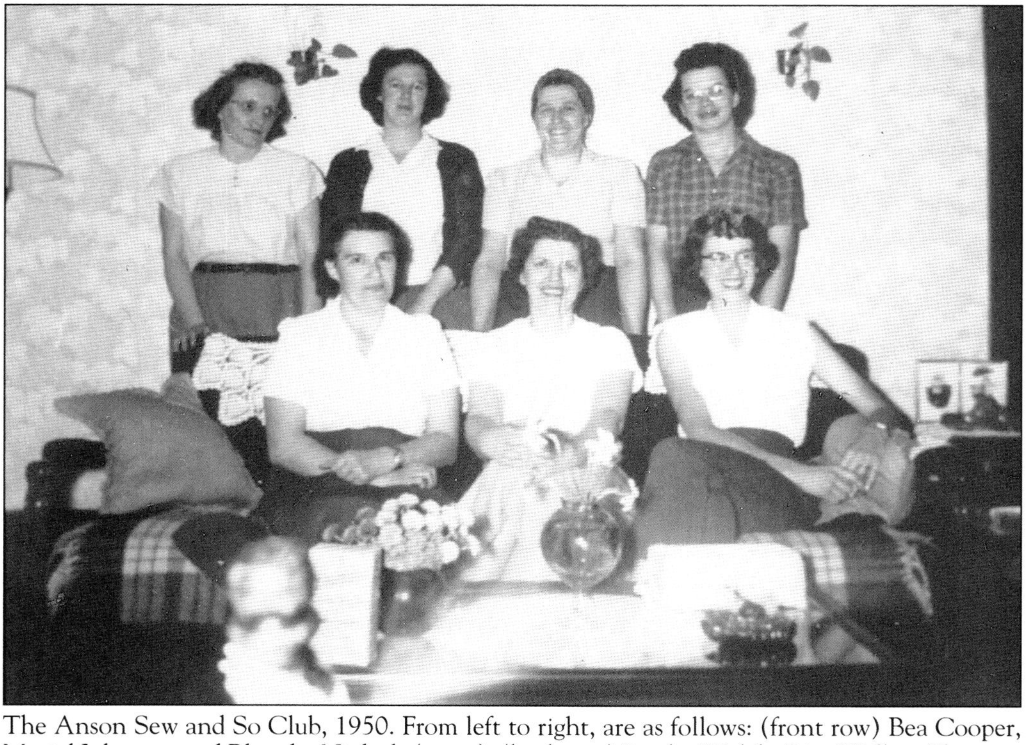

The Anson Sew and So Club, 1950. From left to right, are as follows: (front row) Bea Cooper, Muriel Johnson, and Blanche Nichols (guest); (back row) Bertha Welch, Rita Walker, Florence Welch, and Barbara Hoyt.

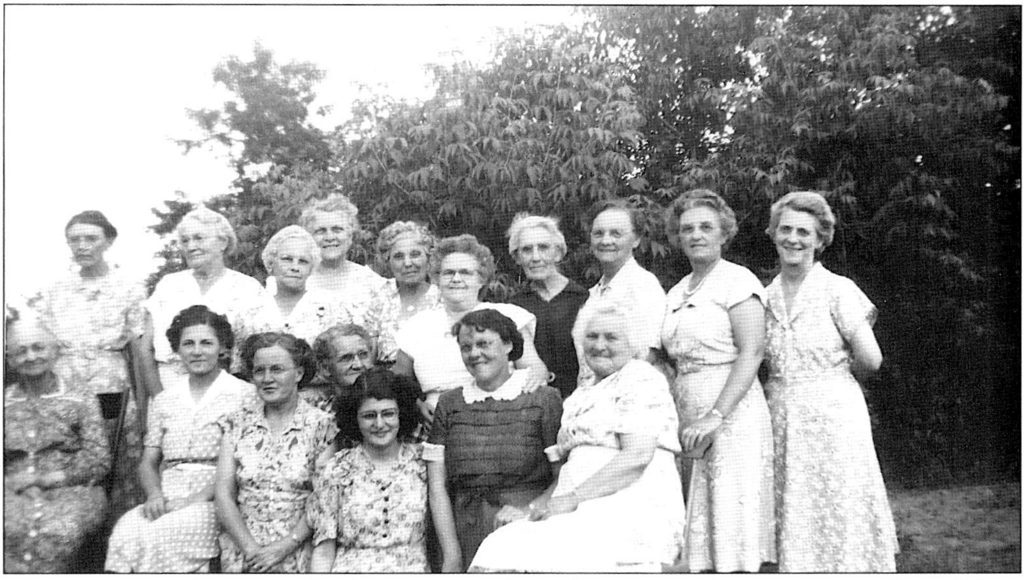

The Anson Rainbow Branch of International Sunshine Society, Inc., c. 1930. From left to right, are as follows: (front row) Mildred Sterry's mother, Eva Sterry Gillin, Nellie Fowke, Lucy Paine, Beverly Sterry Wills, Vera Page, and Harriet Hamilton; (back row) Helen Frost, Olive Robinson, Ida Caldwell, Mildred Sterry Beck, Maude Harding, Ethel Luce, Emma Jones, Etta Weston, Alma Peters, and Martha Nichols.

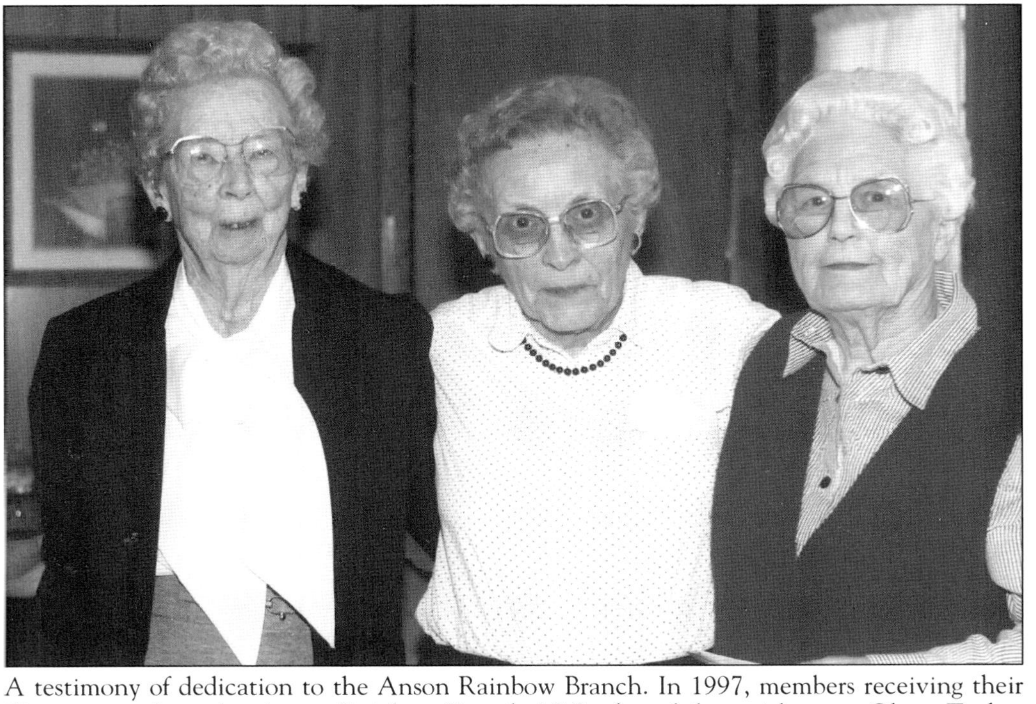

A testimony of dedication to the Anson Rainbow Branch. In 1997, members receiving their 50-year pins from the Anson Rainbow Branch I.S.S., from left to right, are: Olena Taylor, Bertha Welch, and Minerva Buzzell.

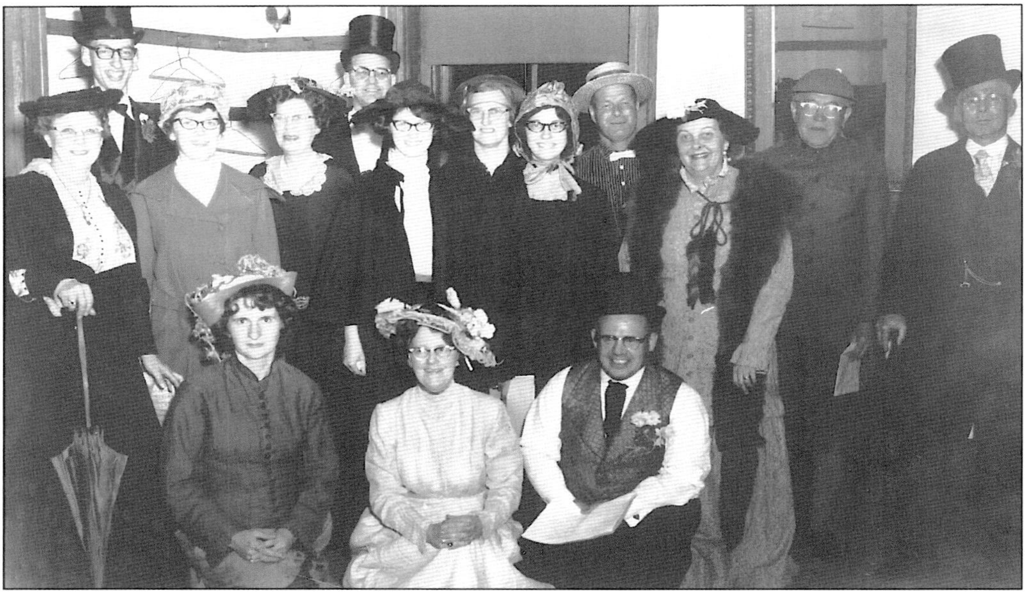

North Anson Church Choir after performing in an Order of the Eastern Star program, c. 1960s. From left to right, are as follows: (front row) Frances Spencer, Anna Pickett, and Everett Wiswell; (middle row) Genevieve Partridge, Janet Grant, Berle Ducharme, Emily Morrell, Natalie Wiswell, Mary Wescott, Philip Webber, Avis Luce, Harry Jackson, and Linton Partridge; (back row) Gene Wiswell and Harold Burbar.

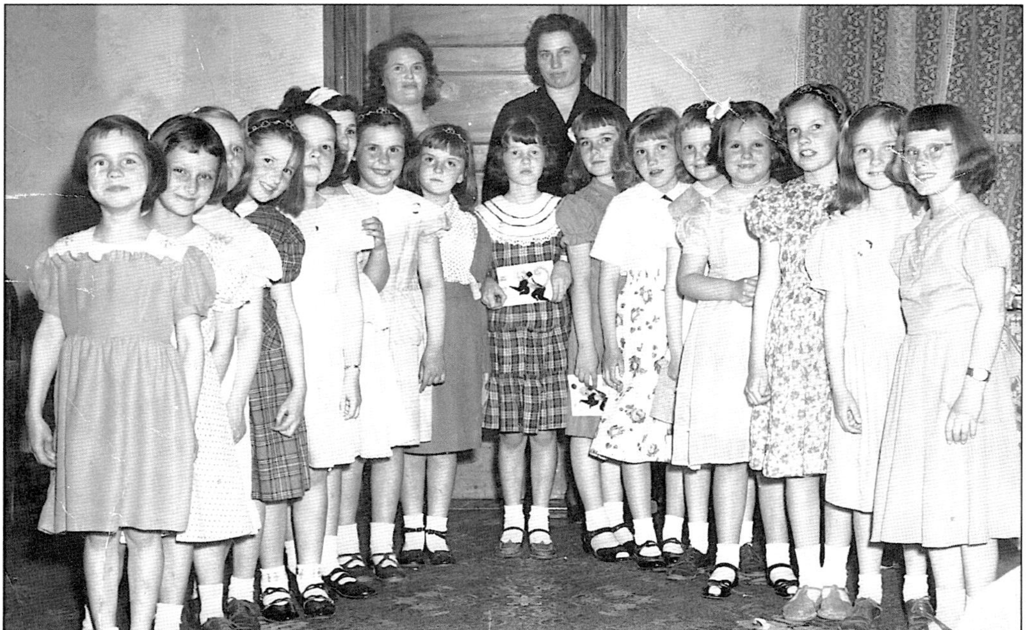

A Brownie Scout Troop, 1950–51. From left to right are: Betty King, Patty Mayo, Lucy Burns, Connie Oliver, Virginia Fletcher, Sandra Homestead, Bobbi Ellis, Connie Lane, Roberta LeHay, Carol Phiney, Peggy Berry, Judy Luce, Verniene Allen, Dawna Heald, Mary Hines, and Sara Jane Mayo. The leaders in the back are Frances Gould and Alfreda LeHay.

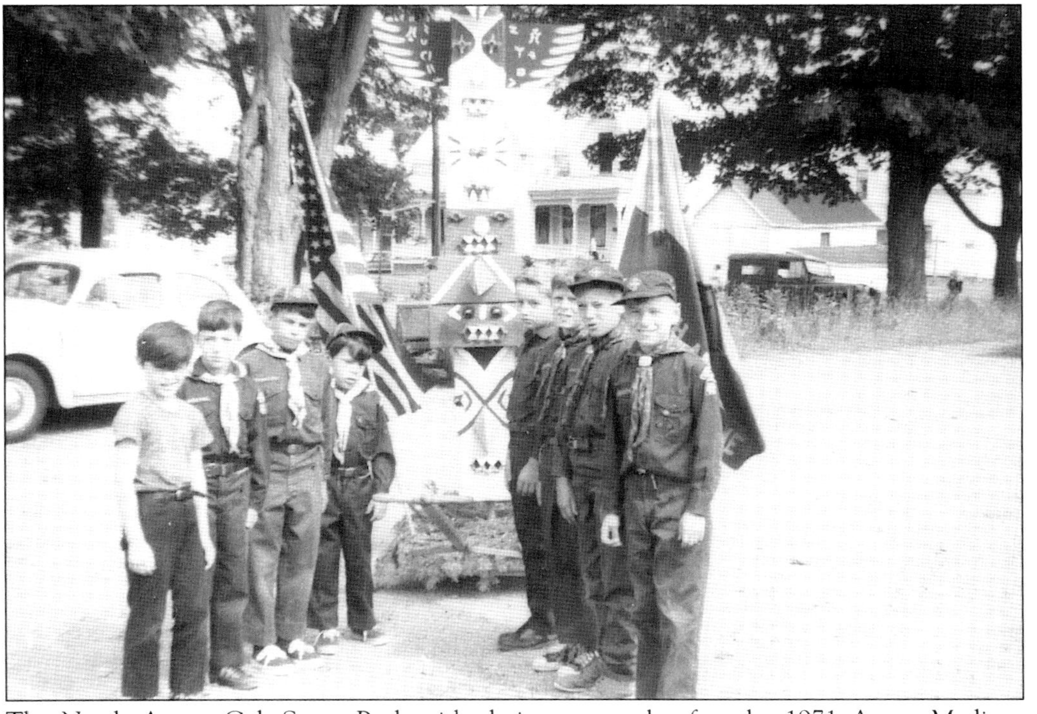

The North Anson Cub Scout Pack with their totem pole after the 1971 Anson-Madison Firemans Field Day Parade. From left to right are: Joseph Paul, Buddy McLean, Greg Tripp, Gerald Jacobs, Wayne Staples, Barry Gray, Clair Adley, and Tom Morrell.

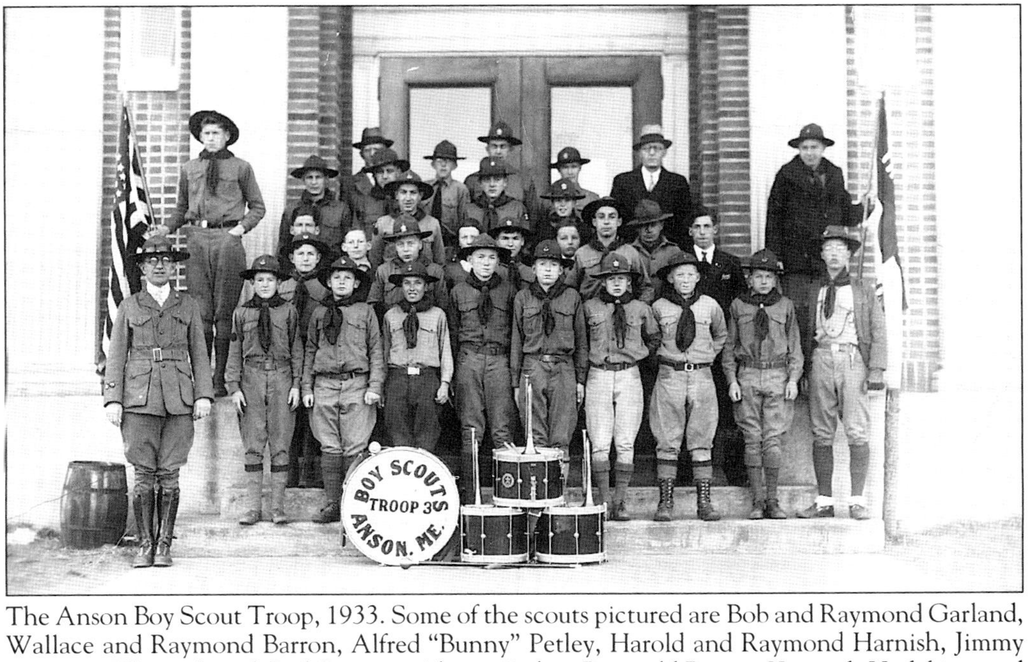

The Anson Boy Scout Troop, 1933. Some of the scouts pictured are Bob and Raymond Garland, Wallace and Raymond Barron, Alfred "Bunny" Petley, Harold and Raymond Harnish, Jimmy Conners, Ellsworth and Carl Spencer, Alonzo Parker, Reginald Bearor, Kenneth Hodgkins, and Scout Leader Willis Hodgkins.

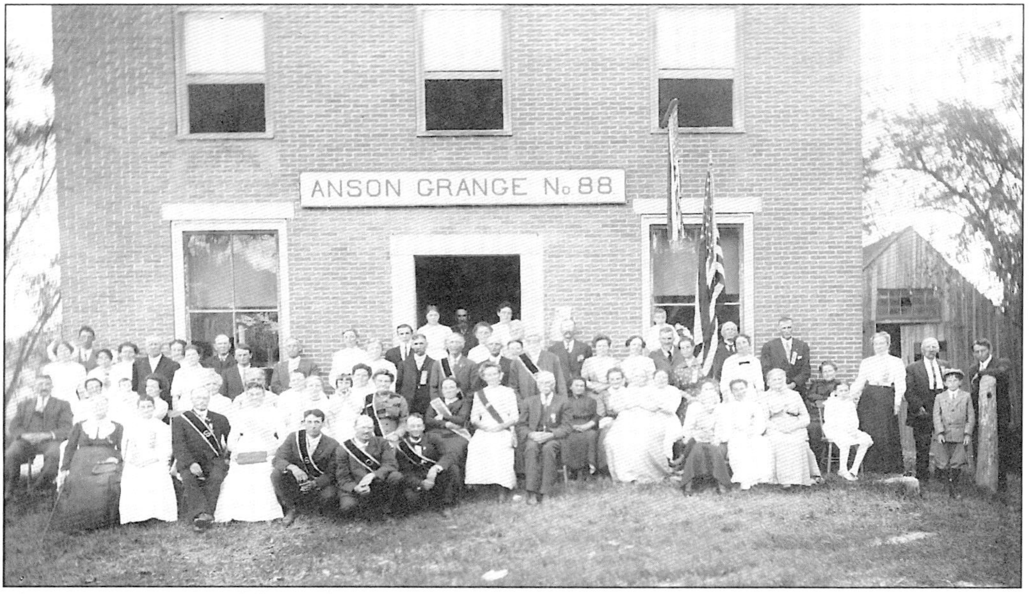

The Anson Grange of the Order of Patrons of Husbandry. Organized in North Anson in 1875, this order existed for three years, was re-organized in 1899, and continues today. Their new building was dedicated in 1906.

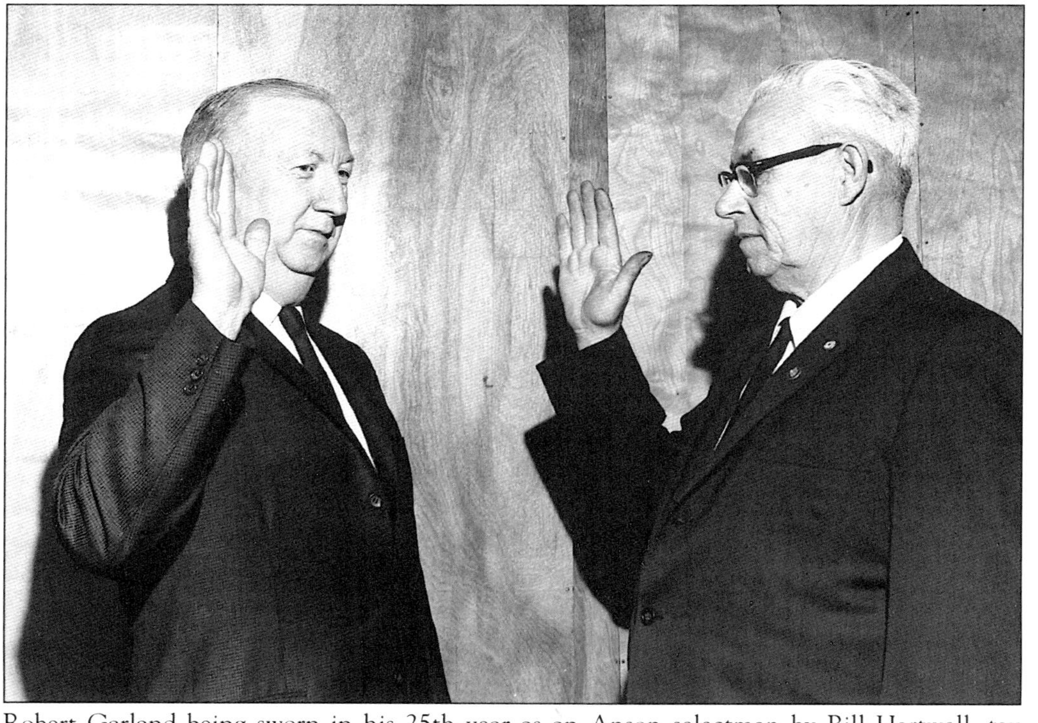

Robert Garland being sworn in his 25th year as an Anson selectman by Bill Hartwell, tax collector and superintendent of the water district, who was serving his 34th year as a moderator for the town. Bill died in 1985. Bob completed 48 years as selectman in 1994 and is still active in town affairs.